LEATHERNECK LEGENDS

CONVERSATIONS WITH THE MARINE CORPS' OLD BREED

DICK CAMP

ZENITH PRESS

This edition published by Zenith Press, an imprint of MBI Publishing Company, Galtier Plaza, Suite 200, 380 Jackson Street, St. Paul, MN, 55101-3885 USA.

Cover photograph: Private First Class Harry Kizierian taking a break from combat on Okinawa.

All photographs official USMC except as noted.

Cover by Rochelle Brancato
Design by LeAnn Kuhlmann

ISBN: 0-7603-2157-4
ISBN-13: 978-0-7603-2157-7

Printed in the United States of America

CONTENTS

PRELUDE

In May 1967 I was assigned as the aide-de-camp to Marine Major General Raymond G. Davis, deputy commanding general, Provisional Corps Vietnam. General Davis was provided a helicopter for his personal use and made it a point to visit as many of the Corps' far-flung units as possible. One day I accompanied him into a remote hilltop-landing zone. The unit was some distance away along a lonely path that meandered through thick jungle foliage. It was almost impossible to see more than a few feet off the trail. Suddenly, the "old man" stopped and peered intently into the undergrowth. All kinds of ugly possibilities flooded my mind—sniper, ambush, enemy soldiers. I brought my rifle up to meet the unspecified threat. Davis turned and looked at me rather pensively before speaking. "You know, Dick," he said, "this place reminds me of my command post on Guadalcanal." I was floored; the 'Canal was in 1942 and I was two years old at the time. Vietnam was his third war! I felt rather foolish standing there ready to do battle when the "old man" only wanted to reminisce about his old Corps experiences.

Davis went on to assume command of a dispirited Marine division, which by sheer force of personality and inspirational leadership he turned into a "lean, mean, fighting machine." In the process, the thoroughly aroused division kicked the pants off the North Vietnamese in the northern I Corps. At the time, I was caught up in the daily routine, and I did not have time to reflect on how he accomplished this phenomenal rejuvenation. In the years following my service with General Davis, I had the opportunity to interview and research other Marine Corps greats, which helped me to understand how he and the others gained their military acumen. I discovered they shared remarkably similar personal and professional qualities:

They were gentlemen, men of the old school, who seldom swore or raised their voices in anger. Their behavior harkened back to an era of genteel manners. This, however, is not to say that if the situation demanded firm action, they would not hesitate to act forcefully. In today's parlance, they could "kick ass and take names," but without the histrionics of a martinet.

They possessed an aura of authority on the battlefield—a presence, a quiet courage that steadied men facing great danger. Theirs was not the bravado of an attention-seeker, but rather the unruffled calmness of a professional sea soldier.

They were not content to pass the time in an isolated command post. They moved forward with the assault, into the front lines, sharing danger with their men.

They kept their fingers on the tactical pulse of their unit. They knew, first hand, the morale of the unit, what they were facing in terms of the terrain, and the enemy situation.

They were technically and tactically proficient. They took advantage of formal schools and informal study to prepare themselves for combat assignments.

They had the courage of their convictions and were able, by force of personality, to impart others with that same high degree of confidence in ultimate success.

They made it a point to know their subordinate commanders, their strengths and weaknesses, and allowed them freedom of action without micromanaging them.

They respected and encouraged other opinions, but when the courses of action had been explored, they did not hesitate to make a decision.

During my many conversations with General Davis, he often spoke of Eddie Craig, an officer who he admired greatly. Craig had been his brigade commander on Guam after the war. I had the pleasure of meeting Lieutenant General Edward A. "Eddie" Craig when he was in his mid-eighties and well into his third decade of retirement. He shared the hospitality of his home with me, and I soon became captivated by his self-effacing account of service in what, for me, was the "Old Corps." One story illustrated the tremendous gulf between his generation and today's politically correct military. Assigned to an outlying post in Nicaragua—miles from nowhere—in the mid-1920s, Craig had an up-close and personal confrontation with a local tough. One afternoon, a hysterically distraught native ran up to him, bleeding severely from a head wound—a missing ear—and pointed out his assailant. Craig shoved his .45-caliber service automatic into his belt and confronted the desperado, who without even a "by your leave," grabbed the pistol and tried to wrestle it away. As the two struggled, Craig yelled for help. His platoon sergeant rushed over, grabbed the goon in a headlock, forced his own pistol into the miscreant's face, and pulled the trigger—no Miranda warning, no attempt to disable, just a quick and final solution. Craig went on to higher command, serving with distinction in World War II and Korea.

Craig introduced me to his old friend and mentor, General Lemuel C. Shepherd, the retired twentieth Commandant of the Marine Corps. As my guest, Shepherd attended a meeting of my junior officers at the San Diego Officer's Club. At the time, he was suffering a host of physical aliments and was somewhat infirm. He struggled up the steps of the club—and I overheard a young officer whisper callously, "Who the hell is that old man?" Shepherd invited the officers to sit down and within minutes totally captivated them with his articulate grasp of military subjects and lucid conversation. "General, what was the worst thing you faced in your forty-two years of service?" one young officer asked. Shepherd did not miss a beat, "Machine guns at Belleau Wood," he answered, referring to the famous World War I battle. There was stunned silence. The officers stared at the old man with a new respect. He was the living embodiment of a Marine Corps legend, for Belleau Wood was synonymous with Marine valor and sacrifice.

General Shepherd shared other experiences with me. He talked of serving under General Roy S. Geiger, the only Marine to ever command an American field army, the Tenth Army on Okinawa in 1945. Shepherd commanded the 6th Marine Division during that hellish campaign. He spoke highly of Geiger's combat leadership, particularly his penchant for visiting the front lines. Shepherd related a humorous story of one such visit. Geiger nonchalantly walked up on a squad of Marines lying prone on the ground in a furious firefight with the Japanese on the next ridge. Almost immediately one Marine shouted, "Get down, you old fool! Do you want to get us all killed?" Geiger sheepishly replied, "Sorry son," turned and sauntered away. Shepherd chuckled as he told me the story.

One morning in the 3rd Marine Division command post (CP) at Dong Ha, General Davis held up a list of officers who were slated for Vietnam duty. "Have you seen this, Dick?" he asked, pointing to a name—Colonel Robert H. Barrow. Barrow was scheduled for assignment to the 1st Marine Division, and General Davis was upset. "He is a fine officer, and I want him." Within days, I noted that Colonel Barrow's orders had been changed; he was now slated for the 3rd Marine Division. Davis assigned him to the 9th Marine Regiment, which Barrow led in Operation Dewey Canyon, one of the most successful operations of the Vietnam War. Barrow went on to become the twenty-seventh Commandant of the Marine Corps in the early 1980s.

Leatherneck Legends: Conversations with the Marine Corps' Old Breed describes the professional relationships among five analogous leaders— Geiger, Shepherd, Craig, Davis, and Barrow—whose collective service spanned the world wars, a host of brush-fire skirmishes, and two bloody, indecisive regional conflicts—Korea and Vietnam. It is an account of gut-level combat leadership—the "lead, follow, or get the hell out of the way" moxie that separates the men from the boys. It is the set-the-example personal leadership that inspires men to assault through murderous German machine gun fire at Belleau Wood, charge across the black sand of Iwo Jima, or fight out of a Chinese trap, against impossible odds, in the dead of a North Korean winter. Above all, it is a story about honor and devotion to duty, as exemplified by the motto of the United States Marine Corps: Semper Fidelis, Always Faithful.

PART ONE

THE WAR
TO END
ALL WARS

CHAPTER ONE

FIRST TO FIGHT

Lem Shepherd

In the spring of 1917, Virginia Military Institute (VMI) was rife with talk of war. Many of the graduating class began to think about applying for a commission in the army. Cadet Private First Class Lemuel C. Shepherd was no exception, although earlier Shepherd had not been particularly interested in pursuing a military career. (Following his freshman or "rat year," Cadet Shepherd had been promoted to the rank of corporal but was reduced to private first class the following year. "I had a little fracas with some fire crackers we set off on New Year's Eve. I was caught and busted.") "I went to see the commandant, Colonel Hodges, and told him, 'I would like to apply for one of the army commissions.' Hodges was sympathetic but told me, 'I'm terribly sorry, Mr. Shepherd. I'd like very much to recommend you . . . but I just gave away the last one of the ten appointments to the army a couple days ago.' " Disappointed, Shepherd blurted out, "What about the Marine Corps?" A year earlier, Major General Commandant George Barnett had visited VMI and made a lasting impression on the young cadet. "General Barnett wore his full-dress uniform and had a very snappy aide-de-camp with him," Shepherd related many decades later. "I grew up in Norfolk and knew that Marines served with the navy, but I had never seen them looking like that. I was keen on the idea of serving aboard ship." Unfortunately, those commissions were also gone, but Hodges held out some hope that the services' rapid expansion might generate additional openings.

On April 6, 1917, Congress declared that a state of war existed between the United States and the Imperial German government. A month and a half later, the size of the Marine Corps doubled. Shepherd's opportunity arrived. "I typed up a letter requesting an appointment to the Marine Corps and went over to the superintendent at one o'clock in the afternoon, to deliver it in person to General [Edward W.] Nichols." All the commissions were gone again, but Shepherd knew that two of the vacancies had been taken by cadets who were not physically qualified. "Could I apply as an alternate?" he asked. The superintendent promised to recommend him and sent a telegram to the commandant requesting an appointment. When the word got around that Shepherd had applied, ten of his fellow classmates followed his example, including one of his roommates, Fielding S. Robinson, who later became an aide-de-camp to the Marine brigade commander in France, Major General James G. Harbord, U.S. Army.

Within days, they received orders to appear before an examining board in Washington. Shepherd remembered, "A dozen of us went down to Lynchburg to catch the midnight train. I didn't have any money, so I had to borrow the price of the ticket. Well, the train was crowded and we had to stand up all the way, which was a pretty good piece. I was a young fellow then and could take it, but it was tiring standing up on this train for six hours. There were six or eight of us, I think, in the group. When we arrived in Washington the next morning, we went down on Pennsylvania Avenue to a hotel, rented a room, washed up, shaved, and reported at nine o'clock for examination. We reported to Colonel Doyen, who was the commanding officer of the barracks at the time and was the president of the examining board."

The young "gentlemen" were turned over to navy Captain "Bobo" Dessez, the senior member of the medical examining board. "He was a rough, gruff old seagoing bull surgeon . . . quite a big fellow." Shepherd was concerned about passing. "I was underweight because I think the minimum requirement was 135 for my height and I only weighed 123 pounds. I ran on the track team and I was pretty thin in those days. After he looked us over, he took our blood pressure and then said to me, 'Get down over there and stick up your ass. Have you ever had a dose of the clap?' he asked, examining my posterior. 'No sir,' I replied rather indignantly. 'Turn around,' he ordered brusquely, ignoring my response. 'Have your ever had piles?'

'No, sir.' 'You pass,' he barked." After completing the perfunctory examination, the students appeared before Colonel Charles A. Doyen, USMC, the president of the board. He swore them in as reserve second lieutenants, just four days after war was declared. Shepherd and his classmates accepted reserve commissions because regular commissions would have taken several months to be approved.

Even though they were newly commissioned Marine officers, they still only ranked as cadets at VMI. This imbalance lasted only a few days. In the third week of April, the superintendent received a telegram from the Marine Corps asking him to graduate the new officers as soon as possible, "We need their services," it said. On May 3, 1917, they received diplomas, two months ahead of the rest of their classmates. "The date stuck in my mind," Shepherd recalled, "because it was on that day, May 3, 1863, that Stonewall Jackson made his great flanking march at Chancellorsville. Just before the attack, Jackson remarked, "I see a number of my commanders are VMI men. VMI will be heard from today." From my cadet days, Stonewall Jackson was my great hero, and I've always felt that VMI would be heard from by those of us who graduated on the third of May and went into the services." Two weeks later, they reported to the Officers School of Application, Parris Island, South Carolina, to begin training.

Parris Island, an insect-infested spit of swampland near Beaufort, was an isolated outpost that could be reached only by boat. One private commented: "I thought they had landed us on an island for the insane, but later I was told it was the old quarantine camp." "PI," as it was called by generations of Marines, was one of four officer-training facilities in 1917. Two were located in California—Mare Island and San Diego—and another at the Marine Corps rifle range at Winthrop, Maryland.

Instruction included infantry drill regulations, bayonet training, bombing (hand grenades), minor tactics, military engineering, administration, military law, lectures on poison gas and sea duty, and a two-week practical course on the rifle range. Shepherd was just beginning the second week on the range when his class of officers was ordered to report to the commanding officer. "We've just gotten a request from the Commandant asking for volunteers to join the 5th Marines (Fifth Marine Regiment)." Shepherd immediately volunteered, along with two friends. "We thought, *Well, maybe we can get out of here; Parris Island was a deadly place. Let's get out of here and go down to Santo Domingo along with our buddies.*" Several VMI classmates had already sailed for the tropics. They told him that duty there was a good deal. "None of us knew where we were going, but we were glad to receive our orders and be on our way to join a regiment."

Shepherd's request was granted, and he immediately caught the train north, with a short stopover in Norfolk to see his family. Before leaving Parris Island, he picked up his uniforms from the tailor and was able for the first time to wear the officer's khaki blouse and trousers. Initially Shepherd and the other newly minted Marine officers had to make do with blue, enlisted men's uniforms. "Our uniforms were supposed to have been delivered upon [our VMI] graduation, but since we had been graduated ahead of the scheduled time, our tailor had not completed them. We just had to take what was issued to the men and put officer's hat cord on our campaign hats. Second lieutenants wore no rank insignia in those days." When he visited his grandmother, a grand old southern lady who had suffered greatly during the "War of Northern Aggression." As he stood in her parlor, she looked closely at him and said, "Well, my grandson, I'm so pleased that you came to see me before you go off to war. But I'm further delighted that you wore your khaki rather than your blue uniform. You know, I never want to see a son of mine wearing a Yankee blue uniform." With that guidance in mind, Shepherd and two other volunteers made their way to Philadelphia, where the 5th Marines were being mustered.

They were assigned to the 2nd Battalion, commanded by the eccentric Major Frederic May "Fritz" Wise, the nemesis of junior officers. General Julian Smith, who had received his appointment as a second lieutenant in January 1909 and went on to command the 2nd Marine Division at Tarawa during World War II, described Major Wise as "a queer combination of ability and hard-headedness. I described him once as a very even-tempered man who was mad all the time. He was always rough on his men." The battalion consisted of four companies: the 43rd (Captain Joseph D. Murray), 51st (Captain Lloyd W. Williams), 55th (Captain Henry M. Butler), and the 23rd Machine Gun Company (Captain George H. Osterhout, Jr.). The new officers soon learned that he was a hard taskmaster, who ruled with an iron fist. "Wise was an old-time Marine," Shepherd recounted. "He entered the Corps before the turn of the century and saw his first action during the Boxer Rebellion." Wise was proud of his ties with the old Marine Corps. "We lived hard, drank hard, and fought hard—there are damned few of us left." Behind his back, the junior officers called him "Fritz" because of his authoritarian, Prussian-style leadership. Wise was unrepentant. "No doubt my ancestry was questioned many times but I was getting my battalion ready for war; in that game no excuses could be accepted." One story about his callousness involved a troublesome Marine who passed away. At his funeral, Wise is reported to have ordered the band to play "He Was Always in the Way." "We entered the service under martinets," Wise expounded. "They accepted no excuses. They required results. They left their mark on us."

Second Lieutenant Shepherd was assigned to the 4th Platoon, 55th Company, and immediately began the process of absorbing the recruits who had swarmed into the recruiting stations under the banner "First to Fight." In those days a Marine infantry company was organized with 8 men in a squad, six squads to a platoon (and several file closers and guides bringing platoon strength to 52 men), four platoons per company, along with a company headquarters section that brought the company's muster total to 250 men. Shepherd recalled: "I stayed up all the first night issuing uniforms to men joining the company. Everything was in confusion. Recruits and old timers were pouring in. . . . Our company was brought up from less than 100 men to 250 men, during a period of a few days. It was quite a job assimilating them."

Many of the recruits were from socially prominent Philadelphia families, who enlisted as privates in the 55th Company. Shepherd called them the "Racket Clubbers," because they were all members of the celebrated Philadelphia Racket Club, which only the prominent families could join. "All Philadelphia seemed headed to the [Navy]Yard," Wise recalled. "My principal job for a couple of weeks was getting the families of those recruits in to see them." Later, in France, Shepherd would have to censor their mail. "I recalled one of them writing, 'Take my Stutz out for exercise.'" Wise turned them over to one of his old-line sergeants. "Put them through the mill," he ordered. "If there's anything in them, I intend to make officers out of them."

Call to the Colors

Educationally, they were not so far out of line with thousands of others who answered the call to the colors. Brigadier General Albertus W. Catlin, former commanding officer of the 6th Marines, wrote, "Sixty percent of the entire regiment—mark this—sixty percent of them were college men. Two-thirds of one entire company came straight from the University of Minnesota." Wise remembered that "They came from universities and clubs, from factories and farms, from garages and shops. Every phase of American life was represented, and all of the best."

The Marine Corps recruiters bulletin for 1918 trumpeted, "Harvard's Football Captain a Marine." Harvard's great Eddie Mahon was accepted for enlistment in the Marine Corps on June 27 in Boston. Mahon led Harvard's eleven against Yale in 1915 and delivered the "Bull Dog" its biggest walloping.

"Crack Yale Athletes Join Marine Corps," proclaimed another headline. "Five of Yale's leading athletes, of whom four captained the Yale teams, are today enrolled for service with the Marines. They are Harry Le Gore, the baseball captain and football star; Holcomb York, of the hockey team; Louis Ferguson, who captained one of Yale's best swimming teams; and Johnny Overton [who was killed in action on July 19, 1918], the track and cross-country team captain and cross-country inter-collegiate champion. All four will receive temporary commissions. Rex Hutchinson, the football center and baseball outfielder, has also joined the Marine Corps."

Enlistment standards required that an applicant "be not less than five feet five inches, nor more than six feet two inches in height; weigh not less than 130 pounds." The standards also prescribed "not less than 18 nor more than 36 years of age; able to speak, read, and write the English language with ease; native born or naturalized citizen of the United States; steady and regular habits; unmarried, with no one wholly dependent upon him for support; of good health, strong constitution, well formed, sound as to senses and limbs, and not addicted to the use of intoxicants or drugs." The new recruits were eager to learn and quickly adjusted, albeit with some degree of trepidation, to the hard-core training methods of the veteran non-commissioned officers. Private Malcolm D. Aitken wrote: "The first day at camp I was afraid that I was going to die. The next two weeks my sole fear was that

I wasn't going to die. And after that, I knew that I'd never die because I'd become so hard that nothing could kill me."

The primary recruit training depots were located at Mare Island, California, and Parris Island, South Carolina. Recruits received at least eight weeks of preliminary training that qualified them for general service. Two of those weeks were spent on the rifle range learning to shoot the bolt-action 1903 Springfield rifle, the Corps' raison d'être. Private Roland Rogers wrote: "Next week we go on the rifle range, and believe me, I am going into it for all there is in me because it means a whole lot to a person if they qualify as an expert rifleman." Upon graduation, they were sent to the Overseas Depot at Quantico, Virginia, for advanced training before shipping out to France. The recruiting effort was so successful that Major General Commandant George Barnett stopped appointing officers from civilian life and instead, filled the officer corps from the ranks. The officer in charge of recruiting was directed to deliver a personal message from the Major General Commandant to the recruiting service: "All officers and enlisted men on recruiting duty are to be congratulated for their zeal. I am well pleased with the results of your efforts." The same officer alerted them that the offices would be shut down for ten days because they had reached their quotas.

The newly minted Marines were joined by several hundred veterans who were brought back from Haiti, Cuba, and Santo Domingo. Wise told his officers: "I don't want a man who has the slightest thing wrong," and they quickly stripped away the sick, lame, and lazy. Many older noncoms were left behind, but those who remained taught the newcomers how to be Marines, including the young officers. Wise relented for one old timer. "He waylaid me in the Yard one day. 'I hear, sor, that you're not goin' t' take me t' France,' he said. 'That's right,' I replied. 'There's room in France for both av us, sor,' he assured me. He was forty-seven, but he was *some* man."

Lem Shepherd

Less than a week after reporting for duty, Shepherd received startling news: "We [were] going on an expedition, but we didn't know where the hell we were going. Everything was in confusion." The transport USS *Hancock* arrived on the night of June 13 and immediately began embarking troops and equipment. The docks were a frenzy of activity as frantic quartermasters struggled to meet her morning sailing deadline. Late the next day she entered New York harbor and dropped anchor for several days, while a convoy formed up, exemplifying the old military adage "Hurry up and wait!" To add insult to injury, the *Hancock* was too slow and was not going with the first convoy. The regiment was ordered to transfer to the newly commissioned USS *Henderson*, named after the Corps' fifth commandant, General Archibald Henderson. Shepherd found out that he would not be joining his friends in the tropics. He was headed for the battlefields of France.

"Transportation Has Been Arranged"

The fact that Marines were going to France at all was solely due to the unremitting effort of Major General Commandant George Barnett, who launched a personal campaign to convince Secretary of War Newton D. Baker to use Marines. Barnett recalled: "We had used the slogan 'First to Fight' on our [recruiting] posters, and I didn't want that slogan made ridiculous." Despite a shortage of trained men, the army did not want Marines and dredged up phony roadblocks, which in the cold light of day proved to be groundless.

Barnett, a socially prominent Washington insider, enlisted the aid of the president. Woodrow Wilson ordered the secretary of war, "in pursuance of the authority vested in me by law," to "issue the necessary orders detaching for service with the army a force of Marines to be known as the 5th Regiment of Marines." The secretary penned a note to Barnett with one last ploy. "I am sorry to have to tell you that it will be utterly impossible for the War Department to furnish transportation for a Marine regiment with the first outfit sailing . . ." Nevertheless, General Barnett had an ace up his sleeve. A friend, Admiral W. S. Benson, Chief of Naval Operations, had "reserved" three navy transports for the Marines. Barnett wrote Secretary Baker rather tongue in cheek: "Please give yourself no further trouble in this matter, as transportation for the Marines has been arranged." Years later, Shepherd acknowledged the commandant's role. "General Barnett deserves great credit for getting the Marines to France, because the army fought it tooth and nail."

Shepherd led his heavily laden platoon up the *Henderson*'s gangway and followed guides to the berthing compartments. Encumbered with rifles, heavy marching order, and web gear, they struggled to negotiate the narrow, twisting passageways. Equipment caught on bulkhead projections, men tripped on the unfamiliar deck, and tempers grew short. For the unwary, hatch coamings (openings between sections of the ship) offered their own brand of torture. The new men who did not duck collided with the steel and found themselves flat on their backs, nursing sore heads and bruised egos. The physical exertion and the heat below decks caused them to break out in sweat, soaking their uniforms and causing even more discomfort. Somehow or other the troops were embarked and supplies loaded and stowed in the holds. Shepherd heaved a sigh of relief after getting his platoon safely aboard. "By God, that really was something, but we did it!"

The newly embarked Marines were faced not only with a new environment but also with an entirely new jargon: deck (floor), overhead (ceiling), ladder (stairway), passageway (hallway), head (toilet), galley (kitchen). They learned other navy traditions about whose origins they neither knew nor cared. The youngsters became the subject of harmless, time-honored pranks, played on them by old sea dogs. The very newness of the adventure, going off to war, made it exciting and somehow strangely romantic.

The *Henderson* got underway on June 14 in a consort with five other ships. The convoy had hardly left port when they discovered *Henderson* was a long way from being ready for an Atlantic crossing. Nothing seemed to work. "The drinking fountains wouldn't function. The green crew didn't know how to operate the oil-burning ranges in the galley; there were no gaskets for the hatches and the steering gear broke," Major Wise lamented. Shepherd had to stand watch in the rudder compartment "to hand-steer the ship when the mechanical transmission didn't work."

The weather was good, but even so, many of the newly embarked Marines were victims of *mal de mare*. Private Carl Brannen wrote that "We were stuffed in like sardines, but I happened to get a hammock hung from the overhead. I got seasick the first day by the time we were out of sight of land down Delaware Bay, and remained sick and miserable the entire thirteen days crossing." The sight of so many landlubbers hanging over the rail gave the old salts an excuse to taunt the "dying" men with visions of pork fat, bacon, and other mouth-watering delicacies. Despite misgivings about surviving, most of the men recovered within a day or two. Shepherd used the time wisely, organizing his platoon and teaching them the new drill. "Because we were attached to the army, we were ordered to change the drill. Fortunately, having been to VMI, I was an expert so it was not difficult."

Three days off the coast of France, American destroyers arrived to escort the convoy through the German submarine zone. Shepherd was assigned lookout duty and took a turn on a gun crew. "It was a very tense time." A hundred miles off the coast, two German U-boats were spotted, but didn't attack. The next day they docked at St.-Nazaire; it was June 27, 1917. Shepherd looked back on his short time in the Corps. "I graduated from VMI on the third of May, reported to Parris Island for duty on the nineteenth, and landed in France with a platoon of Marines on the twenty-seventh of June—all within a period of two months. That's moving!"

Upon arrival, Shepherd was assigned to go ashore and set up camp for the entire regiment. "I never laid out a camp before but I had a couple of good non-coms and we went to work staking out a camp site. When I arrived at the camp site, I found all the canvas dumped on the ground. We had to get the tents erected between nine o'clock in the morning and three o'clock in the afternoon. We got the camp laid out pretty well, although I had never done anything like it before. It just shows what you can do when you have to. By the time the regiment disembarked, we had completed the job and had erected some of the tents."

CHAPTER TWO

JE SUIS AMERICAIN

Second Lieutenant Shepherd listened intently as the highly decorated *chasseur* officer shouted passionately in French, "En avant, tourjours en avant," and then repeated the phrase in heavily accented English—"forward, always forward." The French soldier's fierce declaration struck a responsive cord with the young officer, who thought "the Chasseurs had fighting spirit!" The instructor, Major Toussaint, commander of the 115th Battalion Chasseur Alpine Corps, the "Blue Devils," had taken the Marines in tow and was doing his best to prepare them for combat. Shepherd remembered him as a big man, with a blonde mustache and reddish hair. "He was a good soldier, quite a hero that had been decorated a number of times. Toussaint later became one of the top generals in the French army and headed the Ecole de Guerre after the war." The Blue Devils earned their nickname from their dark blue uniform and beret, with its distinctive French horn insignia. They considered themselves a corps d'élite and were very proud of their war record. Shepherd was grateful for the instruction. "None of us had any combat training. All we knew was squads left, squads right, and extended-order formations. The *Landing Force Manual* was our only textbook." Shepherd remembered that "We continued training all that summer with the French Chasseurs. They were fine soldiers. . . ." In 1917, almost 75 percent of Marine enlisted men were in their first year of service; slightly fewer than 10 percent were regulars on a second enlistment. One private wrote, "To have sent us to the front at that time would have been murder; but we were all willing to go. We were woefully ignorant of the basic principles of the soldier."

The battalion spent the entire summer training with the Blue Devils, who paired one of their companies with its American counterpart. "Fritz" Wise related, "Right after breakfast we marched out to the training area, met the French officers, and the day's work began. We dug a series of trenches . . . took up the new method of bayonet fighting . . . [were shown] how to conduct trench raids . . . put through a gas chamber . . . and given a workout with those damnable French Chauchat automatic rifles. [The French Chauchat automatic weapon, which replaced the Marines' Lewis gun, was described as heavy, clumsy, and inaccurate.] The men looked upon the French instructors as gods, for they knew they were being trained by veteran troops." The French trained the Americans in trench warfare, a highly specialized type of operation that evolved after four years of bloody fighting. Lieutenant General Merwin H. Silverthorn, who was an enlisted man in the 5th Marine Regiment when it sailed to France in 1917, described it: "The troops lived underground in what was called dugouts. Those dugouts had to have a circuitous entrance and exit on account of gas. They were hung with burlap curtains with an air space in between, and then in six to eight feet [there was] more burlap curtain that was heavily covered with gas neutralizing chemicals. There were three bands of trenches. There were the front lines. There were what were called the support positions, which would be some miles to the rear; and there were the reserve positions, which would be some miles to the rear of that. They were heavily fortified by barbed wire—two or three bands of barbed wire, each having two or three aprons—and that barbed wire [was] protected by automatic fire; and it [was] also protected by an artillery barrage, which was called a boxed barrage, which literally would come down one hundred meters in front of you and make a wall of steel." Silverthorn described the conditions in the dugouts: "You slept on some type of a frame that had chicken wire for a spring, and there were no mattresses, and you had your blanket. Now, that was the abode of rats also, and the greatest concern was crawling in with rats, because when you got down there, even if you did have a candle, it cast a very dim glow. You would take your blanket and ruffle it up, you see; and you didn't know if some rat had crawled in there or not. I mean these were great big field rats . . . and the air down there didn't have ventilating systems on account of the gas danger. Of course, the men hadn't bathed. They didn't disrobe; they just lay down in their regular clothes. It was the foulest smelling air!"

Shepherd remembered the training included drill, in French—"Adroit par quatre," squad right; "avant," forward march; and "arretez," halt—until the regimental commander found out. "Well, the word got to Colonel Doyen at regimental headquarters, and he stopped this monkey business." Despite the language difficulties, friendships soon developed, helped along by quantities of *vin blanc* or *vin rouge* served in the officer's mess, or out of the bottle in the field.

Many of the Marine officers attended special schools. Shepherd was assigned to the *chef de section*, French platoon commander's school. "Classes started at eight o'clock and went until eleven. Then we'd have a wonderful French lunch (*dejuener*) with wine and often champagne. When the luncheon was over, we'd go over to an old cemetery and sleep among the graves until school started again about two p.m. That was my idea of a good detail!" Despite the laid-back schedule, Shepherd learned a great deal and thought it was a wonderful experience. Training was interrupted when the Blue Devils were ordered back to the trenches. As they left, their band played the "Star-Spangled Banner."

Late in September, Shepherd's platoon boarded troop trains for transport to the Bourmont training area, the headquarters of the U.S. Army's 2nd Division (Regulars), which included the 4th Marine Brigade (5th and 6th Marine Regiments and the 6th Machinegun Battalion), 3rd Brigade (9th and 23rd Infantry Regiments), 2nd Field Artillery Brigade, 2nd Engineer Regiment, and various service troops. It was their first experience with French boxcars, the famous "40 & 8" (40 men, 8 horses). They were unlike their American counterparts. Light and flimsy, they were about fourteen feet long and equipped with a diabolical arrangement of heavy plank seats, which were convenient during the day, but made it absolutely impossible to get any sleep at night. There was not a spot in the car where a man could stretch out flat. The cars did not have air brakes; just large disks the size of dinner plates, which clashed loudly together when the cars bumped.

Half the men were billeted in old, leaky French barracks and the rest in various farm buildings. Major Robert Denig described his experience: "The whole (barracks) floor is muddy and in one place it's six inches deep.

Water is brought in by wagon and is treated with [a] chemical that makes you sick. Hot water can't be had. To take a bath you stand on your trunk and have someone swab you down in ice-cold water. I am covered from head to toe with thick, sticky mud that dries as hard as a brick. There are narrow wooden walkways, called 'duck walks,' throughout the camp. They are very slippery and hard to negotiate, especially when two people meet—one has to give way and that usually means stepping into the knee-deep mud." Private Alfred Schiani lucked out. "My platoon was assigned to the upper part of a barn . . . a gold mine; it was the storage place for cognac." (Schiani, a twenty-year-old private from New York City was awarded the Navy Cross, Distinguished Service Cross, Purple Heart, and the Croix de Guerre.)

Wise shrugged off the winter weather and ran the battalion through the final grind of heavy training. Shepherd remembered: "I got so damn sick of the place. Colonel Wise really put it to us that winter. We were constantly on the alert. Sometimes at night, we were called out without warning to make a hike in sub-zero weather. Around Christmas, we marched to some mock trenches where we spent three days in simulated trench warfare. It was rugged duty but we learned a great deal, and we became tough as nails."

It was during this time that Shepherd found out a little more about his battalion commander. "I personally learned something about Colonel Wise, whom we all regarded as something of an ogre. He normally addressed me as 'Goddam you, Shepherd!' One night when I was OD (officer of the day), I had to break up a fight between some French and American soldiers in a small café. I did this by sending the Americans to their billets. The woman who owned the café accused me of ruining her trade. She got so mad that she fell to the floor and started gnawing on the rung of a chair. We had orders to report anything out of the ordinary to Colonel Wise, so about ten p.m. I went to his quarters. He heard the story, complimented me on my handling of it, then said, 'Sit down; I want to talk to you.' He said it in a friendly way. I had never heard him talk like that and rather hesitantly took the chair he indicated. 'Shepherd, you've been with me some time now and you know I'm considered a martinet. I know that you youngsters fuss because I insist on meticulous obedience of my orders. Some of them seem petty to you—the making up of the bunks to regulation, the correct uniform, my inspecting every rifle in the battalion. One of these days we'll be in combat and the only way we can win is by strict and unqualified obedience of orders. In combat you won't have time to think and deliberate over an order. You will have to execute it immediately without questioning your superior. When we go into battle this battalion will be so trained that there will never be any question about our disobeying an order or not carrying it out to the best of our ability. It was a talk I remembered all my life. It was the only time he ever showed another side to me, the only time he explained that he had a purpose for being the way he was."

CHAPTER THREE

THE BLOODING

The last days of May brought welcome relief for the men of the Marine brigade. Warm weather had finally arrived, giving them an opportunity to shed their long underwear and dry out after an onerous tour of duty in the trenches. They also got a welcome surprise, a rare day off to celebrate Decoration Day, May 30. For most it was a time of rest and relaxation—a relief from the constant training regimen. It was a time to write letters, catch up on sleep, or for a lucky few, a date with a local *jeune fille*. Lem Shepherd was one of the fortunate ones. He had met "an attractive French girl" and had been invited to dinner at her home—along with a host of relatives, who wanted to look him over. In preparation for the big event, he was "squaring away" his best uniform. His former VMI classmate Fielding Robinson was horseback riding with his boss, Brigadier General James Harbord, U.S. Army, the brigade commander. (General Pershing had relieved Brigadier General Charles A. Doyen, USMC, from command of the 4th Marine Brigade due to Doyen's ill health, and replaced him with General Harbord, who had been his, Pershing's, chief of staff.) The assignment caused some consternation among the Marines because Doyen was well liked and considered to be professionally competent. Pershing gave Harbord the assignment with this admonition: "Young man, I'm giving you the best brigade in France—if anything goes wrong, I'll know whom to blame." Upon taking command Harbord was handed a Marine emblem by the two regimental commanders. Much to the delight of the Marines, Harbord immediately pinned it on his uniform. Sergeant Gerald C. Thomas of the 75th Company was stuffing himself with food at the regimental galley after listening to the chaplain deliver a gloomy sermon on "the ultimate sacrifice." Acerbic "Fritz" Wise was in Paris on a three-day pass with his wife, a hospital volunteer. Floyd Gibbons, the flamboyant correspondent for the *Chicago Tribune*, was also in the city, trying to confirm a rumor that a huge German offensive was bearing down on the "City of Lights."

On May 27, a massive German offensive smashed through the French lines. The attack seemed unstoppable. There were not enough British and French reserves to plug the gap. A hurried call went out on the afternoon of May 30 to the inexperienced American 2nd Division: "March to the sound of the guns." A French general worried that *les Americains* could not hold and said as much to Colonel Preston Brown, the 2nd Division chief of staff. Brown indignantly replied, "General, these are American regulars. In a hundred and fifty years they have never been beaten. They will hold!"

Wise and his wife were at a friend's home, when the telephone rang. "My adjutant, Lieutenant James Hennen Legendre, told me, 'We've been ordered up to the front at once. The *camions* [trucks] will be here at five o'clock in the morning.' 'I'll be there,' I told him." Harbord and Robinson had just finished their ride when "A Sergeant hurried toward us with news of orders to move . . . packing started at a furious pace." Shepherd got the word just as he was climbing on a bicycle to go to dinner. "I was told to turn out my platoon and stand by for boarding *camions*. I knew this meant action, otherwise we would have moved by foot. All I could do was send my orderly with a note of apology to my *Marianne*." A messenger found Thomas and told him to report to his platoon commander. "When I reported to Lieutenant David Redford, a hard-bitten little fellow from Rhode Island, he told me to make sure the men drew ammunition and rations. We were moving out—but he didn't know where."

Wise got back just in time. "The bugle sounded 'assembly' and the battalion fell in on the road, alongside the *camions*. Platoon leaders' whistles blew and the men climbed aboard." Second Lieutenant W. B. Jackson, 6th Machine Gun Battalion, wrote in his memoirs, "In the early morning hours the *camions* arrived and we embarked. Nobody seemed to have any idea where we were heading or why. The *camions* were driven by Chinese coolies, two to a truck. They spoke no English, so they couldn't tell us anything." Others recalled that the drivers were Annamites (Indochinese).

Camions were French army trucks that were notorious for being uncomfortable. They held twenty to twenty-five men, who sat on narrow board seats along each side and another in the middle. The wheels were solid rubber, which jostled the men mercilessly on the pothole-filled roads. Long funnels of suffocating dust engulfed the convoys, adding to their misery. In bad weather, a canvas tarp was rigged over the bed to provide some cover from the elements. Merwin Silverthorn remembered, "Of course, there was no place to stow one's gear. Our heavy marching order had to either stay on our lap or you could attempt to wedge it under the seat. There was no place to lie down. The truck was pretty bumpy—at least the road was bumpy. There were no regular stops for any exercise or water or food or anything like that." The *camions* sped along with reckless abandon, scaring [the] hell out their passengers. First Lieutenant Chester H. Fraser of the 18th Company noted, "Lucky if we don't get killed before reaching the front."

The massive fourteen-mile convoy carrying the 2nd Division skirted Paris and haltingly made its way toward the town of Meaux in central France. General Harbord recalled, "Sometimes it seemed difficult to gain a foot of distance. Trains, trucks, wagons, civilian and farm vehicles of every description, all headed from the front, [retreating from the attacking Germans,] would congest and block the road sometimes for half an hour at a time so that movement forward was impossible." It was the first time the Marines had seen the human cost of the war. Wise noted, "The moment we got outside Meaux, I knew that hell had broken loose. It was the first time I had seen civilian refugees in France. They streamed down the road; old and young; in oxcarts, in horse-drawn wagon, on foot. Some of them trudged along pushing baby carriages in which their household belongings were piled and tied with cord. Old men and old women tottered along. Children walked in groups, too terrified even to talk much. Hundreds carried things in their arms or in bundles on their backs. All looked terror stricken."

The battalion reached its destination on the Paris-Metz road, nine miles north and west of Château-Thierry. A signpost by the side of the road pointed to the right—Paris 65 kilometers. The travel-worn, hungry men disembarked and stood by waiting for orders. The Marines had outrun their field ranges. The only thing they had to eat was the food they carried in their packs. Silverthorn described the field rations: "In World War I our food and supply were pretty much [the same as they were] way back [in] Civil War days. A man carried two days' reserve rations in his pack. Those reserve rations consisted of a package of hardtack . . . like a soda cracker about three inches square . . . some raw sugar . . . salt and pepper . . . and then some bacon in a tin. You might have a can of Australian beef, which for some reason not known to me was called 'monkey meat.' It wasn't very palatable."

Wise was standing beside the road when, shortly before noon, the regimental commander, Colonel Wendell C. "Buck" Neville, roared up in a staff car. He jumped out with a map in his hand. Wise peered over Neville's shoulder as the regimental commander traced a line with his finger. He pointed out a spot about one and a half kilometers north of their current position and ordered Wise to form a defensive line from the northeast corner of Veuilly Wood to a point east and south of Les Mares Farm. "You've got to get out there right away. We don't expect the French to stick, and if you don't hurry up, the Germans will get there before you do. And when you get there, you stick! Never mind how many French come through you." Wise asked, "Who'll be supporting my flanks?" Neville replied, "I'll let you know as soon as I know myself." Buck climbed back in his car and roared off. Wise ordered the battalion buglers to "sound assembly."

Wise was told to tie in with the U.S. 23rd Infantry on the left and 6th Marines on the right, but when he moved into position, there was no one there. His one thousand Marines faced the German onslaught alone. Remnants of French units passed through their lines, in full retreat. "La guerre est finie," they cried. Many *poilus* staggered from fatigue, their ragged uniforms and bloody bandages attested to the hard fought delaying action. They stared hollow-eyed at the fresh-faced youngsters in the strange field green uniforms. The French were quiet, too tired to waste energy on needless conversation. It was enough that these strangers were between them and the Germans. One haggard French officer buttonholed Captain Lloyd "Josh" Williams of the 51st Company. He gestured excitedly toward the rear and, in halting English, ordered the Marine captain to retreat. Williams looked him in the eye and quipped, "Retreat, hell. We just got here!"

(Shepherd's battalion commander "Fritz" Wise claimed credit for uttering the famous retort; however, Shepherd discredited that claim: "There was another company commander from Berryville, Virginia, we all loved by the name of Lloyd (Josh) Williams. He was the one who made the famous remark at Belleau Wood[;] when some French officer told him to retreat he said, 'Retreat, hell, we've just arrived, we're not going to retreat.' " Captain Williams' message of 3:10 p.m., June 3, 1918, seems to settle the issue. "The French major gave Captain Corbin written order to fall back. I have countermanded the order. Kindly see that [the] French do not shorten their artillery range." Shepherd, in a letter to the author wrote, "Colonel Wise tells a good story [in his book *A Marine Tells It to You* (New York: J. H. Sears and Co., 1929)], but in several instances he is inaccurate. Wise claimed that he established the line and visited Les Mares Farm on several occasions. I never recall seeing him in the area.")

The battalion moved out—quick time—and less than an hour later reached a narrow dirt road, its designated defense position. From one end to the other, the sector stretched over four kilometers, about two and a half miles. Open ground on their right front gradually sloped upward to a wooded hill (Hill 165) about a half-mile away. Les Mares Farm stood on their left front, while a checkerboard pattern of woods and fields swung away from them on both flanks. The extended frontage forced Wise to place all four companies on line—18th Company on the extreme left, in the northeast corner of the Bois de Veuilly; 43rd Company next in line; 55th Company in and around Les Mares Farm; and the 51st Company on the right flank, south of Hill 142. Lieutenant Colonel Frederick Wise sent this field message: "2/5 in edge of woods at 142 (hill) and 2 companies properly disposed to hold right of line—12 machine guns from 8th machine gun company on 2/5 left—8 machine guns of Summer's company and 4 of Kingman's company on 2/5 right."

Company by company they moved into position, each taking its share of the four-kilometer sector. Company commander Captain John Blanchfield and Shepherd, now executive officer, led the two hundred and fifty men of the 55th Company into a woodline and ordered a halt. The two officers went forward to reconnoiter. As they left the shelter of the trees, a German artillery barrage drove the last French soldiers from the field.

Explosions and bursts of flame marked its steady advance over the scarred terrain. The retreating *poilus* withdrew in good order, each group firing a few rounds before falling back to a new position. The two Americans saw enough and returned to the woods. Shepherd waited impatiently for the order to move forward, but Blanchfield was overwhelmed by the tactical situation. The older man seemed paralyzed with indecision. Finally, he issued a rather vague suggestion, giving Shepherd the authority to advance the company. Captain Blanchfield was a senior sergeant major who had been promoted due to the rapid expansion of the Corps. Shepherd noted that "Blanchfield was probably one of the best old sergeant majors, as far as clerical work was concerned . . . but he didn't have any leadership. He couldn't read a map, and knew little about infantry tactics. Poor old fellow. Modern warfare was just too fast for him."

Shepherd gathered the four platoon commanders, Lieutenants Tillman, Lineham, Waterhouse, and Lyle, gave them a short briefing, and led the company forward, "at the double," to a "very commanding position overlooking the valley on the nose of Hill 183." No sooner had he positioned the platoons than Blanchfield ordered him to fall back. They were too far forward and could not tie in the companies on either flank. Shepherd withdrew the company several hundred yards and ordered the men to dig in around Les Mares Farm, using the red-roofed house and barn as part of the defensive position. The farm stood on "rising ground, dotted with clumps of woods, with grain fields here and there, and tall hedges."

There were no prepared defenses and there was no time to wait for proper entrenching tools. German shells reached out: 77mm "whiz-bangs," which gave about two seconds warning, and 88mm "quick Dicks," which gave no warning at all. Those men who had them broke out small T-handle shovels. Others used anything at hand—bayonets, mess kits, spoons—to dig into the rich farmland. They dug individual foxholes six or seven feet apart along the company's front. Shepherd described the holes as "little scooped-up hollows similar to a grave but about a foot deep, with earth piled up in front for a parapet," behind a barbed-wire fence. One private wrote, "It's amazing how quickly we dug in, considering we had no shovels. All around me I saw my buddies sinking slowly into the ground, while parapets of soft earth grew steadily up beside them. . . . We were grateful that the Heinies hadn't started dropping their nine-inch 'sea bags' on us." All that night and into the next morning, they were heavily shelled. The plaintive cry "hospital man" attested to the accuracy of the German shellfire.

Shepherd carefully studied the ground in the morning light and selected "a little knoll a couple of hundred yards in front of our lines, which I recognized as an important terrain feature. We couldn't include it in our lines because it was a little too far from where we'd been ordered to establish our main line of resistance." (In a letter to the author Shepherd wrote, "As second in command of the 55th Company, I was in charge of the establishment and defense of the battalion's front line to the left of Belleau Wood on June 1, 1918. Our strong point was Les Mares Farm, which was the closest point to Paris that the Germans reached in their May [27th] offensive.") I suggested to Captain Blanchfield that we ought to put an outpost out there, because of its good field of fire and observation." Blanchfield concurred, and Shepherd led two squads, fourteen men under a sergeant, to the outpost and positioned them with orders to "Hold their fire until the enemy was close and then open fire. When the Germans got too close, the men were to withdraw to our lines."

Later in the afternoon, Shepherd grew concerned about the men in the outpost as the German barrage increased, signaling an infantry assault. The outpost was isolated and could get cut off. He went to Blanchfield and requested to check the small detachment. "John, I'm worried about that outpost. I sent them out there and I think I ought to check them. Don't you think I'd better go back and look after that outpost?" Blanchfield quickly approved. "I must say it was a foolish suggestion," Shepherd recalled, "because they had orders to withdraw but I just wanted to go out there to insure they did." A rolling barrage blanketed the Marine positions with deadly shrapnel. Shepherd nodded to his runner, Private First Class Pat Martin, and said casually, "Let's go," belying the fear he felt. They had just started when "a shell landed about ten feet in front of me. I'll always recall it to my dying day; the dirt flew up and I just stood there waiting for the shell to go off. Thank God it was a dud!" Somehow, the two made it to the outpost just in time to hear the sergeant shout, "Here come the Boches!" The Germans were advancing toward them, only a few hundred yards away.

Blanchfield sent a message to Wise: "55th Company reports enemy advanced about 2 KM in S.E. direction."

The outpost was on the forward slope of the knoll where they had good fields of fire. The small group of Marines took the enemy formation under fire with their Springfield '03 rifles. They picked off the enemy scouts and then concentrated on the Germans in the first assault wave. Their accurate rifle fire halted the advance but exposed their position. Soon a hail of German machine gun fire blanketed the knoll. Shepherd took cover behind the brow of the mound, where he could observe the action. "There were several trees on top of the knoll and I leaned against one of them where I could look over the top and direct the men's fire. All of a sudden something hit me in the neck and spun me completely around. My first thought was, *My God, a bullet's gone through my gullet!* I was gulping air— funny what you do. I spit in my hand to see if I was spitting blood but I wasn't, so I felt relieved. A bullet cut a groove through my neck and just missed my jugular vein. Another quarter of an inch and I'd be dead."

(A year later, Shepherd returned to the exact spot and found the tree that he had been leaning against. "I found it without difficulty as it was the only one on the knoll. The tree was about a foot in diameter and there, in that tree, at the height of my head, I found seven bullet holes. Evidently what had happened was that the Germans had worked up a machine gun up to where it could fire on this outpost. I've always figured that the first bullet must have hit my neck and spun me around, out of the line of fire of the other bullets. There were seven bullet holes in this tree in a space of eighteen inches at the height of my head. Apparently the first bullet swung me out of the line of fire of the next burst, which hit the tree I was leaning against."

Despite the heavy enemy fire, Shepherd's small detachment held the position until dusk. When the Germans started encircling the position, Shepherd pulled the men out in the gathering darkness. They made it back safely, bringing out two wounded. Shepherd accompanied them to the aid station, where he had his own wound dressed. The corpsmen wanted to evacuate him. "Hell no, it isn't bad," he told them and rejoined his company. Shepherd's hometown newspaper headline proclaimed, "Fought 4 days with bullet in his neck, Lieut. Lemuel C. Shepherd, of Norfolk, proves himself a fighter."

The German advance was an arrow aimed directly at Les Mares Farm. Shepherd said, "It was a key position, as we realized, and all we had was a thin red line of Marines, with a man about every ten feet apart. A Marine with a rifle, that's all in the hell we had, but we held our lines." The brigade commander sent a stand-and-hold message: "General Harbord directs that the necessary steps be taken to hold our present positions at *all costs*." German infantry of the 460th Regiment advanced ever closer—five hundred, four hundred, three hundred yards—until they were within one hundred yards of the hastily dug foxholes, where highly trained riflemen waited for the order to fire. The Marines sighted in, each one carefully aligning the front sight blade of his '03 rifle on the target's center of mass—a German chest. Elton E. Mackin recalled the German advance in his memoir *Suddenly We Didn't Want to Die*. "Experimentally, [each Marine] raised his rifle to cover one of those forms. When glimpsed through the small aperture of a peep sight they were nearly identical in outline, the chest-high figures of men, their heads and shoulders rising above the flood of waving grain through which they came." Hours and hours of practice on the rifle range had made them marksmen, but the targets had been paper; now the silhouettes in front of them were flesh and blood. Mackin continued, "Target—the half-drawn breath—a finger pressure—recoil. The German staggered and seemed to sag suddenly, wearily, so close that one could see the shock of dumb surprise on his face."

Wise watched from his post of command (PC): "A long way off over those grain fields I could see thin lines of infantry advancing. It wasn't the mass formation I had expected to see after what I had heard of German attacks. Those lines were well extended. At least six or seven paces of open space were between the men. There seemed to be four or five lines, about twenty-five yards apart. They wore the 'coal-scuttle' helmet. Their rifles, bayonets fixed, were at the ready." "Suddenly," Wise continued, "when the German front line was about a hundred yards from us, we opened up. Up and down the line I could see my men working their rifle bolts. I looked for the front line of Germans. There wasn't any!" The deadly accurate rifle fire stopped the attackers in their tracks. "The Boches fell by the scores there among the wheat and the poppies." The extraordinarily stiff resistance was entirely unexpected by the Germans, who were flushed with victory after having thoroughly trounced the French. They expected it to be a cakewalk to Paris. The first two German waves made repeated attempts to close with the Marines, but every time they came within range, deadly rifle fire forced them back. Dead and wounded carpeted the ground, attesting to the accuracy of the sharpshooters. The third wave withdrew, unwilling to cross the field of death. This unexpected setback caused the enemy to stop, consolidate their positions, and bring up reserves. The riflemen of the Marine brigade had stopped the German offensive. Shepherd observed, "The French, who were in support of the Fifth and at one time thrown into the line, could not, and cannot today, grasp the rifle fire of the men [Marines]. That men should fire deliberately and use their sights, and adjust their range, was beyond their experience."

Shepherd was very concerned about a three-hundred-yard gap "between our company and the next battalion in line. . . . Beyond Les Mares Farm there was a vacant space of several hundred yards between our company and the next battalion in line. . . . The French had been withdrawing through our lines." As the hard-pressed French withdrew, one of their commanders reported to Shepherd. "They were colonial troops, in khaki uniforms. I assigned them to fill in the gap on our left." Just as the Germans started their attack, Shepherd tried to find the French platoon. "I went over to a few trees that were standing on the other side of the farm and looked around, but I couldn't find the French. The Germans opened fire, so I jumped behind a tree, just as the damned missing French platoon started firing. They had withdrawn a couple of hundred yards and now bullets were coming from both directions. There I was, jumping from one side of the tree to the other, trying to keep from getting hit. It was a real hot spot!" Suddenly, his orderly yelped and jerked convulsively. A French bullet had hit him in the foot, shattering the bones and making it impossible for him to walk. Shepherd half-carried the wounded private to a front-line aid station before returning to the company.

Upon returning, Shepherd learned that several grey-coated figures had been spotted creeping through the waist-high wheat. He placed snipers on top of a haystack to pick off the German infiltrators. "The wheat in the field to their front was waist-high, but we could see the Germans moving in the wheat." Shepherd sent out half a dozen men under Gunnery Sergeant

David L. Buford. "Our patrol surprised the German patrol and killed about a dozen of them. Sergeant Buford, who was a wonderful pistol shot, killed seven Germans alone with his automatic. That stopped the infiltration in this area." During the night, a detachment of machine gunners joined the battalion, driving off the enemy gunners. German artillery fire blanketed the farm, causing several casualties and setting one building on fire before American counterbattery fire silenced the enemy gunners.

Shepherd saw them "working around to the left of Les Mares Farm" and called in an artillery barrage. "We'd been impressed with how many hundred thousands of dollars it cost to put down an artillery barrage, so everybody was loath about calling for one, but I said to myself, 'This is the time we really need artillery fire,' and in a few minutes our artillery shells were falling on the advancing enemy."

Major Frank E. Evans of the 6th Marine Regiment wrote the Major General Commandant: "The Fifth bore the brunt of it, and on our left the men raked the woods and ravines to stop the Boche at his favorite trick of infiltrating through. The next day Wise's outfit pulled a spectacular stunt in broad daylight. They spotted a machine gun out front, called in a barrage, swept out behind it, killed and wounded every man in the crew, and disabled the gun."

CHAPTER FOUR

MACHINE GUNS IN THE WHEAT

On the evening of June 6, the company received orders to join the battalion and take up reserve positions in the woods northwest of Lucy. During the move they were spotted by German balloon observers who called in artillery fire. "Gas!" someone shouted. The cry was taken up by others and echoed up and down the Marine lines. A choking cloud of yellowish gas billowed from the exploding shells. Years afterward in an oral history interview Lieutenant General Louis B. Jones related an early morning, four-hour German barrage that rained seven thousand gas shells on his position. Thirty-three men were killed and most of the rest of the company was hospitalized. "I did not know for sure they were gas shells, but when they hit with a thud and no detonation, my fears were confirmed. Soon I smelled the gas, and I gave the alarm to the men, and they put on their masks. By this time there was a steady stream of incoming shells—gas, air bursts, shrapnel, and high explosives." The shells were filled with a liquid, which slowly evaporated, permeating the air with the sharp smell of mustard. It quickly covered exposed skin, leaving burn blisters under arms, between the legs, and around the eyes—particularly if the skin was wet with perspiration. The lungs were particularly susceptible, leaving hundreds of men suffering from torturous fits of coughing.

Just before midnight, Wise received orders to take his battalion along the Lucy-Torcy road toward Belleau Wood. Private Schiani was close enough to see Wise in the dim light: "Colonel Wise had a beard now, and smoking a stub of a cigarette, he looked tired, as we all did by now. I can never forget that scene of desperation as events began to unfold." The battalion stumbled along the road. No one knew what they faced. The French reported the woods were unoccupied. However, Second Lieutenant William Eddy, 6th Marines intelligence officer, had led a three-man patrol close to the woods. He reported "considerable activity" in the woods itself and heard the "distinct sound of [a] heavy wagon apparently moving south through the northern half." William Eddy was awarded the Navy Cross for the patrol. He was later severely wounded and invalided out of the Corps; however, he was recalled in 1941 and served with distinction in the OSS.

Wise recalled, "That was the damnedest order I ever got in my life. I was between the devil and the deep blue sea. If I didn't move, I knew I'd catch hell. If I did move, I knew I was going right down into Germany." It was pitch black. The men held onto the man in front to keep from getting lost. They advanced about half a mile between two high banks when the terrain opened up into sloping grain fields, with Belleau Woods on their right flank. "It was still as a graveyard when we started. Too damned peaceful, I told myself." Wise stopped the column and cautiously advanced another two hundred yards. "Suddenly rifle fire broke out on our left. We could see the flashes in the dark. A couple of my men dropped." Wise thought the rifles sounded like '03 Springfields and called out, "What the hell do you mean by shooting into us! We're Americans!" The shooting stopped immediately—it was a company from the 3rd Battalion—but they warned that Germans were in the woods to the right.

German machine gun fire erupted, scything through the wheat, forcing the 55th Company to take cover from the torrent of automatic weapons fire. German mortars soon found the range and added a deadly barrage, blanketing the field with shards of jagged metal. Wise yelled out, "About face to the rear—on the double." Shepherd, near the rear of the column, "wondered what all the firing was about, then we got the word to 'about face to the rear.' We had been taught never to do that without saying, 'By whose command?' This word now went all the way back up the line and was answered with, 'By Colonel Wise—we're in the wrong spot.'" The battalion scrambled to get back to cover. Wise ordered Blanchfield to dig in on both sides of the road. Shepherd led his platoon to the left, along the edge of the woods. He could plainly see Germans moving through the vegetation. Suddenly a runner scrambled through the rain of shot and shell with an electrifying message: "Captain Blanchfield's been wounded; you're to take command!" Private Paul Bonner saw the captain fall, right on the road. "I rushed across the road, machine gun bullets whipping the air everywhere, and I made [it to] the captain's side. He was still alive. He was twice my size, but I picked him up and carried him back." Captain Blanchfield did not survive his wound. He was posthumously awarded a Distinguished Service Cross for his actions at Les Mare Farm.

The young officer and his orderly left their shallow foxhole and dashed from cover to cover along the edge of the woods to the command post. Rifle and machine gun bullets snapped overhead. Mortar and artillery rounds exploded, shaking the ground with a tremendous concussion. Suddenly the orderly cried out and went down, a Mauser slug in his leg. Shepherd bent down to help the Marine when something walloped him in the left thigh—"like a kick of a mule. I crumpled in a heap, unable to move, not realizing that I had been hit. I glanced down and what should I see on the ground beside me but the bullet which had struck me." Blood was oozing from his trousers. His little pet dog Kiki, who had loyally followed, was on the ground beside him, his head on Shepherd's leg. He was so quiet Shepherd thought he was dead. "Damn it, they shot little Kiki too, and I picked him up and threw him off my leg—but he jumped up and ran right back to me. I was elated, 'My God, my dog's safe.' "

The two wounded men lay in the road until a Marine from Shepherd's platoon ran out and dragged them to the safety of a ditch. In the confusion, Shepherd never learned his savior's name. A hard-pressed navy hospital man quickly slapped a first aid dressing on his leg wound and signaled a stretcher-bearer team to carry Shepherd to the aid station near Lucy-le-Bocage. Kiki gamely followed along. The station was overrun with casualties, and Shepherd was given only emergency treatment before being placed in an ambulance and transported to Hospital Number One. "The field hospital was in a schoolhouse, and I can remember to this day, there were the French mathematical figures still on the blackboard where the school had been hurriedly dismissed a few days earlier on the approach of the Germans." The pews and desks had been removed and given place to litter racks, each with its blanket-draped litter. A portion of the schoolroom had been partitioned off by means of blankets into a resuscitation ward where the heat from several primus stoves was conserved to the maximum. The remainder of the schoolroom was arranged as a dressing room for the seriously wounded. The church was used as a temporary refuge for the slightly gassed and wounded while awaiting evacuation farther to the rear. Shepherd was placed on a litter and prepared for evacuation. "As I was lying on my stretcher in a church yard, some medical man said, 'You can't take that dog with you.' I replied, 'Either you leave me here, or take my dog.'" The aid man relented and Kiki shared the stretcher.

Shepherd was taken outside and gently loaded into one of a long, seemingly unbroken line of muddy ambulances. The interior of the vehicle held four litters, two above and two below, suspended from hooks. As quickly as it was loaded an orderly motioned to the Annamite (Vietnamese) driver and, with a mashing of gears, the vehicle lurched forward, out of the yard. The solid rubber tires jolted over the rough road. The wounded groaned with pain. Shepherd swore the driver went out of his way to hit every pothole and rough spot. After what seemed to be an eternity, the ambulance reached Red Cross Hospital Number 2 in Paris. "After I had been in this hospital for about ten days my doctor told me one morning, 'We want to send you to another hospital further to the rear, you don't seem to be suffering too badly. We have to make room for the Marines still coming in.'"

Shepherd was still in his disheveled, muddy field uniform, complete with bloodstained trousers and blouse with the collar shot away. The doctor gave him permission to go into the city to buy a new uniform and toilet articles—"if you can walk on crutches." Shepherd assured him that he was an expert—somewhat of a stretch, because he had never been on crutches before! People stared at the strange apparition, as he hobbled along in a bloody, disheveled uniform and helmet, with a leashed dog in tow. As luck would have it, he ran into another officer from his company, who had been gassed. The two decided to extend their liberty and have dinner before turning in. As the night wore on, Shepherd's leg started giving him fits: "I just couldn't stand the pain anymore, so I caught a taxi to the hospital. It was a quarter of a mile from the gate to my tent. I had a heck of a time making it back—I was so faint that I had to stop and lean against the fence every few minutes." He was immediately wheeled into the operation room for emergency surgery. Gangrene had developed in his wound. "When I woke up the next morning I was lying on my back with Dakin's Solution tubes in my leg. I couldn't turn over because they had seven rubber tubes in my wound which had been opened up so the Dakin Solution could drain through and come out the back side where the bullet had gone through. . . . I lay there for three weeks without turning over—in that damn hard bed!"

The French had a big Fourth of July parade and, as a courtesy to the United States, invited a platoon from each battalion of the 2nd Division to participate. Private Douglas C. Mabbott, who was later killed in action at St. Mihiel, described the march: ". . . the morning of the 4th found us parading down the Grand Boulevard, the Champs Élysées . . . with the whole population throwing flowers at us and shouting 'Vive l'Amerique' and 'Vivent les Marines' . . . and to see those fine old grey-haired Frenchmen take off their hat to Old Glory as we passed." Shepherd watched from the curb as the troops marched by. "All of a sudden I looked up and there was my [old] platoon marching by! I was so excited that I jumped up and joined them for about twenty yards on my crutches. That was one of the greatest thrills of my life—to march around the Place de la Concorde at the head of my platoon." Shepherd learned of the terrific fight for Belleau Wood from his men. Later, a French general order renamed Belleau Wood as the *Bois de la Brigade de la Marine*.

In the middle of August, Shepherd rejoined 2nd Platoon, after being released from the hospital. "Soon thereafter we began our night marches toward the zone of action of the 2nd Division for its attack on the St.-Mihiel Salient." The salient, which was crisscrossed with miles of trenches that had been dug by the opposing forces, had been a quiet area since the Germans overran the area at the beginning of the war in 1914. "It was raining and cold, and the wound in my leg bothered me a great deal, as I was not in good physical condition for the long marches we had." Shepherd marched all night long, finally reaching the jump-off position a few minutes before zero hour on September 12, 1918. "I shall always recall the tremendous artillery barrage that preceded the St.-Mihiel attack." Wise described: "Mile after mile the American guns stretched, wheel to wheel, beneath their camouflage netting. Behind them for miles the shells were piled by millions."

Shepherd's platoon "went over the top" with the rest of the battalion into no man's land. "For the first several hours of our attack we crossed these trenches with their barbed wire entanglements. It was about noon before we finally got into the open terrain and could make a substantial advance. By early afternoon the 2d Battalion had reached its chief objective and we dug in for the night." Fortunately, there had been only minor German resistance. Major Robert L. Denig saw things a little differently. "Shells were bursting in front, phosphorus fire blazing on all sides, the edge of the wood was on fire." The next morning the attack resumed, and by noon the battalion had seized its objective, "a terrain feature of strength which overlooked the rolling country to our front," Shepherd recalled. "We organized this position for defense against the anticipated German counterattack but none developed in our sector."

American and German air squadrons ranged over the battlefield, engaging in aerial dogfights that often provided the infantry with a ringside seat. Shepherd observed a German Fokker attacking an American Spad. "The German plane was on the tail of the American. . . . As the German plane circled low to the ground after having shot down the American plane, it passed over our lines only a few hundred feet in the air. Every man in the company began firing at the German plane. It was so low that I fired at it with my pistol. Our concentration of fire was effective and the German plane was brought down on the hillside close to our position. The men in my company jumped out of their foxholes and ran over to where the plane had landed. The pilot was dead, apparently having been hit by our small arms fire. Everyone began taking souvenirs. I took the pilot's blood stained goggles and the altimeter from the plane. I managed to obtain a piece of fabric on which was painted the German Iron Cross and the registered number of the airplane. I sent the plane's number back to the Intelligence Section but kept the portion of the fabric on which was painted the German Iron Cross."

The battalion held the position for several days under heavy German shelling before being relieved and sent to the rear for rest and recuperation.

Replacements arrived, bringing the company up to its authorized strength. The older veterans knew this signaled immediate action. Shepherd prepared his platoon to move out. "On September 29th, the 2d Battalion received an order to 'stand by for *camions*.' At 6:00 p.m. we entrained for a move to the front. About midnight we arrived at the shell-torn village of Somme-Py where we detrucked and were billeted in an old French cantonment nearby." Their billet was within striking distance of their objective, the Blanc Mont Massif, a high plateau that dominated the surrounding terrain.

Shepherd described the sector as a "scene of heavy fighting throughout the war." During 1916 the Germans had strengthened their defenses with a series of concrete emplacements in depth, which they named the "Hindenburg Line." In a letter to his parents Shepherd wrote, "We were up in the Champagne Sector. It is north of [Chalons] and west of the Argonne Forest, which you have probably read about lately—an awful sector, one of the worst on the entire front, so the French say. We were with the 4th French Army under General Gourade [Gouraud]. When the French wouldn't go any further they shoved us in. You know the Second Division, which is mine, is supposed to be the best American division." Shepherd included a German report to back his claim. "Here is an extract found on a German officer, from an order from a higher command. 'You must hold on the right at all costs, as the Second Division Americans is on our left and ground captured by them can never be retaken.' " Marine historian Colonel Robert Heinl described the plateau: "The ground before Blanc Mont was a festering charnel house churned by four years' shelling and putrid with the flotsam of lost divisions: 'a place,' commented one Marine, 'just built for calamities.' " The French had been trying to capture the near impregnable heights for four years. The effort had cost them thousands of casualties.

The night before the attack, Shepherd was called to regimental headquarters. "I was informed by Colonel Logan Feland that my platoon would be temporarily detached from the 2d Battalion and assigned . . . as a liaison unit between the 4th Marine Brigade and the 3rd Army Brigade." General John A. Lejeune, USMC, had succeeded General Harbord in command of the 2nd Division. In planning his attack on Blanc Mont the division's scheme of maneuver called for the 4th Marine Brigade to assault the German position by a frontal attack while the 3rd Army

Brigade executed a flanking attack from the right. This way General Lejeune hoped to bypass a large portion of the German Blanc Mont defenses. Shepherd's mission required him to maintain physical contact with the two units and send back hourly reports on their progress. "I confess that I was unhappy about this assignment as it required my platoon to advance through the center of the German defenses that the two brigades were bypassing." The assignment speaks volumes about Shepherd's professional reputation. Out of thirty-six platoon commanders in the regiment, he was singled out, a mark of achievement.

The attack kicked off with a thunderous artillery barrage, blanketing the frontline German trenches with high explosives. The shelling forced them to remain in their concrete bombproofs as the Marines advanced across no man's land. Shepherd led his platoon into the maelstrom of exploding shells and small arms fire. "Initially I kept fairly close to the zone of action of the 2nd Battalion but could observe in the distance the advancing units of the 3rd Army Brigade. About the middle of the morning when we had advanced beyond the front line of German defenses, I took a squad from my platoon, and we worked our way to the right across the area being bypassed without being shot at and I contacted the commander of the 3rd Army Brigade left flank company." Later in the afternoon, the two brigades established physical contact, ending Shepherd's mission and allowing him to rejoin his company for the final assault.

The 55th Company was on the left of the battalion. Shepherd discovered that its flank was exposed to German attack because "The French unit to our left was nowhere in sight. I therefore assumed the duty, with my platoon, of establishing physical contact with the French." He finally located the errant French unit, and by nightfall it was tied in with the Marines on the crest of Blanc Mont Ridge. It had been a tough day for Shepherd, who said rather laconically, "Operating with my platoon alone in enemy territory was rather a hazardous experience!" The attack continued against heavy German resistance, toward the small village of St. Etienne, north of the ridge. Two days later, the company commander, Captain DeWitt Peck, was wounded and Shepherd took command. Captain Peck went on to have a distinguished career rising to the rank of major general and serving as assistant commandant before he retired in 1945.

Shepherd described the action in a letter home:

Blois, France
Oct. 12, 1918
Dear Ones All,

We cut a salient into the German line and held. And this caused the general retreat in the Rheims sector, thus delivering the famous city from gun fire. In the second day's attack, in which my regiment led, we were only two companies wide. This was a most dangerous position as there were Boche on all sides of us and we were likely to be cut off any time. We held there though, and it was worth it, for the praise we got from Gen. Gourade [Henri Joseph Eugène Gouraud]. He said we had done something wonderful. It sounded fine afterwards, but those were seven awful days we spent in the front lines. If there ever was a hell on earth it was up there. In one attack, in fact, most of the time there were Boche on all four sides of us. The country is full of small trees and shrubbery & they would hide in these with machine guns & when we passed, open up. Our salient was so narrow and with no protection on the sides, they easily filtered in around us, and they gave us all the artillery they had. I never have seen so much. My captain was wounded, but I took the company through all right. We were in a reserve position & another outfit had relieved us, when a shell dropped beside me and laid me out. It's very funny indeed, as I had been through those eight or nine days without even getting touched. Our losses were quite heavy. I was the only officer left in my company and the others had only one or two in each. The enlisted personnel were quite shot up also.

The Blanc Mont attack was costly for the 55th Company. Only 70 enlisted men and 2 officers, Shepherd and Voss, were left of the 250 Marines who started the fight. On October 8, the company lost its two remaining officers. "Lieutenant Voss, the only remaining officer in the 55th Company, and I were standing just in the rear of a crossroads near Blanc Mont . . . when an Austrian 77mm cannon whiz-bang shell hit close by. Fragments tore a hole in Voss' stomach and I was hit by a fragment in the leg. We were both evacuated to an army field hospital where Voss died that night."

Shepherd was still in the hospital when the Armistice was signed. He remained in the hospital until December, when he was transferred to a replacement camp, having turned down the opportunity to go home. In a letter home, he casually mentioned the wound. "Well, I am back in the hospital with another wound, but I was as lucky this time as before, only a piece of shrapnel in my right thigh. It was a small piece and went around the bone not breaking it. The doctor cut through from both sides to clean and get it out, so as soon as this heals up I will be O.K. Please don't worry over me one bit, as I will be all O.K. soon. I won't be laid up over two months at the most." Surely this last sentence was of no small comfort to his mother.

In January 1919, shortly following his release, Shepherd rejoined the 55th Company as its commander on occupational duty on the Rhine. "I had the leading company of the 2nd Battalion, 5th Marines, which was the advance guard. The battalion was ordered to jump off at nine o'clock that night when we received word that the Germans had signed and to return to our billets. You know they wouldn't sign, so we started marching and got up to the border of the occupied zone. This move forced the Germans to sign the Versailles Peace Treaty in 1919."

Six months later he was assigned as the aide-de-camp to Brigadier General Wendell C. "Buck" Neville, the brigade commander. In August, the brigade returned to the United States and was formally disbanded at Quantico. However, the brigade chief of staff, Major Charles D. Barrett, asked Shepherd to return to France. "I think we ought to make a map of Belleau Wood because it is of great historical significance because . . . it's the greatest battle the Marine Corps has ever participated in. If I can arrange to return to France to make a map of Belleau Wood, would you like to go with me?" Shepherd jumped at the chance, even though he had spent only a weekend with his parents, after being gone for more than two years. The project lasted three months, which allowed him to revisit the Marine battlefields. He could see that "the trenches were still there. They were quite obvious because the ground was a chalky soil . . . so everywhere there was a trench dug there was a white line." Belleau Wood proved to be a gruesome experience. Shepherd recalled that "when we were mapping the area, we found the skeletons of a Marine and a German in a well; they still had their uniforms, which identified them. We also found bodies of Marines and Germans in the grass and thickets."

The team completed the project and returned to the United States. According to Shepherd, "The (plaster of Paris) relief map was about sixteen feet square and included all of Belleau Wood and an area of equal size to the west . . . Hill 142 and Les Mares Farm . . . and showed every terrain feature in detail—woods, fields, farms, and individual houses [and a scale of] one inch on the map represented one hundred feet on the ground." The map was displayed in the National Museum and later returned to Quantico for storage.

Shepherd was instrumental in erecting a Marine memorial at Belleau Wood. "I sent out a plea to all officers to contribute a dollar each." The 6th Marines contributed more than $1,500, which funded the noted sculptor Felix de Weldon to design the monument.

CHAPTER FIVE

1ST MARINE AVIATION FORCE

W hen the Marine Brigade had been deployed in France in 1917, the Marine Corps turned its attention to winning approval for its fledging air service to join them. By mid-summer, the Navy Department approved the formation of a Marine air unit of "landplanes" to provide reconnaissance and artillery spotting for the brigade. The unit was designated the 1st Aviation Squadron and established in a new facility at the Marine Flying Field, Miami, Florida. A second unit, the 1st Aeronautic Company, formed at the Naval Air Station (NAS), Cape May, New Jersey, for duty conducting antisubmarine patrols. It deployed in January 1918 to the Azores, becoming the first American flying unit to go overseas. Despite the assignments, one major problem existed: the entire Marine aviation component at the start of the war consisted of just four officers and thirty men. A major recruiting effort was launched, but trained aviators were hard to find.

"Rugged Roy" Geiger

Captain Roy S. Geiger hit upon a novel recruiting approach, which helped solve the problem. He located a small, sandy airstrip on the edge of the Florida Everglades that was owned by the Curtiss Flying School and took it over lock, stock, and barrel. The new facility was redesignated the Marine Flying Field, Miami, Florida. A contemporary account described the field: "Marines are still operating at the temporary field at Miami, living in tents, housing the machines in canvas hangers, which are about to fall down, using a landing field which is made of sand so soft that no grass can be made to grow in it . . . the surrounding country is almost entirely wild and uncultivated, making it possible to land machines in only a very few places. . . ."

After a considerable amount of negotiation and smooth talking, Geiger convinced the instructors to join the Marine Corps as reserve officers. He also succeeded in requisitioning the school's entire complement of ancient Curtiss Jennies, a very welcome addition to his aircraft-starved detachment. Prospective aviators continued to trickle in: U.S. Navy pilots willing to transfer, volunteers from the Marines Officers Candidate School at Quantico—anyone who seemed willing, able, and had a reasonable set of credentials. Lawson Sanderson, an early volunteer, remarked, "Well, hell, I thought I can ride better than I can walk. So, I volunteered for aviation. . . . I'd only seen about two airplanes in my life, but I'd rather ride than walk." Geiger's detachment was joined by the 1st Aviation Squadron from Philadelphia, forming the nucleus of the 1st Aviation Force.

Roy Geiger was a mean go-getter, a man noted for making things happen without fanfare or flamboyance. His father died when he was seven years old. Four years later, he stowed away on a train and spent two months riding the rails around the country. He paid his way through college, and at twenty became the principal of a school. He was a lawyer at twenty-two. Doors were opening and a bright future was in the offing but something seemed to be missing in his life: adventure, a sense of purpose. Abruptly, Geiger gave up this budding career for the life of a Marine. He applied for officer candidate school but was promptly rejected. He had flat feet, a heart murmur, acute eyestrain, and, at 140 pounds, was underweight for his height. Geiger tossed off the rejection. "I guess the Corps considered me more dead than alive." To the absolute amazement of his family, he enlisted as a private on November 2, 1907. A year later he was promoted to corporal, a singular achievement, considering the average time for advancement in those parsimonious days was four years. A short time later, he was selected to attend the Marine Officer School of Application at Parris Island. On February 3, 1909, he was commissioned a second lieutenant.

Early in his career, Geiger earned a reputation as a fun-loving, cocky, energetic officer. His contemporaries nicknamed him "Rugged Roy" for his rough and tumble spirit. However, at times he pushed the envelope. While in officer's training, he was caught out of bounds and placed on restriction. He added insult to injury by having a few "belts" with a couple of enlisted men—a serious offense. A senior officer caught him, and he ended up with ten days "arrested in quarters." Luckily, his reputation escaped relatively unscathed this time, because in those days young officers were allowed a certain degree of latitude. Unfortunately, after being assigned to the USS *Delaware*, he made the mistake of matching, drink for drink, a group of British Royal Marines while visiting their ship. The resulting adverse fitness report cited him as being "unfit for duty from the effects of drink." The report failed to mention that he swam from ship to ship in his skivvies, carrying his uniform over his head. In an interview with the author Geiger's son mentioned that his father dressed upon reaching the ladder to the quarterdeck, climbed up, and rendered a hand salute to the officer of the day, as if it was perfectly natural to swim from one ship to the other. Geiger was a powerful swimmer and at one time had been the Atlantic Fleet champion.

Again, Geiger managed to avoid serious damage to his career because several respected senior officers subsequently gave him favorable reports, helping to rebuild his reputation. He served in a variety of infantry assignments, but his first love was flying. When he was nine, he decided to try his hand at it. He borrowed a pair of feathered turkey wings, wired them to his upper arms, and jumped from the woodshed. He fell like a stone, breaking his arm and bringing his first solo flight to a screeching halt. In March 1916, he reported to Pensacola for a second attempt. The syllabus consisted of two phases, aircraft qualification and ballooning—both of which he found to be dangerous.

The first time Geiger took over the controls of a trainer, he ended up in Pensacola Bay. The plane was a total wreck, but Geiger was not seriously hurt. However, one ballooning incident almost got him killed. At the end of the flight, he selected a cornfield to land on and began to unload ballast to decrease his landing speed. Unknown to him, he dropped a sand bag dead center through the roof of an outhouse. An enraged farmer rushed out, spotted the flying menace, and ran for his shotgun. Geiger, realizing that discretion was the better part of valor, heaved sandbags out as fast as he could. The balloon rose, just as the farmer fired several rounds in his direction. Despite these minor setbacks, Geiger graduated, becoming the fifth Marine Corps aviator and only the forty-ninth naval aviator. Captain Geiger cut a dashing figure, wearing highly polished knee-high boots, leather flying jacket, and riding breeches—a true knight of the air.

With almost eight years of commissioned service at the start of the war, Geiger's seniority allowed him to assume command of Squadron A, one of four in the Miami-based 1st Marine Aviation Force. Major Alfred A. Cunningham, its dynamic leader and first Marine aviator, pushed to get the force to France, despite strong army objections. The army was dead set against Marine aviation and stated publicly that if the Marines got to France, they would only be used to run their training fields. Rebuffed, Cunningham proposed another strategy: conducting bombing operations under the British in Belgium and northern France. His idea was approved, and the unit was designated the Northern Bombing Group, composed of two elements: the Day Wing, consisting of Cunningham's four squadrons, and the Night Wing, manned by U.S. Navy pilots. With a mission and an influx of trainees, Cunningham and Geiger struggled to meet training schedules.

Geiger insisted that his pilots fly every type of aircraft at the field. He believed in hands-on experience and threw the navy training program out the window. One of his pilots, Lieutenant General Francis P. Mulcahy, USMC (ret) recalled, "We didn't get any naval training. Whatever training that went on was on our own . . . in all land planes." Normally, the Jenny took fifty hours of flight time to qualify; however, Geiger instituted an abbreviated schedule. Mulcahy found that "It took us a day, maybe two, I guess, to switch from one kind of plane to another, because we flew everything they had—the N-9, R-6, and even a flying boat they called the 'F-boat.' "

CHAPTER SIX

FLYING COFFINS

I n late May 1918, Geiger's squadron finally acquired the bomber it would take to France. Gruesomely nicknamed the "Flaming Coffin," the DeHavilland DH-4 was a highbred British- and American-designed two-seat biplane. The DH-4 earned its nickname because fire was a constant hazard. The pilot and gunner, seated in tandem, were separated by a sixty-seven-gallon unarmored gasoline tank. In addition, a thirty-gallon auxiliary container was installed in the upper wing above the pilot's head. The exhaust manifolds extended along both sides of the fuselage. A mere teaspoon of gasoline hitting this red hot metal would instantly ignite, setting fire to the plane's highly inflammable, dope-covered fabric covering. One well-aimed tracer into the fuel tanks could literally explode the plane in flight. Even a nasty jolt on landing or a sudden dip or turn during an aerial dogfight could cause the gravity feed to slop over and set the aircraft on fire.

Despite the dangers, the DH-4 became the standard American bomber. It was simple to construct and was easily mass-produced. The DH-4 could reach a top speed of 124 miles per hour, matching or surpassing the speed of most fighters of the day. Geiger set the example by flying dozens of hours in an attempt to dispel any fears his men might have had. Mulcahy remembered, "We got a hold of a DH or two—I don't know how—and we got some familiarization in those. I had a wonderful time during all the time we were there. . . ."

Training had hardly begun, when orders came down alerting them to prepare to ship out. A British liaison officer pronounced them fit for combat. However, one of the Marine pilots remembered it differently. "Our gunnery training had consisted of getting into the rear seat and using a Lewis gun, shooting at targets on the ground. None of us had ever fired a fixed gun in our lives. None of us had ever dropped a bomb in our lives. . . ."

Geiger, a member of the advance party, arrived in France in mid-July and reported to the commanding officer, U.S. Naval Aviation Force. The bulk of the force would not arrive for some weeks, so Geiger wrangled an assignment "for training and combat indoctrination purposes" with the Dunkerque-based 5th Group, Royal Flying Corps. The British were plane rich and pilot poor after years of combat losses. The agreement authorized the temporary transfer of Marine pilots and observers to the group's two squadrons, which flew the British version of the DH-4.

On August 9, the first three crews joined 218 Squadron and participated in bombing raids against German supply dumps and airfields. The fledging Marine pilots came to admire and respect their tutors. Marine Karl Day said the British commander taught him what it means to be an officer and a gentleman. After completing three missions, they were rotated out and replacement crews continued the cycle. In addition, six Marine pilots were continually maintained at the RAF pilots' training pool. The agreement paid dividends by giving the Americans valuable combat experience under the tutelage of veteran aviators. Their British hosts did not show them any special consideration. An American described the grim realities of their combat indoctrination saying, "the newcomers [us] were [always put] last on the right, in the 'V,' because if you got shot down, they hadn't lost anything."

For a man of Geiger's physique, the DH-4 was a difficult aircraft to fly. Its fifteen-thousand-foot ceiling required the crew to wear bulky high-altitude clothing, which greatly restricted movement. Geiger, having grown physically since his initial enlistment, was a "bear of a man" who almost had to be a contortionist just to get into the cockpit. Bundled up to his ears in a sheepskin flight suit and bound in a tightly cinched parachute harness, he had to squeeze into the impossibly small cockpit, which was located under the center portion of the upper wing. It would have been impossible for him to get out in an emergency, a fact not lost on him after observing several flaming aircraft whose pilots rode them down.

Geiger's observer-gunner was not much better off, even though it was somewhat easier for him to get into position. Upon takeoff, the gunner raised his jump seat and stood erect, half out of the cockpit, exposed to the icy blast of the slipstream. Leather straps attached to the cockpit ring mount kept him in the aircraft—at least that was what was advertised. On one notable occasion, the gunner was pitched over the side during a wild dogfight. The unnerved man, by a stroke of incredible luck, landed on the plane's tail assembly and then managed to claw his way back, inch by inch, to the rear cockpit—while his plane maneuvered wildly to escape the German fighters!

Unlike many who considered air combat as chivalrous, Geiger looked upon the airplane as a weapon, to be used to destroy the enemy. He liked the DH-4's formidable array of weaponry. It had fixed, forward firing, twin .30-caliber Vickers machine guns that fired through the propeller blades. The gunner/observer manned dual .30-caliber Lewis machine guns that were mounted on a ring, allowing a 360-degree traverse—but "Don't shoot up the tail assembly, please!" The plane could carry up to a ton and a half of bombs. Racks for twenty-five-, fifty-, or one-hundred-pound bombs were attached to the underside of the lower wing and could be released by either the pilot or the gunner.

Upon the arrival of the main body, Geiger's position as second in command evolved into a frustrating administrative role. He scoured the countryside trying to beg, borrow, or steal aircraft to get his own pilots in the air. Aircraft were simply not available. The rush to mass-produce in the United States the British-designed aircraft with the American-built Liberty engine was beyond the physical and technical expertise of the manufacturers, and it was not until late September that the first DH-4 arrived. The rest dribbled in, and it was not until mid-October that enough aircraft were available to launch the first raid.

The eight-plane sortie dropped a ton of bombs on the German-held rail yards at Thielt, Belgium. On their return, twelve German fighters jumped the formation and separated a DH piloted by Lieutenant Ralph Talbot. As the Germans attacked, the gunner, Corporal Robert Robinson, shot down one. Two others attacked from below. A bullet hit Robinson in the elbow, carrying most of it away, and jammed his machine gun. Despite the severe wound, he cleared the jam and continued to fight. Hit twice more in the stomach and thigh, he slumped unconscious in the rear cockpit.

Talbot maneuvered his plane as the Germans bore in and shot down one of the attackers with his fixed machine guns. Seeing an opening, he put the battered DH into a steep dive and escaped. Both men were awarded the Medal of Honor.

Roy Geiger

Geiger was a man of action and chafed under the workload of administrative duties. On the spur of the moment, he decided to take a newly delivered DH-9A for a lone bombing mission on the railway center at Loos, Belgium. He enlisted the aid of Lieutenant Commander Harold B. Grow, USN, to fly with him as tail-gunner. The two flew the brand-new plane to a nearby British field and loaded four 100-pound bombs. As Geiger taxied to the runway, he observed several off-duty English pilots watching him prepare to take off. In a momentary lapse of judgment, he could not resist the urge to show off.

Commander Grow described the scene: "The major advanced the throttle to full power, and took off with a deafening roar. The moment his wheels cleared the surface, he pulled back hard on the stick, and forced the aeroplane into a steep, climbing flipper turn, momentarily forgetting the all important fact that the DH was a good five hundred pounds heavier . . . At the top of the turn, and at an elevation not exceeding 350 feet, the machine commenced to slip rapidly. Belatedly realizing what had happened, Geiger managed to level it off just before the scout-bomber hit the ground. Miraculously, the DH bounced, leaving behind the entire landing gear assembly, the two lower wing sections with their respective bombs, and both wooden blades of the propeller!"

The impact threw the wreck another hundred yards before it plummeted to the ground a second time, right side up, with the engine on fire. The badly shaken pair threw off their seat belts and scrambled out of the furiously burning wreckage. An ambulance roared up, expecting to find, at the least, two badly hurt victims. Instead, the sheepish survivors asked for a ride back to the hanger. The surprised Brits were kind enough to drop them off in front of the officers' club, where the two made their way to the bar and, with studied nonchalance, downed several stiff drinks. An appreciative crowd gathered to congratulate them on their narrow escape.

Somehow, it just did not seem to be the right moment to announce, "The Marines have landed." Geiger's commander was not as appreciative. In a disciplinary letter, he stated, "While it may not be the fault of Major Geiger that [the] DH-9A was crashed, and fully recognizing that he is a competent pilot, I must nevertheless restrict his use of day machines at this time. . . ." Geiger objected—vociferously. Cunningham did not appreciate the unrepentant officer's protest and placed him on suspension for "talking back."

Ford O. Rogers, who won a Navy Cross "for distinguished and heroic service as an aviator in an aeroplane engaged in active operations co-operating with the Allied Armies on the Belgian Front" as a first lieu-tenant and retired as a major general, characterized Geiger's approach as " 'fly it or smash it.' If ever there was a flier who had God as his co-pilot, it was Geiger."

The end of hostilities also marked the end of Geiger's brief restriction. He was restored as the squadron commander in time to attend to its demo-bilization. Geiger himself arrived back in the States on the last day of January 1919.

In its brief combat appearance, the 1st Marine Aviation Force carried out fourteen missions, dropping more than 52,000 pounds of bombs on enemy railway yards, canals, supply dumps, and airfields. Twelve German planes were shot down at a cost of four Marine pilots killed, and one pilot and two gunners wounded. The force earned thirty decorations. Roy Geiger received the Navy Cross "for distinguished service in the line of his profession as Commanding Officer of Airplane Squadron No. 2, in which capacity he trained and led this squadron on bombing raids against the enemy."

Between the Wars
Lem Shepherd

Lem Shepherd came home from France a proven, highly decorated combat leader, with a U.S. Army Distinguished Service Cross, Navy Cross, Silver Star, and a French Croix de Guerre. He was a charter member of the "Marine Brigade," a clique of young officers, linked by personal and profes-sional relationships forged on the battlefields of France, who would leave their mark on the Marine Corps in the years to come.

In the two decades that followed the war, he served in a variety of command and staff assignments; aide-de-camp to the commandant, sea duty, expeditionary duty in China, an independent assignment with the Garde d'Haiti, and command of an infantry battalion in the newly formed Fleet Marine Force. He also attended two service schools that served to broaden his professional development.

Four months after Pearl Harbor, newly promoted Colonel Shepherd took command of the 9th Marine Regiment and prepared it for combat.

Roy Geiger

Geiger returned from France to find the Corps' fledging air service struggling to survive the postwar demobilization. Along with other senior aviators, Geiger fought for permanent status of an air arm in the face of opposition from within the Marine Corps. The opposition stemmed from a doubt as to its usefulness and from a feeling that aviators were not "real Marines." Geiger worked hard to overcome this stigma. He believed that aviation was not something separate, but a part of the Marine Corps.

As Geiger advanced in rank, his responsibilities also increased—commanding officer, aircraft squadrons, East Coast Expeditionary Force; officer in charge, Marine Corps Aviation; and chief of aviation. In the spring of 1941, he was assigned as an observer with British forces in the Mediterranean. The assignment confirmed his strongly held view of the necessity for close coordination between air and ground forces. Upon his return to the States, Geiger was assigned as commanding general, 1st Marine Aircraft Wing. Four months later the country was at war.

PART TWO

BANANA WARS

CHAPTER SEVEN

A DAY LATE AND
A DOLLAR SHORT

Eddie Craig

A somber Woodrow Wilson slipped into a side room off the main lobby of the White House, took pen in hand, and scribbled his signature on the document that lay on the highly polished walnut table. A buzzer sounded in the executive office, and a navy aide, Lieutenant Byron McCandless, ran out onto the White House lawn and semaphored to a fellow officer peering out a window of the Navy Department office across the street. The signal was immediately flashed to every ship and shore installation: "WAR."

The April 6, 1917, newspaper editions proclaimed a call to arms, sending the nation's collective blood pumping. Thousands of young men streamed to the colors. Among them was twenty-year-old St. John's Military Academy student Edward A. "Eddie" Craig. "When World War I broke out I immediately set out to get in the service. I was in school at the time, and on my own. I couldn't get in the Army until I was twenty-one with a commission . . . and twenty in the Marine Corps. Having had ROTC training for four years, I was offered a commission in the Marine Corps and reported to the Marine Corps Recruiting Station in Chicago for a physical examination." He was attracted by the Corps' slogan, "First to Fight." "I'd seen the posters all over, and I wanted to get to Europe with the Marines and see what was going on and help out over there." Craig sent a telegram to his army doctor father. "I'm entering the U.S. Marine Corps. I have a chance for a commission. I received a telegram from him: 'Do not join the U.S. Marines under any circumstance. A terrible bunch of drunks and bums,' signed, Father." His father had gained his dislike of Marines while stationed at Fort Leavenworth. There were several Marines attending school who were heavy drinkers. He changed his mind after World War I and became very pro-Marine.

Despite the admonition, Craig went for the physical. Everything went well until the eye test. "I could not read the chart they had in a rather dark office. I was of course broken hearted, and after some letter writing by my father, and telegrams to Headquarters Marine Corps by myself, I was granted a reexamination. The same light conditions in the same examining room threw me out again." He returned home, resigned to the fact that he could not go to war. "Life to me about that time was pretty black, and my father sensing my disappointment wrote a personal letter to the Commandant asking if I could have another examination." The assistant commandant, Major General John A. Lejeune, responded and gave him one more try. He hopped a train to Washington and was given an appointment with the Corps' leader. "The Commandant, Major General George Barnett, talked to me personally, ending with the statement that if I did not pass the exam this time, there would not be another chance." Craig was vindicated. "I took the exam that same day and passed without any difficulty and was given a commission a week later."

Unfortunately, the delay was costly. "I found that my failure in passing the physical examination had a great effect on my future in the Marine Corps. At the time there were many officers joining in 1917, among them Lem Shepherd and Cliff Cates. But being three months ahead of me, they were almost captains when I was a second lieutenant . . . [which] had a great effect on my position on the lineal list all through my career, just that short period of about three months." In Marine parlance, Craig was a "day late and a dollar short."

"A Bit of Flanders in Virginia"

Craig reported to the First Officers' Training Camp, Quantico, Virginia, for active duty. "I found myself in Company D. This company was already one month through the course but my military training stood me in good stead, and by the second month I found myself a platoon commander." Quantico was nothing more than a whistle stop on the railroad trunk line thirty-five miles south of Washington. In August 1917, Marine engineers struggled to clear the heavily forested land and create a training base. When Craig arrived, "the base at that time was a big mudhole. I remember the day I reported. There were trucks stuck all along Barnett Avenue, and the stumps sticking out all over had not been taken out." Barracks consisted of rough-hewn board shacks that barely kept out the weather. Craig was assigned to one of the poorly built huts that served as officer's quarters. "The cracks had no batting over them, which allowed the wind and rain to come through. When winter came, it was pretty cold . . . unless you sat by the stove in the center of the room. The rooms also had open cracks, which the wind and rain came through."

Quantico's main purpose was to train Marines for combat duty with the American Expeditionary Force (AEF). "The training was rugged," Craig remembered. "Each morning before daylight, we were out for setting up exercises, then rifle calisthenics, and this was followed by a run in company formation under arms to the old railroad station and back. I found that by breakfast time I was so tired that I could not eat very much. Then by nine or ten in the morning I would be ravenous." The training was realistic, and often taught by French and British veterans. "We constructed a complete trench system as learned from the war in Europe." Craig's training company dug miles of revetted trenches, bombproofs, and posts of command (PCs). A miniature battlefield was created, "a bit of Flanders in Virginia." They "practiced" war games, one side defending and the other attacking under simulated combat conditions. Unfortunately, Craig "never did have occasion in my career . . . to put any trench warfare training into practice. However, the pick and shovel work tended to get us into shape physically."

One aspect of the training included boxing. "We had a British officer in this phase and he was tough. A huge man, who had been through the fighting in France, he meant to make everyone learn the art of killing. I was one of those he picked out to box with and he almost knocked me silly." Shortly before graduation, Craig received orders to report to the 8th Marine Regiment as battalion adjutant. His commanding officer had a reputation as a strict disciplinarian. "Major Miller was a tall, fine looking officer but was not well liked, a real martinet." Fortunately, the acting sergeant major took young Lieutenant Craig under his wing. "Wisner was an old timer who had been broken a number of times due to his like of the bottle. However, he was efficient otherwise and had much practical experience." Craig related that Wisner always had a ready answer for the battalion commander, which kept him out of trouble.

During one of Craig's first inspections, Wisner accompanied him. "I had just entered a mess hall when Sergeant Wisner yelled, at the top of his voice, 'Attention.' I snapped quickly to attention and stood there frozen in my tracks, until I heard Wisner whisper, 'Lieutenant, you are the inspecting officer." The young officer and the veteran sergeant major became fast friends. Later in Santo Domingo, Craig attended the old Marine's funeral. "The tropics and rum had been too much for him."

Shortly after his assignment, secret orders arrived directing the regiment to leave for an unknown destination within twenty-four hours. Rumors were rife—"France, here we come"—and the men entrained in high spirits. A few hours later, the train stopped for water and the regimental commander and his staff got off to stretch their legs. While they were at the far end of the platform, the train started up. Craig was in the last car. "I could see them running to catch up. I will always remember the look on their faces as the train pulled rapidly away." The regiment arrived in Philadelphia and immediately boarded the USS *Hancock*. By late afternoon, the ship was loaded and had "singled up all lines," preparing to shove off. The hawsers were hauled in and the transport started to swing away from the pier. The deck was lined with officers and men, including Craig. "It was at that moment that the Colonel and his staff appeared, pounding down the dock at full speed. Jacob's ladders were lowered over the side and, amidst a chorus of cheers and catcalls, they climbed aboard."

Hancock sailed into the Atlantic, her destination still secret. Craig was bitterly disappointed when "we got clear of the land and headed south [and were told that we] were not on our way to France. The 5th and 6th Marine Regiments had already been formed and officered, and that threw me out of a chance to go to France." Three days later the ship docked at Galveston, Texas. "We had been sent south due to trouble in the oil fields at Tampico, Mexico. German agents had fomented trouble there, which was a danger to the oil supply for our fleet." The townspeople turned out to watch the

strange-looking soldiers as they hiked through the city to the army post at
Fort Crockett. They had never seen Marines in green uniforms before and
thought they were Canadians, much to the chagrin of the proud
Leathernecks. In the confusion of unloading the equipment, much of it disappeared, as each unit took what it needed regardless of ownership. Craig
helped himself to transport. "I secured a nice new Indian motorcycle and
sidecar and was driving that around for over ten days until the
Quartermaster, Captain Baugh, saw me hung up on a railroad track. . . . He
came over, and after a severe dressing down told me to turn it in. It was
many months until poor Captain Baugh got most of his property back. . . ."

After some months on the staff, Craig requested duty with a line
company. It was granted and he was transferred to the 105th Company as
a platoon commander. He soon found himself back in the trenches, "a bit
of Flanders in Texas." A large area was made to resemble a typical French
battlefield, with revetted trenches, bombproofs, and sophisticated defensive wire barriers. Sometimes, however, the training was too realistic. Craig
related how the "boys" got a little carried away. "Raids were conducted by
Marines armed with wooden rifles, tennis balls over the bayonets to prevent injury, to capture prisoners from the defenders." Marines being
Marines, exuberance was the order of the day, and "many times the tennis
balls would be accidentally removed. Prisoners were often removed in a
limp condition."

Craig was not immune to a little youthful indiscretion. "I had been
assigned to take a patrol and reconnoiter through and behind our regimental lines. I ran into the overall commander's CP. Sneaking silently towards
it, we cut all the telephone lines and rushed in to find everyone asleep.
When I pulled open a door, the major came out like a tiger, cursing me for
taking them prisoner. He raised even more hell when he found we had cut
the wires." Fortunately, the incident was soon forgotten when the 9th
Marines arrived. The two regiments formed the 2nd Brigade, embarked
aboard *Hancock*, and sailed to Port-au-Prince, Haiti. However, Craig was
reassigned to the 1st Provisional Brigade, "which-was fighting bandits," in
the Dominican Republic.

CHAPTER 8

A PARROT, FOWL WEATHER, AND FIELD DUTY

Craig and six other officers were given passage aboard the USS *Kwasind*, a converted yacht manned by reserve naval officers. Space was at a premium, and they had to bed down on the deck of the wardroom. The captain's beloved parrot perched above, occasionally showering them with bird droppings to their great annoyance. The parrot's noxious muck and a West Indian hurricane, with its high winds and towering waves, made it the voyage from hell. To top it off, the commanding officer, a Captain Blood (whose name Craig thought particularly apropos) chewed them out for littering his wardroom. One of the exasperated lieutenants remarked in a stage whisper, "How about that damn parrot crapping all over the deck!"

Upon arrival at Santo Domingo, Craig learned that he was being assigned to the 70th Company, temporarily attached to the 15th Regiment under Colonel James G. Breckenridge. Before taking command, however, Craig was directed to report to the 1st Air Squadron. "I was to spend a week and make daily flights over the eastern district in order to orient myself and learn the principal trails, rivers, and mountain ranges. This was a most valuable experience and stood me in good stead when I headed combat patrols later." The exhilaration of flight in the backseat of a Curtiss Jenny never left him. He developed a keen appreciation for the potential of aviation. "I became air minded. My interest in Marine aviation and its capabilities never left me from then on."

Craig's company was located in a remote area of the country. He set out to join his new command aboard the only transportation available, a small native boat, known as a "gasolina." "I was the only American on the trip, and practically every available space was occupied by natives. My accommodations consisted of a small space on the forward deck where I was surrounded by a native family, complete with chickens." The natives were friendly, even sharing their meager food with him. He debarked at La Romana, a large sugar estate, which became his base of operations for the next eight months.

The remote camp was located between the town and the sugar estate. Housing consisted of nine-feet-square wall tents for the men. Craig and his assistant bedded down in a wooden building, which also housed their office, storeroom, and sickbay. A small company store stocked a few treats. Craig recalled, however, "We had little time to enjoy the luxuries because the bandit situation was critical. Several large groups were operating in this section of the republic. I found myself in the field inspecting outposts or leading patrols most of the time." Ramón Natera headed the largest bandit group, seventy-five to one hundred men, but it was extremely rare to run into more than a few. "We hit small groups, six or eight at a time; and that was all. And these big groups would operate as a large group only on rare occasions; the rest of the time they were split up and operated against various villages and natives and would rob and burn and what not, as small groups."

Craig's mission could be summed up in a few words, "cover the eastern district," which permitted him maximum flexibility. "As a company commander, I was allowed much latitude in my decisions. I rarely received patrol instructions, and I could find nothing that defined the area I was supposed to patrol. Consequently, I assumed I could go anywhere . . . I desired." The assignment was truly an independent command, one in which Craig thrived, while others did not. The officer he relieved was sent home for a medical discharge because of a mental breakdown.

"Life on patrol was rugged," Craig recalled. "We usually traveled on foot carrying the minimum of gear. Food was prepared over open fires in canteen cups, mess pans, or whatever we could borrow from the natives." His patrol area was lush jungle-covered terrain, crisscrossed by numerous rivers and streams. Dense undergrowth forced his patrols to use the trail network, making them vulnerable to ambush. Casualties were a tremendous burden. Craig did not have enough doctors or corpsmen to accompany every patrol. "We had to use home-made litters with carrying parties of natives who were impressed for the job."

On one patrol, one of Craig's men was shot through the groin, which left a gaping wound in his buttocks. A Navy doctor hiked in and started treatment. Sadly, though, gangrene set in. The wounded man was in terrible pain but the doctor would not let him be evacuated to the regimental hospital. Craig agonized over the decision. "From the odor and the condition of the man I knew he would die if we didn't move him, so I overrode the doctor." The dying man was carried on a makeshift stretcher several miles over narrow mountain trails. "Halfway down, I almost lost my nerve and thought of turning back, but I decided it was the right thing to do. He would die anyway if I didn't make the effort." Native carrying parties replaced each other every few miles to keep up the pace. They finally reached a road where an ambulance picked him up. The doctors performed emergency surgery and managed to save the Marine's life. Craig was told that if he had not acted, the Marine would surely have died. "This was a terrible chance I took at the time, but I was never so happy over a decision in my life."

CHAPTER NINE

DUM-DUMS AND BANDITS

The 70th Company was composed almost entirely of old timers, pre-war Marines who had served in Santo Domingo for more than two years. Craig found them to be "a pretty hard-boiled crowd, but I found they were good, efficient Marines." They had been under the command of a "Prussian"-type officer, who committed suicide rather than face a general court-martial for mistreating the natives. The company had several bad experiences with bandits in the eastern district and was itching to get even. During Craig's first morning inspection, "I found that, without exception, each man had dum-dum bullets in the pockets of his cartridge belt. The tips of the bullets had been cut off." (Dum-dum bullets would cause a larger wound and, as some claimed, increase the stopping power of the round.)

The company occupied two platoon (twenty-four men) outposts, one at Yuma (forty-two miles from the base camp at La Romana) commanded by a Sergeant and the other at Higuey (thirty-five miles from the base camp), under a lieutenant. The only way for Craig to reach them was by horse or mule, with an escort of six to eight Marines. "I would make a regular monthly inspection of the outposts, and at that time it would mean about an eighty-mile hike or ride. We usually carried a couple days' rations. If we were going to stay out longer, we would sometimes take a pack mule. When the rations ran out, we would forage through the country, obtaining what we could from the natives." In one of the outposts, their entire store of food consisted of bacon, flour, canned corn, jam, and cases of sardines. Craig allowed that "Nobody got fat down there!" They obtained fresh meat and vegetables by bartering with the local natives. He had to put a stop to one bartering scheme. Several Marines were trading cans of sardines for "favors" from the local women.

The natives were sometimes friendly and sometimes not. Craig found that "We would find some that in order to obtain favors would be friendly, or if they were employed by the Marines—it meant their jobs. Others, of course, were between the Devil and the deep sea. If they gave information to the Marines, the bandits would kill them; and if they didn't give information, the Marines would sometimes be hard on them." Craig developed a close relationship with a local native guide by the name of Ramón. According to Craig, Ramón was "about thirty-five, wiry, with a drooping moustache and missing his left arm. He always carried a .44-caliber revolver, and with his slouch hat, homemade shirt and blue denim trousers, and leather thong sandals, would have passed for a bandit anywhere."

Ramón accompanied Craig on every patrol and proved to be a loyal and competent guide. "He also brought us many hot tips on the bandits who infested the area." At times, he left camp to visit his wife, who lived several miles away in another village. Craig always worried: "I always hesitated in granting his request for I knew the danger he faced on the fifteen-mile ride down the mountain trails. He had made many enemies as [a] result of acting as a guide for the Marines. The average Dominican was quick to take revenge if the opportunity presented itself." One weekend he requested leave, which Craig granted. "I watched as he mounted his horse and, with his one arm flapping, trotted down the trail." A few hours later, Craig learned that "Ramón had been waylaid and killed. His head was found impaled on a fence post and his body horribly mutilated by machetes."

Then, as now, it was difficult to tell innocent civilians from bandits. At one time Craig received orders that his men were not to fire on any armed man unless that man fired first! Craig found it a senseless order. "These were the most stringent orders I ever received. And, of course, they were very hard to carry out, because if you saw a native with a rifle pointed at you, you had a tendency to shoot first if you possibly could. And I think this is what happened on many occasions." He blamed the orders on the military government, which was out of touch with the situation faced by Marine commanders in the field. "We had a military government at that time, and the military governor was an admiral with a staff up in Santo

Domingo City. During my time . . . I never saw the military governor or any of his staff on any inspections."

Shortly after returning from a mounted patrol, Craig received news from a friendly native that a large bandit force had seized a German store-owner and his wife only six miles away. He quickly organized a twelve-man mounted patrol and galloped to the rescue. As they turned a bend in the trail, two armed bandits jumped up and took a shot at them. Lieutenant Shields, riding ahead of Craig, attempted to fire back with his pistol, but it jammed. Shields was so angry that he heaved it at the bandits, but only succeeded in frightening his horse, which took off at a gallop. The rest of the patrol thundered along behind. Within minutes, they ran headlong into the bandits, who scattered in panic. "Hell of a thing," Craig remembered. "We came thundering right into the middle of them, yelling and shooting. We picked off four of them before they could go to the jungle." The Germans were released unharmed, however, "mad-man" Shields took quite a lot of good-natured ribbing. The troops teased him unmercifully for leading a charge, unarmed.

Shortly after the rescue, Craig learned that Nateras had established a permanent base camp in his patrol area. He learned where it was located and set out with a force of twenty Marines. "I followed a roundabout way and hit the trail leading to the reported site. The area was densely wooded, but the trail was well worn by men and horses. As we proceeded farther into the jungle, it branched out in many directions and became harder to follow." The patrol came across woodchoppers industriously cutting large mahogany trees. Their chopping could be heard a long way off. Shortly after, the patrol found a barrier of felled trees. Their branches had been cut so the sharp ends formed a formidable barrier. They worked their way through it and suddenly "came into a cleared area containing ten or twelve long shacks and many lean-tos—Nateras' camp." The bandits had fled, forewarned by the wood-choppers' clever alert. "In the camp we found three badly wounded bandits and a large quantity of supplies, which we burned. I took great pleasure in reporting the destruction of the camp, particularly since the regimental commander told me there were no bandits in the vicinity."

Craig spoke of the difficulties in fighting a guerrilla war. "Many patrols were fruitless after much hardship, and it was so difficult to come into contact with the bandits . . . this type of duty was most discouraging. Occasionally our patrols would hit small groups and kill one or two, and on a number of occasions we were ambushed by bandits."

After seven months, Craig was transferred to a mounted detachment stationed at Chicharrones, a railhead at the end of a macadam road that led to regimental headquarters. The detachment sergeant was a former cowhand and a member of the Canadian cavalry named Bill Hensley—a wizard with horses. The mounts were Puerto Rican, much larger than the native mounts. They were fed on oats and hay and were well cared for, or "Sergeant Hensley would know the reason why." Craig described the sergeant as "a typical Marine of the old Corps, every inch a soldier. He was well over six feet in height, powerfully built, straight as a ramrod, and always wore a mustache. He was one of the finest Marines that I have ever served with." Like all good sergeants, Hensley took care of his officer, even saving Craig's life. "I was riding my favorite horse, Sublime, a big Palomino stallion, when he bogged down up to his belly in mud and fell on his side, pinning my right leg. His movements pushed my head and shoulders down and I couldn't breathe. Suddenly I felt like a tractor was pulling me through the mud." Hensley had grabbed his pistol belt and suspenders and pulled Craig out from under the horse. "He saved me from possible death."

On another occasion, Craig's patrol had surrounded a cluster of jungle shacks. "It was bright moonlight night and I had just stopped a native who had come from one of the houses and was headed for the jungle. As I questioned him, he appeared surly and edged toward me." Just then Hensley came around the other side of the shack and, without even a "by your leave," butt-stroked the native on the side of the head with his '03 rifle. It happened so fast that Craig could only look on with amazement. "I was surprised when he clubbed the native over the head. As the man dropped, Hensley reached down and grabbed a razor-sharp knife from his hand." Hensley had seen the flash of the knife in the moonlight and instinctively reacted. "Bill Hensley and the moon shining on the knife gave me the break I needed."

On one of the few occasions Craig was in camp, his "boy," a hired man who did housekeeping chores, dashed up screaming hysterically. Blood streamed down his face from a ghastly wound on the side of his head. A piece of mutilated flesh was all that was left of his ear. "My God man, what happened?" Craig exclaimed. The terrified man pointed to a tough-looking native across the street and, in halting English, explained that the man had cut his ear off because he worked for the Marines. Craig "picked up my automatic pistol, which was lying unholstered on the table, and slipped the lanyard over my shoulder." As he strode across the street, he yelled "for Sergeant Hensley to get his gun and follow me. My intention was to apprehend and arrest the native before he could escape." Craig approached the desperado and started to question him. "He suddenly reached forward and grabbed my pistol, which I was holding cocked in my right hand, pointing at the ground." The two struggled, but the bandit was too strong and succeeded in turning the pistol toward Craig. At that moment, Hensley ran up, grabbed the goon in a headlock, forced his own pistol into the miscreant's face, and pulled the trigger. "As the man fell dead, he pulled me over with him," Craig related, "covering me with blood and brain matter. Hensley's quick reaction saved me from being shot by my own gun."

One of the more macabre missions Craig ever had to perform was to take the body of a dead Marine back to the regimental field hospital. "The rainy season was in full swing and trails were slippery and deep in mud as I started with my patrol down the mountainside. Natives [who] we had commandeered were carrying the body on an improvised stretcher." He reached a road, where the body was placed in a wooden coffin and loaded on an old truck. "We had reached a point about three-quarters of the way and were traveling through deep mud in the pouring rain, when the truck stopped." They could not get it started; the battery was dead. "I decided the only thing to do was to break open the coffin and place the dead Marine's body across a horse and continue on foot." Craig had orders to deliver the body by morning.

The road ran through thick jungle, and the overhanging trees shut out any light. Craig did not have a flashlight and had to work in the pitch-blackness. "I had only the driver and one other Marine with me. As we ripped off the lid of the coffin, a sickening odor hit us in the face. The tropics had begun to work on the corpse. The driver became sick, and it fell on the other Marine and me to lift the body out and secure it across the horse." Rigor mortis had set in, making it difficult to lash the body across the horse.

"Every mile it seemed the gruesome load would shift and we would have to tighten the lashings." They finally reached another road where they were relieved of their grisly responsibility.

However, the successful delivery did not end the incident. Weeks later, Craig received a letter accusing him of losing the dead man's bayonet. "I often thought that if the regimental commander had been present when we arrived, completely covered with mud, hungry, tired, and carrying what we could salvage, he would have relented in his desire to make me account for the bayonet."

Craig was hardened, mentally and physically, by the constant patrolling and privation in the field. "Everything I owned, I carried on my back. My quarters were a 9x9 wall tent without a deck. I slept on a field cot . . . with a small ration box as a table, the light of one oil lantern, when I had kerosene—a candle when I did not. I had no sheets or pillowcase and my pillow consisted of my musette bag filled with my extra underwear and socks. My blanket was the only covering, except for a poncho—and the nights were cold and damp in the mountains. If I wanted to bathe, I had to go some one hundred yards into the jungle, where there was a cold stream running over rocks into a deep pool. The presence of bandit groups made it desirable to lay your pistol within easy reach. My eating utensils consisted of a GI spoon and knife, a mess tin, and [a] tin can to drink out from." Craig echoed an age-old lament of the field soldier: "It always seemed to me that the troops chasing the bandits and living in the far-flung outposts should have been the ones who received the best, but it was just the opposite. The ones in garrison were the ones where comfort was the rule."

After two years of field duty, Craig received orders back to the United States. He looked back on those days with a sense of accomplishment. It was professionally rewarding, although "it was rugged duty, and the methods we used were not always those of the book. Most of the men had never been trained in jungle warfare, and it was necessary to train them on the march and bivouac." He was an experienced jungle warfare expert, joining a core group of junior officers who would subsequently rise to command positions in World War II.

CHAPTER TEN

FRAUGHT WITH DANGER

Nicaragua was going through one of its periodic revolutionary upheavals when Major General Commandant John A. Lejeune passed through on one of his periodic inspection visits. Craig, his aide-de-camp, accompanied him. "We traveled to all parts of the republic, and at this time, I became interested in the Guardia Nacional de Nicaragua (Nicaraguan army). It had only been recently organized by the Marines, and all [of] its officers were detailed from the Marine Corps." The Guardia was organized in 1927 as a combination native police force and national army, commanded by Marines but separate from the Marine brigade. Officers were "loaned" to the Guardia, advanced one grade, and paid a stipend, in addition to their regular military pay. Even with this incentive, there were not enough volunteers. Selected non-commissioned officers were brevetted to lieutenant in order to make up the shortages.

Craig liked what he saw. "Duty with the Guardia looked different from the regular Marine Corps, and I believed that I could be of some help, as volunteers for the outfit were not too plentiful." Shortly after returning to the States, General Lejeune retired. He gave Craig an opportunity to pick an assignment. "I asked him if I could be detailed to duty with the Guardia. He agreed, and said [it] would give me good professional experience and training." In the months to come, Craig had cause to doubt Lejeune's prophesy. "I found life in the Guardia much different . . . the good American food was gone, equipment was lacking, and the native troops were still not completely trained and in many cases were unreliable and dangerous." Craig found that "In some instances the Guardias had mutinied and shot their officers, and desertions were frequent."

Initially assigned as the executive officer of the 1st Mobile Battalion, Guardia Nacional, Craig found the duty interesting but wanted something more exciting. He requested assignment to a newly formed company slated for duty in a remote part of the country. "My company was composed of drafts from the other companies of the battalion. On the morning of our departure, men released from the brig filled up the vacancies in the company. It was a mongrel outfit." With some degree of trepidation, Craig and his second in command, Second Lieutenant Kurchov, Guardia Nacional (corporal, USMC), marched his "crack" troops into the jungle. Craig remarked rather dismissively that "Being the only Americans among these native troops, with only a poor command of the Spanish language, could be a nerve-wracking experience." He had every right to be concerned. Just a few hours after starting out, one of the wrongdoers tried to shoot Kurchov. Unfortunately, for him the lieutenant nee corporal wrestled the rifle away and brained the man with his own weapon. The bashing quickly ended the abortive mutiny.

Soon after reaching the post, Craig received word that a Guardia detachment had mutinied and kidnapped their officers. It was expected that others might go over to the bandits. "At the time Kurchov was out on patrol, and not knowing my men too well, I was pretty nervous when I turned in that night." Craig slept with a Browning Automatic Rifle (BAR) under his cot. The next day one of the sergeants asked if the detachment could serenade him after work. "It was not unusual to serenade people in Nicaragua, but I thought it strange under the circumstances. As darkness set in I became more nervous when they did not appear. About eight o'clock there was a knock on my door, and when I opened it, every man who was not on duty was standing there." The men requested to come in. Craig really did not have a choice. "I thought to myself, *Well this is it, they have me cold!*" They squeezed in and arranged themselves around the small room. A small kerosene lantern provided a weak light as the hard-looking group crowded around Craig. "To say I was afraid would be putting it mildly." Finally, a man started strumming his guitar—and the whole group broke into song. "The group loosened up when I passed out cigarettes and coffee. They cracked jokes and smiled. I finally understood, they were showing me their loyalty. I never had trouble with the men after that, and always felt secure when with them."

Craig "found that life in the Guardia was one crisis after another. They were good soldiers and loyal, if they were treated like men and only punished when they understood that they had committed an offense. However, punish one of them unjustly and your life was in danger." Craig was in his small office one morning when a shot rang out and a bullet thudded itself in the wall beside his head. "Seems a Guardia who had just enlisted let his rifle go off while on guard in the tower. He deserted the next morning and I never did find out if the shot was accidental or intentional."

"In the Department of Chinandega we had an average of two or three machete-fight killings between civilians each month. The winner of the fight became a hunted man, and many joined the bandits or went over the border to Honduras." After one of the fights, the "winner" was arrested and incarcerated in the local hoosegow. Unfortunately, for the miscreant, the jailer was a relative of the victim. Craig was notified that a riot had developed after the prisoner was savagely murdered in his cell. "I found a milling crowd of some two thousand Nicaraguans in front of the Cuartel (jail). The body of the murdered man lay on the street, guarded by four Guardias. I could see a dangerous situation was in the making and ordered an interpreter [to] tell the mob that I would investigate . . . and in the meantime stay calm." While the interpreter talked with the crowd, Craig telephoned for reinforcements. Just as the situation was turning critical, ten Guardias carrying a machine gun roared up—in the best tradition of the cavalry. "When they had set it up, the mob began to disperse, and in twenty minutes the last one had disappeared."

The Guardias were tough and they had to be, according to Craig, in order to deal with the bandits and criminal elements. "I remember on one occasion, I gave orders to a Guardia to arrest a murderer. Later on in the day, I heard a loud thump outside my door. A Guardia came in and handed me a large pearl-handled .44 revolver, and told me the prisoner was outside. I said, 'Bring him in.'" The Guardia went outside and came back in, dragging a body by the legs. "It seems the man was armed and the Guardia, not wanting to take any chances, fired first. The thump I heard was the body being dropped from the Guardia's horse."

Craig found that he had to be always on the alert for brutality. "In a country where killings, water cures, and hot pepper enemas were routine questioning techniques, one had to be on the watch to prevent excesses on the part of the Guardias." He had a burly Nicaraguan first sergeant who always seemed to be able to extract information from prisoners. "I was passing a small roof off the sallyport and found his method was to have a Guardia hold the prisoner, while he grabbed his testicles and twisted. Being a powerful man, it seems only a few twists were necessary."

The government started a road-building program to support the economy and, at the same time, increase security in the remote areas by keeping potential bandits gainfully employed. Craig laid out the route for a two-lane road and hired three hundred natives at fifty cents a day. "Many of the men I employed were part-time bandits, and when most of them did not show up for work, I could always count on increased bandit activity while they were away." He never knew how to take his workers; sometimes they would be sullen and at other times smiling and contented. In an effort to improve morale, Craig decided to throw a big party. He was "rather nervous" about attending because of the threat of bandit attack. "I asked my head man whether he thought the bandits would interfere. He laughed and put his arms around my shoulders and said, 'Never worry, there are too many of them right here. You will have no trouble at all!' "

Craig sent two of his men out dressed and armed as bandits. "They encountered two of my workers on a side trail, and identified themselves as members of [guerrilla chief Augusto César] Sandino's Army." The undercover Guardias asked the workers to guide them in an attack on Craig's post. "The two immediately gave the information and stated they would help in the attack, if given rifles, as they hated the government and the Guardia." The two were arrested and Craig was surprised to find they were among his best workers. "Sometimes between my Guardias and my workers, I had a hard time deciding who to trust."

CHAPTER ELEVEN

CLOSE CALLS

Shortly after taps one night, bandits attacked Craig's post. "The bandits took up positions around the town and fired into our barracks. However, we had made plans for just such an emergency. Certain Guardias manned defense positions while the bulk of my outfit formed an attack force. We fanned out through the village and the bandits fled to the bush." At first light, Craig's men searched the village but found nothing except hundreds of expended cartridges.

Craig was always thankful for Marine aviation. "Each day one or two planes would come over to check and would not leave till they had received an official code acknowledging that all was well." The planes would also deliver and pick up mail. The pilots were not adverse to a little gallows humor. "One of the tricks they pulled on me was to drop colored advertisements taken from magazines of chocolate cakes, puddings, baked hams, etc. They knew we yearned for such things [which] were impossible to get. Rather a perverted sense of humor I thought at the time."

Normally, when Craig supervised the road gangs, he rode with four to five Guardia escorts. One day, however, he sent them on ahead, and almost immediately regretted the decision. "I was rounding a sharp curve. A deep valley dropped away on one side and a ridge looked down on me from across it. A bullet smacked against the stone cliff, missing me by inches, and I heard the report of a rifle." Craig put the spurs to his horse and bounded to cover before the hidden rifleman could fire another shot. On another occasion, while he was with the road gang, twelve bandits waved at him with their rifles. "They stood and watched us for some time but offered us no resistance and finally left. I had only two of my Guardias with me at the time and did not feel that we should start a battle."

A political leader urged Craig to take his brand new Ford touring car to one of his outposts. Craig took two men and completed the first half of the tour without difficulty. On the way back, however, "We had no sooner started than a terrific storm came up. The further we went, the worse the trail became. It was pitch dark and the rain was pouring down with much lightning and thunder." The car skidded off the road, rolled down a gully, and got stuck at the bottom. The driver knew the way to a ranch house. "It was after midnight when we reached the house. A sudden flash of lightning revealed a long porch where several men were asleep. Leaning against the wall behind them were rifles." Craig knew they could not be Guardia and signaled the others to hit the muddy ground. Quietly, they slithered back the way they had come, thanking their lucky stars that the storm covered their getaway. "If the bandits had a sentry posted, the story might have had a different ending."

After two and a half years in Nicaragua, Craig received orders to report to the embryonic 1st Marine Division at San Diego. The orders directed him to travel via a navy oil tanker. After all the hardships he had suffered, Craig requested to proceed at his own expense and come home in style. "Accordingly, I boarded the SS *Columbia* of the Panama Mail Steamship Line on September 3, 1931." After several stops along the coast, the ship docked at Mazatlán, Mexico, where the passengers went ashore for a celebratory party. "Returning to the ship, we continued to party in the bar. The general air of festivities must have been catching, as I saw many trays of drinks going up to the ships' officers near the bridge." After getting under way, the ship encountered rough weather and high winds. Craig went below to his stateroom. "What a relief to have a clean cabin, hot shower, and all the comforts of home. I lay down and relaxed on my bunk and thought how smart I had been to travel in this luxury."

Craig dropped off to sleep. "I was awakened when I found myself on the deck. The ship was at an angle and the door to my stateroom was slanted over me. At first, I thought that it might be too many drinks." He soon realized the ship was in trouble and grabbed some personal articles and headed topside. "I could clearly see that we were aground. The ship was getting lower in the water and canted at quite an angle. The captain gave orders to abandon ship." The lifeboats were swung out and all women and children were successfully loaded—but with great difficulty because of the canted deck. "When my turn came to leave, I had to climb down a Jacob's ladder. As I was about halfway down, crude oil spurted from a seam in the side of the ship and covered me and everyone in the lifeboat." About eight inches of the heavy crude covered the bottom of the boat. Craig manned an oar, along with some of the crew, and started to pull away from the ship. "The captain, known as "Whispering Oakes" because of his name and loud voice, yelled down, 'Don't light any matches or it will burn up.' The engine room crew, who were not too fond of him, yelled back, 'Shut up you old son of a bitch. We hope you go down with the ship.' "

The lifeboats milled around for some time, as the various boat officers argued about the best course of action. Craig was finally able to convince his still-tipsy officer to head for the open sea because of the jagged shoreline. "Sometime later we spotted a steamer on the horizon. We sent up rockets from most of the boats, but the steamer continued on its way." The bedraggled passengers quickly succumbed to *mal de mare* in the rough seas. "I could feel someone on the bottom of the boat every time I pulled on the oar. When daylight came I found it was a German who was so sick that he would not even sit up." Late that morning, the SS *San Mateo* rescued them, ending their *Titanic*-like saga. An investigation revealed that *Columbia* had skirted the coast too close to Cape San Lucas and hit a submerged rock. Craig bemoaned his loss. "I lost all my clothing and personal gear, including a fine collection of some thirty-five beautiful revolvers. The only things I saved were my Zeiss field glasses, my Colt pistol, and my wallet. I landed in a pair of dungarees."

Craig alternated between staff and command assignments during the 1920s and 1930s. During this twenty-year period, he served almost nine years in foreign stations, to include the Philippines, China, and Nicaragua. Like his old friend Lem Shepherd, he became the aide-de-camp to the Major General Commandant and commanded infantry in the Fleet Marine Force. In 1939, he was assigned as the intelligence officer, Aircraft Battle Force, aboard the fleet carriers USS *Yorktown* and USS *Enterprise*, stationed at Pearl Harbor. He was transferred to San Diego just before war broke out. In March 1942, he joined the 2nd Marine Division.

CHAPTER 12

PLUCKING THE CACOS

While Craig rooted out bandits in Santo Domingo, his brother officers clashed with the Haitian Cacos on the western side of the island. Haiti, it seemed, was constantly lurching from one crisis to the next, as one political faction or another drove government after government from office. Colonel Littleton W. T. Waller, who commanded a Marine brigade, commented that "The Cacos have been the controlling element in all revolutions; they were purchased by first one candidate and then another. Finishing a contract with one man, they, having put him in power, would immediately sell their services to the next aspirant and unseat the first." The name Cacos came from a Haitian bird that preyed on weaker fowl. Because human Cacos lived off the weak, the name was a logical outgrowth of native folklore.

General Smedley Butler, "Old Gimlet Eye," described the political scene in Haiti. "Revolutions followed a definite procedure in Haiti. They always started in the north near the Dominican border so that the rebels could skip over to the sister republic when the odds were against them. The first battle was invariably fought at Kilometer Post 17 on the railroad to Grande Rivière. Don't ask me why. That's the way it used to happen in Haiti." In the winter of 1919, the political situation returned to what in Haiti was the norm, full-scale rebellion. Washington received a frantic request: "Call in the Marines!"

The 1st Marine Brigade deployed, reinforced—almost as an afterthought—with an attached aviation unit, without any clear-cut guidance as to what their role would be. One aviator summed it up: "We were there and they used us, and they used us to their advantage, and consequently we became a useful and integral part of the Marine Corps." In the spring of 1919, the 1st Division, Squadron E, arrived in Port-au-Prince, Haiti, to help "pluck the Cacos."

Roy Geiger

In the autumn of 1919, Geiger took command of the squadron, which was located three miles east of the capital at Bizoton, a Haitian navy yard. The squadron consisted of 10 officers and 60 enlisted men, well short of its authorized strength of 162 officers and men, and included two types of aircraft: land planes and seaplanes. The inventory comprised five JN-6 HG Jennies, six DH-4B de Havilland land planes, and six HS-1 seaplanes. However, aircraft losses decreased the inventory. In one ten-month period, October 1919 to July 1920, the squadron lost six aircraft and had several crewmembers injured. Major General Louis Earnest Woods recalled that "In Haiti when you took off you had to get wherever you were going because there were no fields to get down on in an emergency or otherwise. The level spaces were invariably covered with tall tropical grass."

Geiger was not immune to emergency landings. "On one trip," Woods related, "Geiger was coming back from Camp Haitien and his engine quit. He landed somewhere along the coastal region. I went out to see him and he was highly elated. He said how good an aviator he was, sitting down and not damaging the plane at all. I laughed and said, 'Have you walked over the field?' He said 'No.' I said, 'Walk over it.' He put his wheels down exactly twenty feet over a ditch that must have been ten feet deep, with grass coming up over it. In other words, if he'd set it down twenty feet sooner, he'd have smashed it up into pieces. . . ." Unpredictable weather, unmapped mountains, and a jungle-covered countryside inhabited by bandits made flying hazardous. During Geiger's two-year tour as commander, he was fortunate to lose only one officer in a plane crash.

Woods was philosophical about pilot losses, "In those days the two classes of aviators that were killed most often were, first those who were, shall I say, the poorest, and the second, the very best. The average ones lived longer because first, they didn't take chances that the best ones did, and they had more ability than the poorest ones had." In today's parlance: "There are old pilots and there are bold pilots, but there are no old, bold pilots!"

The squadron's high operational tempo was difficult to sustain. Geiger did not have sufficient personnel to support fully the brigade in the field. In a report to the Major General Commandant dated July 1920, he noted that "The squadron has had only about one-third of its authorized enlisted strength during this period. It has been through the cheerful, capable, and hard work of these few men that the Squadron has been able to care for its equipment." The squadron's mission was to provide aerial reconnaissance, message and mail pickup and delivery, medical evacuation, and the primary task of providing close air support (CAS).

The concept of close air support was in its infancy in the 1920s and 1930s. Airplanes in World War I and the Caribbean operations offered an opportunity to refine techniques. Geiger, an early supporter of CAS, insisted that his pilots work closely with the infantry. On many occasions, infantry officers flew in the backseat as observers. Geiger reported that "Raids were made upon bands of outlaws located in places which could not be reached by troops before the outlaws would have time to note their approach and escape." A combat report dated August 1920 discussed CAS. "Two DH-4B planes arrived there at 6:15 a.m. Visual communication was established with Captain Henniken on the ground. The planes were directed to the proper locality by him. They flew over it at an altitude of about thirty feet. About twelve hundred rounds of mixed tracer and full charge ammunition were fired into the various clumps of trees and into all defiles, etc. . . . that would be likely to furnish shelter. The planes were handled well and directed their fire apparently with good effect, producing the desired moral effect. The operation demonstrated that airplanes are a success in such affairs."

One of Geiger's pilots, Lieutenant Lawson H. M. Sanderson, pioneered an innovative bombing technique. Sanderson fixed a makeshift bomb rack to the underside of his aircraft and secured a mail sack to it. Then he tied off the opening with sash cords, which could be pulled open by the pilot. Using a rifle barrel as a bombsight, he lined up the plane with the target, leveled off at an altitude of 250 feet, and dove at an angle of between 30 and 45 degrees. By using this method of attack, he measurably increased accuracy. Geiger immediately directed all squadron pilots to be trained in this application.

During his two-year tour, Geiger maintained a demanding schedule, flying many of the same type missions as his pilots—and taking the same risks. He was a "hands-on" commander, who was simply not content to issue orders and wait for them to be carried out. Geiger was a take-charge officer—"Lead, follow, or get the hell out of the way!" He earned the respect of juniors and seniors alike and built a solid reputation of professional competence. He left Haiti as a permanent major, with a plum assignment, commanding officer, First Aviation Group, Marine Barracks, Quantico.

PART THREE

WORLD WAR II

CHAPTER THIRTEEN

AIR RAID, PEARL HARBOR

Ray Davis

Pipe down," an excited voice shouted, as an announcement blared from a short-wave radio. "We interrupt this program to bring you a special news broadcast. Pearl Harbor has been bombed!" The word went out. Men gathered around the few radios in the tent camp. First Lieutenant Ray Davis, an antiaircraft (AA) battery commander in the 1st Special Weapons Battalion, 1st Marine Division, remembered: "Everybody was up all night listening to the news and thinking about getting ready to go [to war]." Training at the huge New River, North Carolina, base took on a new importance. War scares were rampant, however, and Davis' battery was called out to defend the base. "Reports of a hostile German airship over the Atlantic led to an organized AA defense around our camps. Our guns were deployed and dug in, and I performed my only engineering project in the Corps . . . I supervised the building of a low bridge so that we could move our guns wherever they were needed." The report soon proved to be false, and training continued until the following summer.

Bob Barrow

The *Yazoo Herald Banner* headline screamed, "Japs Bomb Pearl Harbor!" Nineteen-year-old Louisiana State University sophomore Robert H. Barrow grabbed a newspaper and scanned the report of the shocking attack. "I was in Yazoo City, Mississippi, when I heard about Pearl Harbor. The attack clearly left an impression on me: I was angry. It was a dastardly act, beyond anything one could realize. The attack propelled the overwhelming number of Americans to be fully committed, no doubts, no mistake. If the Japanese hadn't bombed Pearl Harbor, I doubt we would have gone to war because we weren't too far removed from the horrors of World War I."

Barrow went back home to St. Francisville, Louisiana, to weigh his options. He skipped a semester at LSU to work for an oil exploration company in the swamps of west central Mississippi. However, events in the Pacific stirred his sense of patriotism. The *Baton Rouge Morning Advocate* ran a series of reports on the Marine defense of Wake Island, and when a Marine officer came to the campus, Barrow signed up for the Marine Platoon Leaders Class (PLC). "In the summer of '42 I got antsy about the war and wanted to be a part of it, so I exercised my right to resign my PLC status and enlist. I quickly found myself in San Diego."

Upon arrival at the Recruit Depot, Barrow was assigned to a training platoon. "Half the platoon was made up of men from Detroit and the other half was "Zoot Suiters" from Los Angeles, who dressed in colorful, flamboyant clothes. The sight of those colorful youngsters was almost beyond belief for a boy who had never been out of Louisiana." San Diego was on a war footing, jammed with recruits in various stages of training. The syllabus was shortened to six weeks to meet the insatiable manpower requirements of a rapidly expanding Corps. Barrow was awed by the experience. "I had some vague understanding of the Marine Corps but I didn't get the full flavor until I became a part of it." He found the training hard and tough, however. "I liked it enormously the first day I joined; the structure was very appealing. I liked the discipline," he said. Marine recruit Frank Chadwick joined the Corps at sixteen. "I changed my birth certificate," he admitted, and soon after found himself in basic training. "In boot camp there were sixty-four man platoons, run by a corporal. They called him, the DI, the little colonel. One DI per platoon. That little son of a bitch had more authority than the colonel that ran the place."

Barrow excelled and, upon graduation, he was retained as an assistant drill instructor (DI). "My senior, a staff sergeant, taught me a great deal about the Corps. I worked with him for three platoons. It was a great experience." While serving as a DI, Barrow was selected to attend Officer's Candidate School (OCS). "I was sent with twenty-four others to Quantico in February 1943. There were 236 in my class, all of whom were college graduates; I was the only exception. The eight-week OCS course was much more difficult than boot camp. There was special emphasis on map reading, employment of weapons, tactics, and the use of supporting arms. I had a love affair with the Marine Corps; I wanted to excel. It's what I wanted to do with my life."

Upon graduation, Barrow was offered a regular commission, one of only five that were offered to his class. He remained at Quantico for another ten weeks, attending the Reserve Officers Class (ROC). Finally, after twenty-four weeks of training—boot camp, OCS, and ROC—he received orders to Sea School at Portsmouth, Virginia. "The day before we were to report, the orders were cancelled because the school had a backlog, so each of us was ordered to the nearest USMC activity closest to home. I went to the ammunition depot at Bell Chase, New Orleans. The small barracks was commanded by Major Frank Kennedy, a tough old timer, who had enlisted in 1910 or 1912. He took me under his wing and taught me what the Corps was really like, after all the schools I had attended. However, I was getting impatient to go to war. Most of the detachment's men had been sent home from the Pacific to recover from wounds or sickness. It made it hard to see folks who had gone and come back."

Barrow got his wish when headquarters realized that he was a regular officer who had not yet been overseas, and assigned him to a replacement battalion at Camp Lejeune. While there, he was suddenly ordered to Washington for special duty in China. "I was picked to be a volunteer by my superiors because this duty was so unusual and attractive; it should [have gone] to a regular officer. There was a great deal of mystery about the assignment but I had heard about the China Marines, so I volunteered without any knowledge of what the duty entailed. I went to Washington and reported to a navy lieutenant commander who fixed his eyes on me and asked quite sternly, 'Want to go to China, live in a cave, and eat fish heads and rice?' I leaped to my feet and answered emphatically, 'Yes, sir, I want to go to China!' I found out later that he had never been to China and didn't know what he was talking about." Barrow soon learned that he was being assigned to the Sino-American Cooperative

Organization (SACO, pronounced "socko"), the brainchild of Captain (later vice admiral) Milton E. "Mary" Miles, USN, and Lieutenant General Tai Li, head of the Chinese Bureau of Investigation and Statistics—China's dreaded secret service. As a young officer Miles had spent a great deal of time in China and had gotten to know Tai Li, who had agents in every town and village of China and in the Chinese army as well. Miles had gained the Chinese general's attention due to his interest in and respect for the Chinese.

Created in April 1943, SACO's mission was to train Chinese in guerrilla warfare, sabotage, and subversion, and to establish weather and radio-intercept stations. Barrow was one of a handful of Marines who were assigned to the secret unit. "I learned that SACO had been formed the previous year by an agreement between President Roosevelt and Generalissimo Chiang Kai-shek. The organization was dominated by the navy because it was interested in establishing stations in China to be able to forecast weather for its Pacific Fleet operations. The Chinese were willing to cooperate but wanted something in return: U.S. supplies and equipment for its guerrilla forces. The navy looked to the Marine Corps to provide the leadership."

Barrow waited for several weeks before boarding the *General A. E. Anderson* on June 26 with two other Marine officers, Second Lieutenants Frank Dent and James Witt. "Getting into China was no easy task. We had to wait for special arrangements. There was great secrecy surrounding the mission."

Ray Davis

Ray Davis, with three and one-half years of service, was a hard-charging antiaircraft specialist. He developed a strong interest in gunnery while serving aboard the USS *Portland,* a heavy cruiser. Davis recounted that "When you go to sea and live with Marines on those 5-inch guns and the antiaircraft (AA) battery for fifteen months, you get excited about what you are doing. Aboard ship, I was asked about going back to the Base Defense School . . . and that had some appeal."

Assigned to the Marine Corps Schools, Quantico, Davis found that his strong technical background from Georgia Tech stood him in good stead. However, he learned that gunnery school graduates were assigned duty with defense battalions stationed on some remote Pacific Islands, and he looked for a more exciting venue. One day he ran into one of his Basic School instructors, the legendary Lewis B. "Chesty" Puller. "Puller said to me: 'Well, I'll tell you, Old Man (he always called me "Old Man" throughout our two long careers), there is a billet down in the 1st Division at Guantanamo Bay (Cuba) where they need an antiaircraft officer."

Davis hot-footed it over to the school's commander and volunteered. "Davis, you're the first one to ask, so you've got it," he was told. In the summer of 1941, he received orders to join the 1st Antiaircraft Machine Gun Battery, 1st Marine Division, Cuba. Initially assigned as a platoon leader, he was reassigned as executive officer just prior to returning to Camp Lejeune, North Carolina. Shortly afterward, he was designated as the division antiaircraft officer. "I dealt with the Operations Section of the 1st Marine Division and contributed to various plans and schemes to administer AA training. I ran a division AA school, where we had airplanes pull target sleeves across Onslow Beach for all the truck drivers and others with machine guns. They all took a shot at the sleeves at least once, so that when we went to war, they had some experience under their belt." In June 1942, Davis' unit received secret orders to deploy, objective unknown. He later confessed , "We had no idea that our destination was Guadalcanal."

O'er the Seas, Let's Go Men
Ray Davis

Davis boarded the SS *Erickson*, a converted passenger liner, at San Francisco for the month-long trip to Wellington, New Zealand. "This ship was not prepared for the load of troops and supplies. . . . We had trouble with the food; some of it was bad. People were vomiting all over the ship, and there inadequate head [toilet] facilities." The men were fed two inadequate, poorly prepared meals a day, less than 1,500 calories. The embarked troops lost between sixteen to twenty-three pounds per man. The cooks used oil substitutes in place of cooking oil, causing a round of "green apple quickstep." Just prior to sailing, the ship attempted to load rancid butter and condemned eggs. They also gouged the troops by selling items at exorbitant prices. Davis heard, "There were threats against the crew and even rumors that Marines were ready to throw them overboard." Ore J. Marion, a career Marine who served on Guadalcanal with Company L, 3rd Battalion, 5th Marines, had harsh feelings about the navy. "Each time we went aboard ships (I counted fifty-four large ones in my career) we were always made to feel like unwelcome relatives. Usually we were treated like crap—fed crap. I couldn't believe it: time after time. It was always a pleasure getting ashore, even under fire."

Bob Barrow

The *Anderson* was not a luxury liner, as Barrow soon found out. "We had a great number of soldiers on board; it was crowded as hell. The ship did not have an escort. She sailed at high speed, setting a zigzag course to throw off any submarine threat. We wore life jackets the entire time. It took us forty-five days to reach Bombay." Barrow and a handful of other officers took an old British-style train across the breadth of India, arriving in Calcutta a week later. Along the way, they had to shoo the ubiquitous cattle off the narrow-gauge track, as well as combat the mind-numbing boredom of the slow, old train. They were trucked to a forward airfield. "I flew the Hump in a C-46 with an Australian pilot and American co-pilot. We had to fly a circuitous route to avoid Japanese planes. It was awesome to fly at 18,000 feet, our maximum altitude, through passes and still see mountaintops 7,000 to 8,000 feet above the aircraft." A jeep met Barrow as he landed and took him to Naval Unit 2, Chengyuan, in Hunan Province.

Ray Davis

Upon arrival in Wellington, Davis "learned that the Japanese were building an airfield in the Solomon Islands that would have endangered U.S. shipping routes." He was designated the transport quartermaster and had to stay aboard the "Good Ship Vomit" for an additional six days. *Erickson* had been commercially loaded and all the cargo had to be offloaded before it could be reloaded in other ships in a combat configuration. Davis remembered: "It rained constantly and all the cardboard packing boxes and all the paper items on the dock got wet, melted down, and trampled over." An eyewitness described the scene: "The dock was covered with drifts of mushy cornflakes, thousands of rolling C ration cans, and cases of water-logged cigarettes and pogey bait." The ships were finally loaded and the division sailed for Guadalcanal, the first offensive of the war.

Looking back on those experiences, Davis reflected, "As a battery commander sailing for combat . . . I was launching the building of what I hoped would be a distinguished record. . . . Some of my less fortunate Quantico classmates sat out the war as prisoners of the Japanese or in the drudgery of defending various pieces of real estate on small Pacific isles."

CHAPTER 14

OPERATION SHOESTRING

The 1st Marine Division's capture of Guadalcanal should have been tagged "Operation Shoestring." It was launched by a "snake-bit" navy command, which was loath to place its ships in harm's way, and when the chips were down, sailed off into the sunset, leaving the Marines to fend for themselves. Ore Marion of Company L, 5th Marines, described his feeling toward the navy saying, "We were surrounded and abandoned all the way down the line. . . . The goddam[n] navy brought us here." Finally, the Marines had to depend on their Japanese adversaries for much of their support, including captured vehicles and food stocks. Ray Davis noted that "There were problems with chow and health. After the Japs drove our navy off, we had few rations. Japanese rice with raisins (to camouflage the bugs!) became the staple diet at times." Intelligence of the island was practically nonexistent. The most recent chart dated from 1908. Colonel Frank B. Goettge, the division intelligence officer, scrambled to gather information, "here, there, and everywhere, from traders, planters, and shipmasters who had visited or lived on the island. The resultant tactical map of the Guadalcanal landing area was little more than a mimeographed battlefield sketch."

Guadalcanal's ninety-mile length is serrated by three mountain ranges, rising in one place to eight thousand feet. The island is a jumbled carpet of green ridges, foothills, and thick jungle, intersected by streams that flow to the ocean. A wide belt of grassy plains runs along the northern coast. Most of the population lives here, in clusters of native huts. Copra plantations, with their well-ordered coconut groves, provided the population with a source of income. Heavy rainfall, coupled with temperatures in the high eighties, resulted in a humid, unhealthy climate. Malaria, dengue, catarrhal "cat" fever, and fevers "of unknown origins" sapped strength and vitality. Fungus infections grew rapidly, causing sores that refused to heal, further weakening immune systems.

The division's health deteriorated quickly in this tropical "paradise." Hundreds of men came down with malaria and dysentery. Davis was no exception. "We were overrun with malaria. With inadequate protection and an unbelievable mosquito population, the situation simply got out of hand. I had both types, plus a severe hepatitis jaundice attack. . . . Fortunately, I had a friendly surgeon who kept me out of the hospital and on my feet. . . ." The division's medical log showed that in the three-month period just prior to leaving the island, six thousand Marines were admitted to the hospital, most for contracting malaria. "In addition, we had dysentery following our first major ground battle with Japanese forces. We killed over seven hundred of them in one small area and it took several days to get them buried. This delay brought a deluge of flies, which was overwhelming—really awful." Ore Marion vividly remembered the dead: "All I can say about decaying bodies in the jungle is that the stink sticks to your body, to everything; your eyebrows, your gum line, and [the] ball[s] of your feet. The stench is unbelievable."

The V Ring
Ray Davis

The first Higgins boats carrying two battalions of the 5th Marines touched down on Beach Red at eight minutes past nine. The Marines stormed ashore. Much to their relief, the beaches were undefended and they landed "standing up." Ray Davis went ashore an hour and a half later. "As we loaded into boats and were heading for shore, a formation of Japanese torpedo bombers attacked us. This was the first engagement for these American ships, and shot and shell were flying. . . . The sky was full, just full of bullets. I felt very uneasy out there with the Japanese aircraft strafing and bombing, and our own ships firing machine guns and AA guns. It seemed like everybody was shooting at everybody and everything. Indeed, I was happy to get ashore." By nightfall, the Special Weapons Battalion, including Davis' battery, was deployed around the half-completed Japanese airfield, soon to be named Henderson Field for Major Lofton R. Henderson, who had been shot down leading Marine dive-bombers at Midway. They were to provide low-altitude antiaircraft protection for the airfield.

Before leaving Camp Lejeune, the Special Weapons Battalion had been equipped with new types of antiaircraft guns to combat Japanese air power. "It was decided at the last minute that we would keep all of the .50-caliber heavy machine guns and take along a bunch of 20mm (Oerlikon) plus 40mm (Bofors) automatic guns received in crates from the factories in Sweden. Consequently, we went in equipped with three complete sets of weapons." These extra weapons were quickly deployed, a welcome addition to the airfield's defensive firepower. "We had a mechanical fire-control computer for the 40s. We also had 20mm and .50-caliber guns. For anything above four thousand feet however, we had no accuracy. Three weeks later, the 3rd Defense Battalion came in with 90mm guns, and we were subordinated to them. Fortunately, we had some Marine fighter squadrons (VMFs) to deal with the (Mitsubishi G4M) Betty bombers." Guadalcanal veteran Fred Heidt described the Japanese bombers: "The worse thing were these big flights of medium bombers we called 'Bettys.' They'd usually come about noon. You could just about set your watch by them. They came in vee formations. There might be twenty to forty aircraft in flight. You could hear them throbbing off in the distance. . . . When they came over at about 20,000 feet, you could see the bombs drop very clearly."

Occasionally a Japanese Zero would swoop down to strafe. "Two or three were shot down, and of course, my guys claimed them. One thing is for sure, my guys enthusiastically shot [at] any Japanese who might have been in range." Marine fighter ace Joe Foss thought they did better than that: "On the twenty-sixth of October, antiaircraft gunners pointed out with some pride that they had shot down twenty-six planes during the month—one for every day. This was roughly one for every eight shot down by fighter planes and represented a highly effective showing. Don't think we didn't appreciate it." Guadalcanal veteran Bud DeVere was stationed in the communications center: "I would listen to the Wildcat pilots talking over the radio. Someone would say something like, 'Hey Joe, there's one on your tail.' And you'd look up and see some fighter on Foss's tail."

Davis established his CP, a deep slit trench covered with crisscrossed coconut logs, "alongside the upper end of the airstrip, in a coconut grove, just a hundred feet off the edge . . ." During the first few nights ashore, the green troops were a little "trigger happy," prone to shoot at shadows, noises, and imaginary Japanese attackers. One of Davis' men fell victim to the fear. "A sergeant of mine, sitting in my command post, raised up to shoot an approaching enemy in the darkness. I managed to knock his Tommy gun up just in the nick of time, as I recognized our Battalion Commander, Bob Luckey (Luckey was lucky!)." Passwords and countersigns were used to avoid these intramural firefights, but even they did not reduce the firing. "One night the password was something or other, and the response (from the incoming man) was 'Hallelujah!' The entire night was filled with endless shooting and shouts of Hallelujah; it sounded like a Holy Roller meeting on the 4th of July!" The commanding general solved the problem by requiring that all rear-echelon troops carry unloaded weapons, with bayonet fixed. Davis followed this same procedure in all his subsequent landings.

Henderson Field acted as a magnet for Japanese attacks. Eighteen to twenty-four Mitsubishi G4M Betty bombers, escorted by up to twenty A6M Zeke fighters, arrived punctually at noon. Their perfect V formations flew too high for Davis' battery of light antiaircraft weapons. Occasionally, however, a foolhardy fighter pilot would make a low-level pass, much to the delight of the gunners.

For six months, Davis was caught in the V ring, the bull's-eye of the Japanese attacks to defeat the Guadalcanal Marines. "Enemy troops were trying to capture that airstrip by attacking overland. . . . They also sent airplanes over every day, and sailed warships down to shell us. During the month of October, there were thirty-one consecutive days during which we were bombed from overhead with the Betty bombers every day at noon. Also, we were shelled at night, every night, from battleships, cruisers, and destroyers offshore. It was a very busy time." Davis' men dug in—deeper and deeper. "We had a rule that there would be two men in a foxhole. In a deep, narrow foxhole, there would be two guys, so a direct hit would never get more than two Marines." Bud DeVere remembered what it was like to be caught in a bombing raid: "When you start[ed] hearing the bombs come down . . . you kept your head down. And I mean down. There was a lot of shrapnel in the air, and any part of your body that was exposed might not be there when the planes left."

Thayer Soule, division assistant intelligence officer for photography, was close to one of Davis' emplacements. "The luckiest group was the 20mm gun crew nearest to us on the airfield. Their gun was dug in. About thirty feet away, in a fit of energy, they had dug in their sleeping quarters so that their cots were below ground level. One night a plane slipped in and dropped a bomb on the gun, destroying it. If the crew had had a minute's warning, they would have been manning it. Two days later, during a major attack, when they were manning a replacement gun, a bomb hit their sleeping quarters. Sergeant Fitch said, 'Our numbers just weren't up.' "

Despite weeks of heavy bombing and shelling, Davis' battery had relatively few casualties. They learned quickly. "We could see the enemy bomb bays open and hear the clicks of the bomb release before we jumped into our holes. At night, we absorbed fire from ships . . . [that] were out of range of my guns, but we watched carefully to see the ships' gun flashes because they would signal the time to go for the holes." One very dark night Davis found himself on the horns of a dilemma. "I dived into my hole to come face-to-face with a large screaming bat. I told him, as I recovered from the terror and shock: 'Buddy—yell all you want—I'm staying!' " Bombs won over bats.

There were so many Japanese air attacks that Davis got a little blasé. "We got so 'salty' that we would wait until the bomb bays opened at a certain point in the sky before we got into our holes." He did not realize that a regimental CP had moved in across the runway. Lieutenant Colonel Clifton B. Cates, its commander and World War I hero, was a stickler for taking cover. "If people didn't get low enough in their holes during an air raid, he'd shoot toward them with his pistol." Davis played his usual game, but this time several pistol rounds cracked over his head. "I went tearing across that runway to straighten out whoever the hell it was shooting at me with a pistol. I ran headlong into Clifton Bledsoe Cates for the first time! He told me exactly what was going on. In short, if I'd been in my hole, there would've been no chance of my getting shot. I said, 'Aye, Aye, sir!' to the future Commandant of the Marine Corps, and moved out smartly."

Japanese fire was not the only hazard Davis faced. Bombs and ammunition were haphazardly scattered throughout the area and then forgotten as the fast growing Kunai grass covered the lethal piles. The first Japanese bombing attacks set the grass on fire. Davis, as the local commander, had to put it out. "I would rush my troops out in order to extinguish the fires. On one occasion, I lost a boot while running. Minutes later I found myself standing with one shoe on and one bare foot, on top of a five-hundred-pound bomb, beating out fire around it to keep the fire off the bomb!"

Davis thought October was the toughest month. "At that point there was no food, and we had to eat captured rice. The cook said that the black spots in the rice were weevils, but some of us ate them, too, as a source of protein. The cook put a few raisins to camouflage them. Fishing boats came in from the West Coast with food. We were sick with dengue, malaria, and dysentery. Our medical supplies were lost. Vice Admiral Robert L. Ghormley said he had to withdraw the fleet and that we had his permission to surrender if we needed to. The Marine commander, Major General Alexander A. Vandegrift, refused." Ore Marion remembered the dark days of October saying, "We know now Vandegrift had been told he could surrender . . . we little snuffies who fought the war, not those assholes in Washington, Pearl, or Australia, let it be known that 'the goddamm Navy brought us here and when those bastards are ready to take us off this island—that's when we'll go.' That's how we, just kids, felt: and that's what we did."

Cactus Air Force
Roy Geiger

The R4D Skytrain transport had trouble finding the darkened field through the clouds. There were no searchlights to guide it in. The 1st Marines sent up flares as a field expedient. Finally, the hum of the plane's motors could be heard over the runway. Antiaircraft gunners of Ray Davis' Special Weapons Battery tracked the twin-engine aircraft as it approached Henderson Field in the gathering darkness. "Hold fire, friendly aircraft" was passed over the telephone circuits. The R4D finally touched down on the battered runway and braked to a stop. A crewmember opened the hatch. Stocky, white-haired Roy Geiger appeared in the opening, took a quick look around, and climbed to the ground. That small step marked a turning point in the fortunes of the Cactus Air Force, a moniker derived from Guadalcanal's code name for the island's embattled air squadrons.

Geiger, now a brigadier general, brought an energy and optimism that raised the spirit of the battered collection of squadron survivors. Medal of Honor recipient Joe Foss remembered that the "Old Man" "often sat at fighter headquarters, watching patrols take off. One dawn an unlucky pilot, with his eyes blurry from sleep, taxied into a bomb crater and wrecked his prop. When the young lieutenant came up, the general glowered at him and snapped, 'Was that necessary?' It was all he said, but it was enough." Marine Brigadier General Samuel B. Griffith, II, characterized Geiger as "curt, cold, and some said, ruthless. He certainly was determined to squeeze the ultimate ounce of performance from men and machines." In an April 1995 *Marine Corps Gazette* article Brigadier General F. P. Henderson described the traits that made Geiger a great leader: he was better educated than any Marine general; intelligent, a quick learner; able to function in adversity; and demanded excellence in his staff. Colonel Walter Bayler watched Geiger during an air raid. "The General didn't seem perturbed by what the Japs had to offer. . . . Right up to the last judicious second he stood out in the open, chewing his cigar, resisting all attempts on the part of his staff to entice him into a foxhole."

A waiting jeep drove Geiger the two hundred yards up a small hill to the "Pagoda," a wooden-sided structure built by the Japanese. The forty-by-fifty-foot coconut-pole building became the command post for the commander, aircraft, Guadalcanal (ComAirCACTUS), and Geiger's new command. The Pagoda's distinctive shape—the roofline had an oriental profile—was a familiar landmark as well as an aiming point. However, it was close to Geiger's airmen, so he chose it despite its vulnerable location. From here, he controlled the desperate air defense of the island. Henderson Field was the focus of the campaign—whoever controlled Henderson controlled Guadalcanal.

The building served as a combination sleeping and operations center. The sleeping area, two rows of cots placed end to end, lined the north wall. Camouflaged mosquito nets protected sleepers from the voracious insects. One wag said they were so large that one landed on the runway and was filled with five hundred gallons of high-octane fuel. Miscellaneous field gear and clothing were scattered about, giving the area more of a college dorm look than military barracks. "Operations" consisted of two desks, numerous EE-8 field telephones, and a jumble of American and Japanese equipment. Two watch officers and their enlisted assistants manned the desks.

Lieutenant C. C. Colt, USN, assistant intelligence officer, described his workspace: "We had a couple of desks, a very poor map of the Solomon Islands tacked up over one, and miscellaneous intelligence gear, most of it useless, distributed on the desks and on top of the heaviest steel map filing case and command chest, anywhere, ever carried to the scene of the war." Geiger often used this area for conferences. On one occasion, he wanted more intelligence about the Japanese troop night landings. Soule attended. "Geiger made a suggestion that startled everyone. 'Let's send up a plane and take flash pictures of the landings. They could be developed right away. We'd know where they were and could respond at once.' We sat in stunned silence. It was a crazy idea. Major Michael Sampas, Geiger's intelligence officer, looked straight at me, but his face was blank. I was trying to decide how to be as polite as possible, when Mike saved me. 'General,' he said, 'that is pure, unadulterated horseshit!' We gasped in relief and astonishment. Geiger, taken aback, said, 'Now, Mike, simmer down. It was only an idea.' That was the end of it."

Colt closely observed Geiger's daily routine in the Pagoda. "Here General Geiger reigned supreme, though with considerable informality. By day, he was usually to be found sitting on a cot in the central, railed area, talking with his subordinates. He could walk out the door and survey his planes as they took off or landed. In the evening, the general usually had sessions with the senior man on his staff and his air group and squadron commanders. The general was a man of few words, and his subordinates did most of the talking. But he made the decisions, and he had plenty of suggestions. His was the final word, and he never tried to avoid taking responsibility. At night (and it was unusually early), the general would pull off his shoes and shirt, and possibly his trousers, and turn in on one of the cots. He slept, when the Japanese permitted us to sleep, with ease and vigor. General Geiger's snoring was great in volume and of sustained intensity. It could easily be distinguished from the others . . . by its deep tone and belligerent character."

On the day of Geiger's arrival, Cactus Air Force, consisted of just sixty-four flyable aircraft, a mixture of Marine and navy SBDs (Douglas

Dauntless dive-bombers), F4Fs (Wildcat fighters), TBFs (Grumman torpedo planes), and three lonely, outclassed army P-400s (Aircobra low-level pursuit planes). Henderson Field, their landing strip, was a raw, unfinished bomb- and naval-gunfire-cratered 2,400-foot gravel runway, with an additional thousand feet covered with Marston matting, pierced steel planking (PSP). This rudimentary strip was sited in the middle of a large, cleared field, bordered by a sea of green coconut palms, which made it stick out like a sore thumb—a bombardier's dream. The field ran generally northeast-southwest, paralleling the coast, and close to Vandegrift's thinly held defensive positions. At night, the pilots could see machine gun tracers and hear the distinctive crump of mortars and artillery—a constant reminder that the Japanese were only a banzai away. Hastily dug, inadequate aircraft revetments lined its perimeter.

The strip was in such poor condition that it caused almost as many losses as enemy action. In the baking tropical sun, it threw off clouds of black dust that plagued radial engines. When it rained, the field turned into a muddy goop that mired the planes in six inches of liquid muck. Even jeeps found it difficult to negotiate. VMF-223 pilot Marion Carl claimed, "It was widely held that Guadalcanal was the only place on earth where you could stand up to your knees in mud and still get dust in your eyes."

Support facilities were almost nonexistent—no fuel trucks, hangars, or repair facilities. Damaged aircraft were cannibalized for spare parts. There were no bomb hoists; ground crews had to muscle the five-hundred-pound bombs into place. Fuel, always in critical supply, had to be hand-pumped out of fifty-five-gallon drums into twelve-quart buckets before being poured into airplanes. At one point, Geiger was informed there was no gasoline after Japanese shelling had destroyed the fuel dump. He pondered the news for a moment and then demanded, "Where's Gray?" Captain Jack Gray, his aide, stepped forward. "Gray," Geiger mumbled, "we haven't got any gasoline. We need it to get the planes off. You get in a jeep and don't come back till you find some." To Gray's everlasting credit, he found a hundred drums that had been overlooked, enough to keep Cactus planes in the air until the next resupply.

Living conditions verged on the primitive. Squadron commander Lieutenant Colonel Richard C. Mangrum, who had led twelve dive-bombers of VMSB-232 from the USS *Long Island* to Henderson Field on August 20, 1942, claimed somewhat tongue in cheek that "The general concept of Marine Corps operations envisions rough field conditions, but just how rough is sometimes a bit shocking even to Marines!" Pilots lived in mud-floored tents in the habitually flooded coconut plantation called "Mosquito Grove." The general health of the aircrews and headquarters personnel steadily deteriorated. Sanitary conditions were lacking, and, as a result, dysentery, fungus infections, dengue fever, beriberi, and malaria were commonplace. The men lived on two meals a day, built around Spam or cold hash—and sometimes captured rice. Colt commented, "Geiger took whatever was offered with good grace, usually canned hash for breakfast, and canned hash, dehydrated potatoes, and canned peaches at any other meal. He usually drove down to the "area," a Quonset hut in the middle of a large coconut plantation, and ate with his staff and some of the Marine flyers. He had a table at one end of the building where he "held court." Jack Cram recalled that "It was a sight to see [General Geiger] carrying his mess gear walking in the mess line for his food. He'd walk to the river every four days to wash his own clothes. He drove his own jeep and slept on a wooden floor."

Major General Stanley Larsen, USA, who served on Guadalcanal commented, "The war we confronted on Guadalcanal is, in my opinion, almost impossible to comprehend because the terrain, the climate, the physical nature of the battlefield is beyond the experience of people who were not there to see it."

Backs to the Wall

The men desperately needed a respite from the constant enemy shelling. Japanese artillery, ships, planes, and even submarines bombarded the Marine positions, sending men scurrying for the dubious safety of slit trenches and bomb shelters. A sign over one shelter read, "Beneath these portals pass the fastest men in the world." Henderson Field, known affectionately by its defenders as the "bull's-eye," was singled out for special attention. "Washing Machine Charlie," a Japanese float plane named for its unsynchronized propellers, dropped small bombs at well-spaced intervals. This nighttime intruder seldom hit anything but interrupted desperately needed sleep. Thayer Soule, assistant intelligence officer, described the effect. "It was not the planes that did the damage but the hours without sleep and the terror when the bombs fell. In itself, each night was little more than a nuisance, but night after night, week after week, month after month, the attack built tension."

More seriously, heavy combatants of the enemy's fleet sailed down "the Slot" to pound the airfield at night, providing cover while Japanese transports landed troops. "Louie the Louse" dropped the first in a series of brilliant flares over the airfield. Lieutenant C. C. Colt, the junior officer of the watch, manned the desk. "At around 10:30 . . . the telephone rang and the radar watch told us a bogey was on the screen, closing. We woke up the General (Geiger), who moved slowly down the hill with most of his staff." Colt sounded the alarm. "I was busy cranking the siren, when out over Lunga Channel a plane started dropping flares. It was a fine sight—a perfect line of flares, beautifully spaced, lighting up the beach and the channel." He and another officer moved to cover. "As we started down for the tunnel, there was a colossal bang, directly overhead, and an enormous flare—or star shell—burst directly over Henderson Field. It was followed by eerie whistlings, and then a roar as if an express train were coming in our direction. We dove into a radio dugout, reasonably deep . . . in which were three or four highly nervous enlisted men. . . ."

The Bombardment

On the night of October 13, two Japanese battleships and their escorts methodically shelled the field with more than seven hundred rounds of heavy caliber ammunition. For the men who lived through it, the shelling was simply called "the bombardment." Soule was asleep in his tent when the shelling started. "The Pagoda siren wailed Condition Red. Outside, a thousand rockets burst in the sky. The tent snapped taunt. The blast blew me from my bunk. Another crushing blast! A heavy salvo landed on the other side of the ridge. Trees snapped." He scrambled into a bunker, "a nine-foot-square hole. The roof was logs, steel plates, and sandbags. . . . The earth heaved. Heavy pieces thudded on the roof. My stomach caved in. My head swam. The light went out. Or was I blind? I choked on the dust now thick in the air. We all coughed, gasped, coughed again, and sat there dazed. Nobody spoke."

When the gunfire temporarily lifted, Colt and another officer made a run for shelter, a tunnel dug into the side of Pagoda Hill. "We found the general and most of his staff in the chamber, literally sweating it out. It was steaming hot and crowded with men." The shelling started again. The general, in a bold act of defiance, lay down on a cot and "went sound asleep, snoring magnificently." Colt thought he awoke once, when the Japanese fire stopped, and mumbled, "Is it over?" and dropped off again. At dawn, Geiger viewed the destruction. "In the early light, he could see holes in Henderson . . . where 14- and 16-inch shells had hit. Over south of the field, where some transient B-17s were parked, and to the north where most of the fighters were located, the sky was red with flame." Black smoke marked a blazing oil fire. An ammunition dump exploded with a roar. The runway was rent and torn, the steel matting twisted and bent like a pretzel. There were nineteen shell craters along the straightaway. The Pagoda had taken six heavy caliber hits, which snapped the coconut pylons like matchwood.

Geiger, clad only in muddy skivvy shirt, khaki pants, and shoes, looked at the utter devastation for several minutes, then turned to his operations officer and said hoarsely, "Well Ray, let's get some planes in the air." Colt remembered that Geiger "sat down heavily on the edge of a trench. . . . He looked tired, despite a heavy sleep. He mopped his face with a dirty handkerchief, tipping back his steel helmet." Major Joe Renner, Henderson Field's operations officer, lamented how bad things were. "They've got our backs molded into the wall. The F4Fs can't meet all the [Japanese] raids. We haven't enough gas or ammunition to send them up each time. . . . If they ever try to break through what's left today . . . God help us . . . it'll be bad."

Geiger's air patrol reported a fleet of six Japanese transports, loaded with soldiers, escorted by several destroyers headed for Guadalcanal. The bombardment was intended to knock out his Cactus Air Force to permit the safe landing of the reinforcements. Geiger scrambled everything that could fly in a desperate attempt to squash the landing.

Saga of the Blue Goose

Japanese Zeros took station over the landing area. A mixed bag of American F4F-4s, SBDs, and TBFs scrambled from the damaged field to intercept the transports, but there were not enough. The Japanese were landing reinforcements just a few miles away, and the Cactus Air Force was desperately short of torpedo planes to sink them. The general's own plane, the *Blue Goose*, a dark-blue Consolidated PBY5A amphibian, was still serviceable. On Geiger's orders, two torpedoes were attached to the underside of the wings, with a manual release jury rigged in the cockpit. Geiger reasoned that "If Navy flyers could carry torpedoes at Midway, by God, a Marine flyer like (my) own pilot, Jack Cram, can do it."

Major "Mad" Jack Cram, Geiger's pilot and junior aide, volunteered, although he was not convinced the experiment would work. Colt wrote an account of Cram's attack. "He got off Henderson and made his attack on a transport circling off the beach. His torpedo ran true and exploded against the side of a Japanese transport, sinking the *Sasago Maru*. It was a fabulous exploit, for the big lumbering plane had to make a straight run in to the attack, launch close in, and get away as best it could, under AA fire for much too long." As Cram came off the target, five Japanese Zeros began firing passes, one at a time, spraying the lumbering *Blue Goose* with machine gun fire. The PBY's crew returned fire with a vengeance. Cram jinked and roller-coasted, trying to make the plane a poor target. As he barreled over the end of Henderson Field, a Zero played its wing guns and cannon over the fuselage. A damaged Marine F4F casually pulled out of the landing pattern and shot the Zero down, without retracting his wheels. Cram was able to safely land the general's badly shot up aircraft. The PBY was riddled, the starboard engine hit, the fuel tanks holed, the tail surfaces almost shot off, and the port gunner's blister shattered.

"Geiger was enormously pleased," but cooked up an elaborate prank. He sent for Cram, who arrived to find the Old Man glowering. "Understand you got that plane shot up," Geiger snarled. Cram, still shaken up, replied, "One hundred and seventy-five holes, sir." The general launched into sham harangue, threatening Cram with everything but a firing squad at dawn. Finally, one of the witnesses uttered a belly laugh, which cracked Geiger up. "Jack, that was a damn fine job," he said, and immediately wrote Cram up for a Navy Cross.

Charles McMurtry interviewed Cram for a Honolulu newspaper. The flyer was quick to praise his boss. "When you work for General Geiger, all your experiences are exciting. He's the kind of person who wants to be at the front lines. He's always into something. You never know what it will be, but you can be sure it will be exciting. One night, in the midst of Japanese shelling, he asked if I'd take him up. The weather was stinking, with storms all night, but General Geiger detected two Japanese forces coming down. As a result, we sank two destroyers with aerial bombs that morning."

Setting the Example

Aircraft losses, inadequate food, primitive living conditions, and sickness robbed the surviving pilots of their fighting spirit. One pilot lamented, "We were fired upon by Japanese troops as we landed. We were always under fire on takeoffs and landings." Morale plummeted and seemed to come to a head when several new pilots complained the runway was unusable. The fifty-seven-year-old Geiger simply walked down the strip to the first serviceable Dauntless dive-bomber, climbed aboard, and took off. He found a Japanese antiaircraft battery and attacked it with a one-thousand-pound bomb. After pulling out of the dive, he reversed course and landed thirty minutes later, weaving in and out over the cratered runway. Several young pilots witnessed the landing, which effectively ended the grousing about the runway's condition. Joe Foss heard about the exploit. "I don't believe he ever gave a thought to his personal safety. Once, just for fun, he loaded a thousand-pound egg onto a dive-bomber and went up over the hills to bomb the Japs on a ridge. He got a good hit, too." Geiger remarked to his tough chief of staff, Colonel Louis Woods, "Oh, I guess I just did it for spite." Woods was more outspoken. "They've got to keep flying. It's better to do that than get a Jap bayonet stuck in the ass!" Merwin Silverthorn remarked on Geiger's dedication. "Old timers in aviation also recall the many, many instances of determination and flying skill wherein he displayed his ability and willingness to fly any mission which he assigned to another."

One morning, just at dawn, a large explosion brought Geiger and crew out of the Pagoda at double-time. Two SBDs were preparing to take off, when two more explosions erupted close behind them. It was the consensus that the Japanese must have landed one or more large-caliber artillery pieces, later named "Pistol Pete." Colt found the intermittent shelling exasperating. "Early in the morning, just after dawn, once or twice in the middle of the day, and along toward dusk, it would open up. There would be a rumble and a crack. The first shell would bring the occupants to their feet. A second or third, however, precipitated action." One morning, two very close bursts sent everyone scrambling. "General Geiger, for all his years, was no slow mover. He was pumping down the hill when suddenly he drew to a halt . . . he shouted over to his aide, Lieutenant Colonel J. C. "Toby" Munn, 'Toby, we've got to quit this damn running. It's interfering with our work.' From then on . . . we didn't leave the Pagoda."

Geiger developed a system of air raid warnings based on radar and/or sightings by the Coastwatchers, a network of British Commonwealth observers that monitored the Japanese. There were three conditions: "Green," no threat; "Orange," a raid was due in half an hour (a Japanese rising sun flag was run up the flagpole in front of the Pagoda); and "Red," which signified an imminent threat (a duty officer would crank up a siren). Warnings were not sufficient to keep the Japanese from making life miserable for the Pagoda's inhabitants. It became more and more obvious that they were using the building as a target. Colt noted, "One day, at least two of three raids plastered bombs too close to the Pagoda. Senior members of the staff pleaded with the general, insisting we should move." That night the building was gone. Colonel Walter Bayler watched its demise. "They knocked it down, converted it into a heap of rubble, then romped on the heap till it was flattened into one more scar on the much scarred hilltop." Colt wrote an entry in the much-battered log of the 1st Marine Air Wing. "Pagoda destroyed—by bulldozer."

Shortly after arriving on the island, Geiger met Vandegrift at the division command post. He carefully lowered a heavy canvas bag on the older man's desk. "Fan mail from Admiral Nimitz," he said, in answer to Vandegrift's quizzical expression. Geiger opened the sack, exposing a case of Scotch, a rare gift on Starvation Island. Geiger was soon promoted, making him equal in rank to Vandegrift. There was no friction, however, because the two were old friends and worked hand-in-hand in defending the island. Geiger concentrated on air support, while Vandegrift worked out the ground defense, but both were cut from the same cloth. When the navy decided to pull out and leave the Marines to their own devices, Vandegrift vowed to fight on, taking to the hills if necessary. Geiger exclaimed, "Archer

[Vandegrift's middle name], if we can't use the planes back in the hills we'll fly them out. But whatever happens, I'm staying here with you!" In late October, Vandegrift designated Geiger as his deputy when he flew to Noumea, New Caledonia, for a meeting with Admiral William F. Halsey, newly installed as commander, South Pacific (ComSoPac). During his absence, the Japanese launched a furious assault against the perimeter, which was beaten back by Geiger's timely employment of the division's reserves.

On November 7, Geiger received orders to assume regular duties as commanding general 1st Marine Air Wing on Espíritu Santo. Both he and Vandegrift opposed the transfer, but Halsey, who wanted Geiger to work more closely with his navy air staff, overruled them. Accordingly, the next day he and his aide climbed aboard a patched-up *Blue Goose* and flew off the island. For his "extraordinary heroism and distinguished service" on Guadalcanal, Geiger was awarded the Distinguished Flying Cross and a second Navy Cross. His exemplary performance also marked him as a comer, one slated for increased responsibility.

Ray Davis

"I pulled out [of Guadalcanal] in January 1943, just as the army units were coming in, and I was subsequently promoted to major. The 1st Marine Division was shipped to Australia to get replacements and equipment. We were out of action for eight to nine months—about 5,000 to 6,000 Marines were down with malaria. Guadalcanal changed a lot of minds, though—it proved that our guys could defeat the Japanese."

CHAPTER FIFTEEN

OPERATION CHERRY BLOSSOM

It's not what you know . . . it's who you know.
—Eddie Craig

In February 1942, Craig was assigned as the commanding officer, 2nd Pioneer Battalion, 2nd Marine Division, which was forming at Camp Elliott, near San Diego. "I made arrangements to have some very fine and highly qualified men transferred to my battalion, and before long I had a well-trained outfit, of which I was very proud." One day his old friend, Lem Shepherd, came down to observe training. "My men were trained in both shore party and engineer work, and in addition I had them well trained as an infantry battalion. They put on a good show." Shepherd liked what he saw. "When he left, he said, 'I'm going to have you transferred to the 9th Marines as (my) executive officer. I hated to lose the battalion, but I was very glad to get into an infantry outfit and especially with General Shepherd, whom I had known for a good many years." Shepherd's request brought Craig into a high-visibility combat assignment that led to increased responsibility and advancement.

Shortly after Craig joined the regiment, it was transferred to the new base at Camp Pendleton, forty miles north of San Diego. "We marched early one morning under full combat equipment and with all motor transport. Colonel Shepherd believed in having a complete CP set-up, including a folding head [toilet] for his personal use." The plywood one-seater outhouse was painted an appropriate Marine Corps green. However, "Even when folded, it was a rather a huge thing, and its purpose could not be disguised." Craig detailed an old-time sergeant to ensure Shepherd's potty reached the new bivouac site. Later that night, Shepherd roared, "Where the hell is my head?" Craig jumped in a jeep and backtracked along the line of march. Soon enough, he found the NCO stranded alongside the road, trying to thumb a ride. "What a sorry sight he was, a very military looking old timer, complete with handlebar mustache and full field equipment—and a folding head!" By darkness, Shepherd had his crapper.

Craig admired Shepherd. "Colonel Shepherd was a fine officer, who was always on the job and demanded perfection in training." He was particularly keen on all types of field training. "I'll never forget the first field problem we had. We were about to go home at 5 o'clock in the afternoon, when he announced that we would leave at six that night for a field problem." Promptly at six, the entire reinforced regiment, more than three thousand men, marched to the field. That night, orders were prepared to seize the Pendleton airfield. "At daylight, the regiment jumped off, hauling everything over those hills, including their machine gun carts and everything else, and took the airfield as scheduled. I was just about whipped, but the training was thorough and it paid off later on when we got into combat."

Heartrending Farewell

Embarkation was fast approaching, and Craig faced a heartbreaking farewell. "My beloved wife was ill with an advanced case of TB. We both knew that a cure would be a miracle and the doctor gave me little hope." Craig had met his wife, a British citizen, in Shanghai. "She was a beautiful and wonderful person and we were very close. I never realized the extent of her character or bravery until the time arrived for my departure for war." Major General Charles D. Barrett, Craig's division commander, knew of his wife's critical condition and visited her in the hospital. He offered to transfer her husband to another command, if she wanted him to stay behind. Barrett told Craig her response: "My husband was a Marine, and had trained for years for just this occasion. It was his duty to his country, and her duty as an American to send him under the circumstances. She said that the effect on her as an individual was small compared to the needs of his command."

The night before Craig's ship was to leave he spent at her bedside. "We talked all night—of our life together; of the future and our happiness despite her sickness." At dawn, his driver arrived to take him to the ship. "Betty maintained her composure till the very last and as I closed the door to her room, she had a smile on her face and said her last goodbye. I walked a few steps down the hall, but I felt I must see her once again. I turned, went back, and softly opened the door. She had broken down completely and lay sobbing on her bed. She would not have wanted me to see her in that condition. . . . I turned and quickly left. I will never forget that moment."

A few weeks later, Craig received a letter from the doctor stating that his wife's condition had worsened and advised him to fly home. "I showed the letter to General Barrett, who said there was no reason that I should not go for a short visit, as the division would not be in combat for some months." However, Major General Clayton B. Vogel, commander of Amphibious Corps, Pacific Fleet, to which the 3rd Marine Division was assigned, refused to approve the leave because "there was a war on." "I found out [later] that General Vogel dispatched a four-motored R-5D plane to the United States two days later with orders to pick up a load of liquor and a portable bar." Several staff officers went along and visited their families. "This made me sick to my stomach. He was one of the very few Marines who I could not respect or like. General Vogel was relieved of his command shortly after as he could not carry his command."

Craig was on Guadalcanal and had just assumed command of the 9th Marines from Lem Shepherd when he received a note from Mrs. Shepherd. "She had just been to my dear Betty's funeral. This was the first word that I received of her death." He later received a letter from a navy chaplain with the official notification. "I continued to receive letters from her for many days after, due to the slowness of the mail. In her last letter she indicated that she thought the end was near. . . . It was still a very brave and cheerful letter." Choked with emotion, Craig dove off by himself to find some privacy. "I finally ended up at the end of a trail. I got out and walked up and down the beach for hours, trying to compose myself and make some sense out of things. I finally realized what Betty would expect of me and how in her last letter she had told me to carry on, no matter what happened."

Chilly-eyed Marine's Marine

Early in October 1943, tragedy struck the staff of I Marine Amphibious Corps (I MAC) as it was planning for Operation Cherryblossom, a major amphibious assault on the island of Bougainville. Its commander, Major General Charles D. Barrett, died in an accidental fall, leaving a gaping hole in the chain of command. Lieutenant General Alexander A. Vandegrift, selected to be the next commandant, was hastily recalled with the promise that he would be relieved as quickly as possible. Admiral William F. "Bull" Halsey thought long and hard on who would replace Vandegrift. He carefully considered a host of officers he had observed since becoming commander, South Pacific (ComSoPac). One name emerged, Roy Geiger, whom Halsey knew from the darkest days on Guadalcanal.

Geiger had earned Halsey's respect. "Pilots, worn out by too many missions, sleepless nights, and poor food, on returning from battles that were still raging, sometimes tumbled exhausted out of their cockpit and crawled sobbing under the wings of their planes. Brigadier General Roy Geiger, with seemingly iron nerves and tireless muscles, forced them back into their planes, slapping and kicking, if necessary. Rough measures, but necessary to save Henderson Field and the pilots themselves." Halsey quickly approved the selection and Geiger was ordered to report as soon as possible. *Time* magazine of November 22, 1943, described Geiger as "thick-set, poker-faced, chilly eyed . . . another Marine's Marine."

Striking Ninth
Lem Shepherd

In March 1942, Lem Shepherd was assigned to form the 9th Marine Regiment (Striking Ninth) at Camp Pendleton, California. "When I took command of the 9th Marines we only had one battalion. The regiment was subsequently brought up to strength by reserves and recruits from the MCRD [Marine Corps Recruit Depot] at San Diego." Lieutenant Orville Freeman was one of the first who reported. "I came under the command of one of the truly great Marines of all time, then Colonel Lemuel Shepherd. I don't know any Marine, enlisted man or officer, who served with Shepherd who doesn't agree with that statement." Shepherd had a leadership style that encouraged the best in his men. One day, Freeman was directing his platoon on a field problem when he ran into the "Old Man." "I turned around and there was a grinning Colonel Shepherd. 'Freeman,' he said, 'you keep going just the way you are and someday you'll make a fine Marine officer.' Naturally I felt great about the whole thing."

Shepherd also had a tough side and could "kick your ass if he felt you deserved it." Freeman recited a story about one of Shepherd's officers who transferred to the Raiders. The transfer came in while he was in the field, ten miles from camp. The officer made the mistake of asking Shepherd for transport back to camp. "What?" Shepherd roared. "You got yourself transferred out of my outfit, which is about to be the best regiment in the Corps, and you expect me to get you a jeep? You son of a bitch; you think you're so tough, you can hike back!" Enough said. The crestfallen officer hitched up his gear and stepped out. Freeman never forgot Shepherd's admonition about an officer's responsibility. "Rank not only has its privileges but it also has its responsibilities. You are an officer. When you are in the field, you don't eat until your men have eaten and at night you don't get into your hole until the men are in theirs."

Shepherd revamped training because "Everybody was trying to do the right thing, but some just know how to train better than others. So, for a period of two months, I said, 'We're going to stop all battalion and company training, and every man in this regiment is going through a prescribed course of basic training under a competent instructor.' It really paid dividends." Shortly after assuming command, Shepherd learned about Guadalcanal. "The news came out in the newspapers, 'Marines land on Guadalcanal.' It was the first offensive move during the war, and it was a wonderful thing for the Marine Corps." Training took on a new meaning; the regiment would soon join their brothers in arms across the seas.

In January 1943, the 9th Marines, as part of the 3rd Marine Division, sailed for Auckland, New Zealand. Shepherd was billeted on the same ship as the division commander, Major General Charles Barrett, and his chief of staff, Colonel Alfred Noble. The three spent the entire voyage working on a standard operating procedure (SOP) for unloading supplies during an amphibious operation. The 1st Marine Division's trouble with supplies was fresh in their minds. Shepherd commented that the U.S. Navy "thought the Jap fleet was approaching, so they all shoved off and left the 1st Division without their supplies." Under General Barrett's direction, Shepherd and Noble produced an SOP for unloading supplies that was used throughout the Marine Corps and formed the basis for present doctrine.

Upon arrival in Auckland, Shepherd's regiment was billeted near the town of Pukukuli and immediately started conducting field exercises. "Of course there was difficulty because it was farming country and the farmers didn't want extensive maneuvers conducted over their cultivated land. However, they were very much afraid that the Japanese might land in New Zealand, and they welcomed us with open arms." Soldier Scott Wilson of the 25th Infantry Division loved New Zealand. "The best three months in the army were R and R in New Zealand. We ate wonderful food. The country was so beautiful. Most of the people were extremely friendly and many invited soldiers to their homes."

If Shepherd could not maneuver the men, he could certainly keep them in good shape. "I remember we made fifty-mile marches in three days living on reduced rations. While we were making this march, each man was issued a sock of rice with a piece of bacon, some hard tack, and some raisins. We subsisted on that and it worked out fine." This was before the development of packaged rations and "proved that you don't have to have a whole lot of different kind[s] of rations."

In June the 9th Marines, as part of the 3rd Division, sailed for Guadalcanal. Shepherd remembered that "We were billeted in that big coconut grove near Henderson Field, [where] we conducted a number of prolonged exercises. There were still Japs on the island, and it gave us an incentive for active patrolling. We occasionally found one. It was very interesting and instructive training." In mid-July 1943, Shepherd was promoted to brigadier general and assigned as the assistant division commander, 1st Marine Division. "I remember going to General Barrett and saying, 'General, it's wonderful to be made a brigadier, but the 9th Marines, I just love this outfit and I want to lead them in combat. We were making plans at that time to go to Bougainville. He said, 'You'd better take it. You've been promoted. You'd better take it now.' So, with great reluctance I left the 9th Marines and turned the regiment over to Eddie Craig, who'd been my executive officer, a very fine officer of the highest type."

Eddie Craig

At the change of command, Craig pledged to "carry on the traditions of the 9th Regiment, which I know, in the days to come, will defeat the Japs." Three and a half months later, Craig embarked on the attack transport ship (APA) *American Legion* for Operation Cherryblossom, the amphibious assault of Bougainville, the largest island in the Northern Solomons.

The landing plan called for the simultaneous landing of two regiments abreast. The 9th Marines, reinforced by the 3rd Raider Battalion, was assigned the left flank of the beachhead, 3rd Marines on their right. Intelligence estimated Japanese strength at one thousand in the immediate vicinity of the landing. Eight APAs and four AKAs (attack cargo transports) carried the Marines to the objective area. Craig, his headquarters, and one infantry battalion were embarked aboard the *American Legion*. "The 9th Regiment consisted of some 5,500 men counting the attached units, and we were all combat-loaded. We sailed for Éfaté, where we carried out a practice landing, simulating the one we were to make later on Bougainville."

On D-day, the attack transports followed the minesweepers into Empress Augusta Bay and anchored in line, about three thousand yards from the beach. General Quarters was sounded at 5:00 a.m., two and a half hours before H-hour. Many of the embarked troops lined the rails and watched as dawn broke bright and clear, in a beautiful sunrise. An hour later, they mustered on deck at their debarkation stations. At 6:45 a.m., the command "land the landing force" was signaled, and the Marines clambered over the sides, down cargo nets into Higgins boats. At this moment, Craig observed, "Jap planes came in to bomb us. Our air cover made short work of them and one dropped right near our ship." Craig and his small headquarters section boarded one of the "free boats," a landing craft that was not assigned to a specific assault wave and could land at the direction of the ranking officer aboard.

As Craig's landing craft made its run for the beach, he observed that "Bougainville looked beautiful but sinister in the distance with a large volcano lying among the low hills and mountains. On the way to the beach an air attack hit us. . . . We had our first casualties . . . an officer and two enlisted men. Looking ahead, I could see a steep and narrow sand beach with the surf piling up on it and knew we were in for trouble." The rolling surf played havoc with the unwieldy landing craft, vehicles, and personnel (LCVPs). More than eighty of the valuable craft broached and were left stranded on the beach, which caused severe problems in the general unloading phase of the operation.

Craig's assault battalions landed against light resistance and pushed rapidly inland to establish a night perimeter. The 3rd Marines on his right "ran head on into machine gun emplacements and took some casualties. My flank patrols were engaged during the night but my main line of resistance was not hit. The Raider Battalion, which was attached to my regiment, landed on Puruata Island and suffered heavy casualties in capturing that place." After checking the lines, Craig returned to his CP and had just opened a can of C rations when, "I received a radio from the division commander directing me to report to headquarters for a conference. I thought it rather unusual that I should be called all the way to division and presumed that there must be something in the wind."

Craig started out on the hazardous trip just as it was getting dark, which could not have been worse timing. The men were "trigger happy and had orders to shoot at anything moving during darkness. There were no roads or trails through the jungle. . . . I did not know exactly know where the division headquarters was." Somehow, he made it to the beach and flagged down an LVT (landing vehicle, tracked), which took him along the coast to an opening in the jungle where he was supposed to meet a guide. "I proceeded into the jungle and walked blindly toward what I hoped was the CP. I had several close calls but finally found the general." After exchanging pleasantries, "The general wanted to know how the day had gone! I was surprised to find out that the conference was only a routine matter."

A guide took him back to the same LVT and it proceeded in the pitch black to its original destination. Several times, they were shot at. After going ashore, Craig "groped my way along the beach trying to find the small trail leading to my CP. A shot rang out and I yelled at the top of my voice, 'Colonel Craig, coming through.' I finally reached my CP. I was a little shaken, to tell the truth, and decided right then and there never to call a subordinate to my CP under conditions of darkness and confusion, if I could ever help it."

Bloody Mire

As was Craig's habit, he went forward to observe the unit that was most heavily engaged. "I had left my CP to go to visit the Raider Battalion where it was engaged with the Japs, and because of the deep mud and lack of roads it was impossible to use a jeep. After a tiring hike through the mud and jungle, I finally reached the front lines and talked with Lieutenant Colonel Fred Beans, the battalion commander. I gave directions for the battalion to continue the attack . . . and (started) on my way back when I passed what I have always thought was the most gruesome sight that I witnessed during the war. A light tank going to the rear with wounded strapped to the outside was mired down in a swamp off the trail. It could not move, and I could see bandaged men with blood dripping down the side of the tank lying there helpless. They were serious cases or a tank would never have been used to get them back. To make matters worse, snipers had pinned the crew inside the tank and the wounded were lying in the open, unable to help themselves. It was a most pitiful sight!" Craig could do nothing and agonized over leaving them to get help. "I notified the Raider CP and had them send a platoon out to rescue the tank and wounded."

Among the Dead

Craig always established the regimental CP close to the front lines, relying on headquarters personnel for close-in security. One night they made the mistake of setting in at a well-known trail junction and were bombed. "I took shelter under one of the LVTs with my exec and orderly. As we lay there, I thought, *Here we are lying under an LVT loaded with hundreds of gallons of gasoline. . . . What would happen if we get hit.*" Vehicle traffic had churned through the mud and unearthed several Japanese dead. "I will always remember one huge-looking Jap who was sitting right up in the mud with his face turned our way. Early the next morning, my orderly brought me a helmet with water in [it] to wash by. I splashed the water on my face and immediately smelled the terrific odor of dead Jap. He had dipped the water from a pool full of dead Japanese without knowing it."

The next day, as Craig returned from the front lines, an LVT stopped to give him a lift. "On climbing up the side, I found it was filled with dead Marines. The odor was terrific but the LVT had got underway and I was afraid to jump down, so I sat on the side and held on." The vehicle plowed through the thick undergrowth and he failed to see a large branch that knocked him into the cargo hold among the rotting corpses. "I was well acquainted with the dead by the time I debarked. There were fourteen of them piled on one another, and seemed to be in complete equipment even to their helmets."

Divine Intervention

Toward the end of the campaign, Craig received orders to launch a final attack on Christmas Day against a strongly held Japanese position. "I felt very deeply that my men should not be killed or wounded on that day. The matter worried me considerably." He planned for massive artillery preparation fires, "as I wanted to save the lives on this Christmas day; that is, the lives of my men." After doing all he could to prepare, Craig issued the orders and the men moved out to their assault positions. "I went to my tent and sat down and worried. The whole thing just did not seem right. We were scheduled to go back aboard ship in a few days, and on Christmas day, I must lose men, the men I had lived, trained, and fought with for so long. On an impulse, I got down on my knees and prayed to God that none of my men would be killed or seriously wounded." After some time he lay down, feeling that he had done all he could. "Sometime around three in the morning, my telephone rang and division informed me that forward patrols had reported that Japanese fire had ceased and they were pulling off Hill 600A." The attack was canceled. "I closed my eyes and thanked God for a seeming miracle."

CHAPTER SIXTEEN

OPERATION STEVEDORE

Roy Geiger

With operations on Bougainville wrapping up, I MAC headquarters relocated to Guadalcanal, Geiger's old stomping grounds. The island had changed little since his Cactus Air Force days. Lieutenant General Merwin H. Silverthorn, his chief of staff, described Geiger's CP: "They were rather primitive headquarters, under canvas, in a jungle grove of miscellaneous trees—very thick, not near any town of any kind. General Geiger lived in a tent. I guess you'd call it a storage tent—maybe twenty feet by twenty feet." Geiger invited Silverthorn to move in with him, which greatly benefited their association. Silverthorn recalled that his "office tent was of the same size and was about fifty feet from his [Geiger's], and the other staff officers were in similar tents with a bunk in their tent that they slept in. So their working quarters and their living quarter[s] were synonymous."

In the spring of 1944, I MAC changed its name to III Amphibious Corps (III Phib Corps). Silverthorn stated that "III Phib Corps was always a field organization and never did have a roof over its head, until it established a headquarters near Naha, Okinawa, in May 1945." At this time, Geiger received a warning order to commence planning for Operation Stevedore, the assault of Guam, scheduled for June 14, 1944. He was to command the Southern Troops and Landing Force (STLF), consisting of the Army's 77th Infantry Division (Reinforced), 3rd Marine Division, and the 1st Provisional Marine Brigade, under Lem Shepherd. Geiger loaded the staff into his command plane, an R4-D, and flew it to Pearl Harbor, arriving there on May 29. The aircraft, according to Silverthorn, "was a

DC-3 (air force designation) with two motors and an auxiliary gas tank. It had one cot braced to the bulkhead . . . one desk . . . and maybe about eight seats. And whenever we moved by plane, the general would take his principal staff officers aboard this plane."

At Pearl, Geiger "bunked" with Lieutenant General Holland Howlin' Mad Smith at his Makalapa quarters, while they worked out plans for Operation Forager, the landings on Saipan and Guam. Smith commanded the Northern Force, V Amphibious Corps, while Geiger's III Phib Corps controlled the Southern Force. Howlin' Mad, not one given to hyperbole, described Geiger, "as a heavyset, bear-like and totally fearless man. He was someone who could only have happened in the Marine Corps. He had flown and commanded almost every kind of aircraft or aviation unit that ever existed. Like all Marine officers, however, he had always kept his feet on the ground."

Geiger was given the mission, the general scheme of maneuver, and the names of his opposite numbers of the navy's attack force. He learned that Rear Admiral Richard "Close-in" Conolly—during the Roi-Namur operation, Conolly ordered the USS *Maryland* to "move really close in," and was hung with the nickname from that time on—commanded the Southern Attack Force (Task Force 53) that would support the landing. "Admiral Conolly had established a reputation for himself in the Mediterranean. He was an old amphibious sailor." Geiger and Conolly developed a close personal relationship that encouraged their staffs to work in harmony. Conolly remarked, "That's the best relationship I ever had, anywhere, anytime, during the war with any other service. It was partly due to the fact that Geiger and I got along very well together, and due to his personality. He was forceful and at the same time very cooperative and human, a wonderful man—very knightly character. In a 1996 biographical study of the general, Major Timothy Quagge wrote, "Everybody liked Geiger. However, he was no 'popularity jack,' he was a good tough Marine."

The navy planning staff was invited to join their Marine brethren "in the field." Silverthorn recalled that "Admiral Conolly and his group arrived by air and went into camp with us. And that's one of the finest circumstances that developed in all my professional career—that naval force living ashore in tents with the Marines, getting to know their opposite number, the naval gunfire people and the transport loading people and the operations people, and getting to understand the Marine problems; and altogether the planning proceeded without a hitch. By the time the ship (*Appalachian*) arrived and the group left us, we were real friends." Conolly for his part felt the same way. "I worked wonderfully well with Geiger. He was a marvelous man. Of course, we got to know each other very well."

The Guam Problem

The recapture of Guam had been a long-standing student exercise at Marine Corps School, Quantico. Generations of Marine officers had passed through the demanding course—and many were now heading for Guam and the "final graduation exercise." General Geiger asked Silverthorn if he knew the island. "I assured him that we knew Guam like the inside of our hand—that I had lived on Guam for two years; I had taught the Guam problem; that General Noble, the ADC of the 3rd Division, taught the Guam problem, and the commanding general of the brigade and 3rd Division, General Shepherd and General Tunage, both knew all about the Guam problem." Lem Shepherd also worked on the Guam problem. "I had prepared a study for a landing on Guam at the Naval War College and so I knew the island pretty well. I wrote an estimate of the situation on this island. At that time the only place you could land without crossing the reef was at Talofofo."

However, the school solution they had spent so much time teaching was not used. The landing occurred on the side of the island that was considered unsatisfactory by the instructors—resulting in a grade of "U" if the student chose the incorrect beach. Shepherd agreed with the instructors. "It was obviously not a suitable place to land due to the limited width of the passage through the reef and the ease with which their areas could be defended." The introduction of the amphibious tractor (amtrac), which could cross the fringing reefs, made the old plan obsolete. Shepherd changed his mind. "Unfortunately, when we landed on Guam there were only enough amphibian tractors to boat the first few waves. After landing the troops on the beach, the tractors which had not been knocked out by Japanese gunfire returned to the seaward edge of the fringing reef, where they met boats from the ships on what was called the 'transfer line.' "

Guam became a territorial possession of the United States in 1898, as a result of the Spanish-American War. The island was considered strategically important, because it was located in the Japanese Central Pacific defensive cordon. Unfortunately, at the start of the war, it was practically undefended. On December 8, 1941, Japanese planes bombed the Marine Barracks. Corporal Martin Boyle described the island's air defense: "We soon learned that a rifle is useless as tits on a boar hog when pitted against even the slowest moving airplanes. It takes a damn lucky shot to do any good, and we weren't very lucky that day." Two days later, a Japanese force of six thousand men landed and quickly overwhelmed the garrison of only 153 Marines and the eighty-man Insular Force Guard, native Chamorros under Marine NCOs. The population of twenty thousand Guamanians, all loyal American nationals, found themselves under the tender mercies of the Japanese army.

The island, thirty-five miles long and nine miles at its widest, was rugged and mountainous in the south, while the north was more rolling and jungle-covered. The most approachable landing beaches were located along the west coast but posed a special tactical problem because ridges that gradually rose to form mountains backed them. This high ground, properly defended, could be murder for the assault troops. With only fifteen miles of usable beaches available to the Americans, the Japanese quickly decided to orient their formidable defenses toward the west.

The Japanese 29th Division and various naval base and defense troops, some nineteen thousand men, garrisoned the island. They were well supplied with coast defense artillery, antiaircraft guns, and field artillery, which were heavily camouflaged and cleverly emplaced to disrupt and destroy an enemy landing. The western beaches were studded with mines and antiboat obstacles. Machine guns and mortars were sited to provide covering fire. The Japanese commander knew the Americans were coming and pushed his men hard to prepare. "We have an excellent opportunity to annihilate him on the beaches."

Geiger's operation plan called for the twenty-thousand-man 3rd Marine Division to land three regiments abreast on Asan Point, to capture the high ground immediately inland. Shepherd's nine-thousand-man brigade was tasked to establish a beachhead in the vicinity of Agat, and then drive north to cut off the Orote Peninsula. The army's 77th Infantry Division commanded by Major General Andrew D. Bruce, would follow up the brigade's initial landings and fight alongside the Marines in the drive north. The three infantry elements were to be backed up by Brigadier General Pedro A. del Valle's heavy guns of the corps artillery. Rear Admiral Richard L. "Close-in" Conolly, who told Geiger, "My aim is to get the troops ashore standing up," coordinated the pre-invasion bombardment. "You tell me what you want done to accomplish this, and we'll do it." As a result, Guam received the most devastating preliminary bombardment of the war. Silverthorn remarked that "There were many coast defenses on Guam, and we would pick those out like a person with a nut picker working on a hickory nut—just blaze away at them."

During the operational planning, Geiger became fascinated with the work of the underwater demolitions teams (UDT). Three teams conducted reconnaissance of the boat lanes, destroyed Japanese antiboat obstacles, and even examined the actual shoreline, under cover of darkness. One particularly gutsy team even went so far as to plant a sign on the beach: "Welcome Marines—USO This Way." Against the advice of his staff—and to their utter consternation, Geiger accompanied the navy frogmen on several of their dangerous missions. He made several daylight forays in a free boat, right under the enemy's nose, on a personal reconnaissance of the boat lanes.

Unexpected resistance on Saipan kept III Phib Corps near at hand as a floating reserve, until the fighting on the island swung in favor of the Americans. Guam's day of liberation was postponed almost a month, which turned out to be a piece of good fortune. The delay allowed Geiger, Conolly, and their staffs to confer with the victorious American commanders from Saipan and alter their plan based on the latest intelligence and the hard-won tactical lessons, particularly how to defend against the Japanese penchant for a final banzai attack. Geiger toured Saipan and got a firsthand look at the Japanese integration of defensive works into the terrain. His observation convinced him that additional naval and air bombardment was critical. He also learned that captured enemy documents indicated there were eighteen thousand army and navy personnel on Guam, almost double the estimated number. As a result, the 77th Division was added to the invasion force.

Aboard ship, the embarked Marines received a final mail call. Master Technical Sergeant Alvin M. Josephy, Jr., observed them. "When it was given out, the men moved away by themselves, opened the letters with tender care and read them slowly, again and again. Before H-hour, they placed the letters in their packs and dungaree pockets, to carry into combat ashore as their most treasured possessions." Reveille sounded before dawn in the troop compartments, rousting the sleepers for the traditional prelanding steak and eggs—more than one surgeon denounced the breakfast because it made sewing up perforated guts damn difficult. With full bellies, they made their way to the debarkation stations, where the sights and sounds of war gave them a quick reality check—and loose bowels.

Bursts of light marked the naval cannon of "Close-in" Conolly's gunfire ships, while aircraft roared overhead, as navy and Marine fighters and bombers headed for beachfront targets. Suddenly the bulkhead speakers came to life with the voice of Roy Geiger: "You have been honored. The eyes of the nation watch you as you go into battle to liberate this former American bastion from the enemy. The honor, which has been bestowed on you, is a signal one. May the glorious traditions of the Marine Corps esprit de corps spur you to victory. You have been honored." As Geiger's voice died away, a stirring rendition of the "Marines' Hymn" blared from the speakers, sending the assault force on their way.

Silverthorn watched the landing through binoculars aboard the command ship. "It was a strange feeling to lay off the coast a few miles, recognize places on the beach, particularly when we went around to the Agana side. There I spotted a house I lived in and observed it being demolished by our own shell fire. I spotted the parade ground where we used to play baseball and the hospital that was only a block away. It was quite a strange feeling to see the houses go up in smoke and debris."

1st Provisional Marine Brigade
Lem Shepherd

On April 16, only two months prior to the landing on Guam, Lem Shepherd assumed command of the 1st Provisional Marine Brigade, consisting of the 4th and 22nd Marine Regiments. "It was on Cape Gloucester on Easter morning, 1944, that I received orders to return to Pearl Harbor to command the 1st Marine Brigade. When I received these orders, I was really sunk. I hated to leave the 1st Division. So it was with tears that I left. . . ." Upon arrival in Hawaii, he was briefed and formally assigned the command by the acerbic Howlin' Mad Smith, commanding general, Fleet Marine Force. While there, Shepherd was able to observe one component of his brigade, the veteran 22nd Marines, which was refitting and training on the big island after returning from seizing the islands of Engebi and Parry in the Eniwetok Atoll. Shepherd spent a few days in Honolulu before sailing for Guadalcanal with the regiment, where they would link up with the 4th Marines.

The 4th Marine Regiment was rather unique. The men of the original regiment were languishing in Japanese prison camps, after being captured when the Philippines fell in April 1942. The "new" regiment was reconstituted by combining the Raider battalions, after General Vandegrift decided they "were divisive to the Corps because they fostered the concept of elitism." Initially the Raiders were unhappy that their organization was broken up. Shepherd thought that "they were all individualists," but turned into one of the best in the brigade under the strong leadership of Colonel Alan Shapley. "He did a magnificent job on that, and they worshipped him."

Upon landing on Guadalcanal, the brigade was assigned a training area on the extreme western end of the island, some ten miles beyond Henderson Field. Shepherd thought the training area was excellent. "We had three beautiful cul-de-sacs where we could conduct three battalion maneuvers at the same time, with hills between us, and could actually conduct firing exercises at the same time."

Shepherd had only a short time to mold the two disparate units into a cohesive team. "I found it to be a gigantic task, as each regimental commander had his own ideas on how he thought his regiment should be employed, rather than working jointly with the other regiment of the brigade." He thought his hardest job was dealing with subordinate commanders. "The greatest problem of a commander is keeping his subordinates happy and working together." Shepherd, ever the southerner, cited Robert E. Lee's problem with his commanders: "He was able, by the force of his personal leadership, to take a man like Stonewall Jackson, who had a difficult personality, and inspire him to work with others. I had somewhat the same problem to keep my individual commanders all oriented in the right direction and imbue them with the spirit to fight for the division, the Marine Corps, and not just follow their own individual desires and aims."

Another problem Shepherd had was getting enough officers for the brigade. "I went to General [Allen] Turnage who was a very good friend of mine and said, 'I need a few lieutenants badly. I don't have sufficient number to command my platoons and you have them stacked up in the 3rd Division three deep, in every job. Won't you let me have a few of the boys I trained in the OCC? . . .' 'Oh no,' General Turnage replied, 'We might need them when we go into Guam.' Frankly, I was quite annoyed as I knew the 3rd Division had an excess of officers and the brigade was understrength." Shepherd could not resist twisting Turnage's tail. "When the brigade landed on Guam, we were to make a junction with the 3rd Division at a point called X on the map." He ordered his leading battalion commander: "You get to that point first. Don't come back to me if you don't get there ahead of the 3rd Division!" Needless to say, the "positive" motivation worked and the point was captured ahead of schedule. "When I arrived there I wrote General Turnage a message, 'I am at point X, where in hell are you?' I don't think he liked it."

Despite the organizational and staffing difficulties, Shepherd deeply immersed himself in the planning for the Guam operation. Although "the limited staff provided [to] the 1st Brigade and lack of an adequate headquarters organization placed a heavy load on the brigade commander and his chief of staff," the brigade was ready on time. "With customary Marine sagacity, however, plans were completed and units readied for embarkation on schedule."

Fighting Spirit

Throughout training, Shepherd imbued his men with a fighting spirit. "You must instill a hatred of the enemy in order to get your men to fight. It's a psychological thing. You've got to hate a man and want to kill him or else you won't kill him. Any feeling that they might have about killing a human being must be dispelled. You've got to pound into them that desire to overcome the enemy regardless of anything else. Consequently, when our troops went forward and saw Japs, they shot them." Master Technical Sergeant Alvin M. Josephy, Jr., commented that "From the early days on Guadalcanal we had learned not to trust the Japs who wanted to surrender. There had been too many cases of treachery. In face-to-face encounters we knew that the man who shot first won—and lived." In the front-line units, it was kill or be killed. No one wanted to risk his life waiting to see if the enemy wanted to surrender. Shepherd was more succinct because he detested the Japanese. "Killing a Jap was like killing a rattlesnake." Marine Donald Fall described the savagery of combat: "You get a nasty frame of mind in combat. You see what's been done to you. You'd find a dead Marine that the Japs had booby-trapped . . . and they mutilated the dead. We began to get down to their level."

It was a given that very few Japanese would surrender. In fact, most of those captured early in the war were physically incapable of resisting, being either wounded or unconscious. Josephy landed in the assault wave on Guam. "We found a Jap sitting on the beach, dazed by our D-day bombardment. We also captured many wounded Japs during the fighting . . . men who were too injured to put up resistance." Shepherd was matter of fact: "The Japs seldom gave up, and consequently there was no opportunity to capture large groups of prisoners." Shepherd pointed out, "When a Jap was ordered to hold a position, he stayed there." In addition, Shepherd thought that "Their religion was to die for the emperor. They glory, theoretically, in death on the battlefield, because that's what's been imbued in the Japanese for centuries . . . to go out and fight and die for their emperor." Vandegrift wrote after Guadalcanal: "I have never heard or read of this kind of fighting. These people [Japanese] refuse to surrender. The wounded will wait until the men come up to examine them and blow themselves and the other fellow to pieces with a hand grenade."

Shepherd found that later in the war, more Japanese surrendered. "I think it was on Guam, we captured some prisoners and on Okinawa we captured more prisoners, as they came around to the idea that they'd save their own skins." Master Technical Sergeant Murrey Marder recalled an extra-small Japanese soldier. "His uniform hung limp like a scarecrow's trappings. A Marine on Orote Peninsula asked him why he surrendered. 'My commanding officer told us to fight to the last man,' the prisoner answered. 'Well,' queried the Marine. A look of wounded innocence spread over the Jap's face as he declared, 'I was the last man!' " "

Japanese Myth

Japanese victories after Pearl Harbor earned them a superhuman reputation as jungle fighters. Shepherd was familiar with this common perception. "I think that at the beginning of the war, the Japs made very remarkable advances—down the Malay Peninsula, Singapore, and all through the Southwest Pacific islands—and they built up a reputation of being wonderful jungle fighters. It became something of a bugaboo to all of us. I mean, we just thought Japs could swing from tree to tree in the jungle." However, Shepherd did not believe it. "I found in my experience that our Marines were better jungle fighters than the Japs were. They were cunning; they were determined. And they were painstaking in their digging—you know, they loved to bore, they were always digging and organizing the ground, but they certainly didn't have much imagination, and I don't think that their units were too effective. But they were good fighters; there wasn't any question about that." However, he did not think the Japanese were as good as "the more intelligent European." "Where the Europeans saw that they were going to be defeated, they gave up. But the Jap was so imbued with the idea that he must never give up, he must fight until the last drop of blood for the emperor . . ."

Death is Lighter Than a Feather

The Japanese believed in the military code of *Bushido,* or the way of the warrior. Article 2 of the Japanese Imperial Army Military Training regulation stated: "The duty of the military is to sacrifice their lives for the emperor's country." The individual Japanese soldier believed that if he surrendered, he lost all honor and brought disgrace to his family. His paramount duty was loyalty unto death: "Duty is weightier than a mountain, while death is lighter than a feather." "Faith is strength," was his credo, and, for the most part, the Japanese soldier carried out his duty without reservation—even in the face of certain death. The infamous banzai charge was perhaps the embodiment of this self-sacrifice.

American researchers concluded that the banzai was a "mutual exhortation which started between unit members and increased to the point of mob hysteria. (But) this was a spontaneous affair and not maneuvered by the commanding officers, who merely explained the tactical situation and placed the challenge before the men." Colonel Hiromichi Yahara, senior staff officer, Japanese 32nd Army, described the assault as "Masses of Japanese soldiers wearing frantic, weird expressions, brandishing swords, throwing grenades, and stabbing with bayonets, charge ceaselessly, jumping over the dead bodies of their fallen comrades while screaming 'banzai.'" One Marine said the preparations "sounded like New Year's Eve in the zoo."

Under Fire Again
Eddie Craig

Guam was no Bougainville. Craig's assault battalion, 3/9, came under a deluge of Japanese small arms, mortar, and artillery fire as soon as it came within range. Several amphibious tractors were hit as they crawled over the coral reef that surrounded the island. Craig directed his free boat to land immediately. "My boat officer, a brand-new ensign, refused to carry out my orders and insisted that he stay in a landing wave. I told him, 'If he didn't carry out my orders, he'd be over the side.' About that time, one of my sergeants jumped up and said, 'I'd be delighted!' So this ensign decided to change his orders." At the reef line, Craig and his command group transferred to an amphibious tractor for the final run to the beach. "It was just at this moment that mortar shells started to fall around us, some of them too close for comfort. Fire was also coming from the right flank at Asan Point. . . . I saw two tractors hit and we decided to keep our heads down." Craig made a mental note to check the area of the Japanese fire when he had a spare moment.

The tractor reached the beach and the command group piled out and dashed forward through a tangle of fallen palm trees and demolished houses, to several bomb craters, where they set up the CP. Craig went forward with his adjutant, Captain Charlie Henderson, to find the battalion commander, Lieutenant Colonel Walter Asmuth. Heavy small arms and automatic weapons fire swept the area, forcing them to take cover behind a low mound. "I was looking through my glasses at the ridge ahead when he [Henderson] suddenly toppled over across my knees, shot through the throat. I lay him out behind the mound and yelled for a corpsman." Craig continued forward after the severely injured adjutant was evacuated and "found Asmuth had just been wounded in the arm." As he returned to his CP, "Some stretcher bearers passed me and I recognized Captain Harry Barker, one of my best company commanders, lying on one of them dead. Waiting for me at the CP was my runner, who reported that my good friend Jaime Sabater (executive officer) had been wounded a moment after he landed and had been evacuated."

During a short lull, Craig remembered the Japanese gun that had hit the two amphibious tractors as they came over the reef. "I was sure it was from a hidden gun emplacement on the ridge. . . . Sure enough, I saw a light puff of smoke on the side of the ridge, and it came from a spot which looked liked a natural hillside, not over 150 yards away." He spotted two 75mm half-tracks and pointed out the camouflaged position. "The second and third rounds hit the target exactly and I could momentarily see parts of the gun and Japs intermingled in a depression on the side of the ridge." Another round hit above the position, causing a small landslide that covered the site." Two months later, Craig happened to be in the area and noted a large group of men gathered around an old Japanese position that had been uncovered. "There in front of me was what remained of a very modern anti-tank gun together with four or five very ripe Japs well mixed up with it. I wondered how many good Marines these dead Japanese soldiers had accounted for before they were knocked out."

Blood on the Reef
Lem Shepherd

Amphibious tractors with Lem Shepherd's assault waves crawled out of the sea onto the wide, fringing reef that fronted the brigade's landing beach. Lieutenant Thomas R. O'Neil, a platoon commander in the 22nd Marines, wrote, "The Jap anti-boat gunfire was quite heavy. I chanced to look and counted six amtracs burning in the water. There was a sudden explosion. The heat and acrid smell of powder was still in the air. We had taken a hit on the port bow, the port track had been blown off, and she had taken about a 20 percent list and the driver's compartment was on fire." The Japanese beach defenses were well organized. Concrete pillboxes, machine gun emplacements, and an elaborate trench system protected the enemy from the initial bombardment, and when the landing craft came within range, the defenders opened up with everything they had. Ten of Shepherd's amphibious vehicles were knocked out. Japanese crossfire raked Yellow Beach 2, a three-hundred-yard strip of sand, killing seventy-five men of the 22nd Marines.

Unfortunately, "Close-in" Conolly's naval bombardment did not destroy all the Japanese gun emplacements. Shepherd watched as his first assault wave surged toward the shore. "The Japs had a block house on Gaan Point. That gun gave the brigade a lot of trouble. We lost some good boys—not too many—but there were casualties coming in. I think it knocked out something like nine boats, and one very nice boy whom I personally knew was killed in one of those landing boats, Adams was his name." Shepherd noted the Japanese defenses "were strongly organized in from the beach in the vicinity of Agat town and across the neck of the Orote Peninsula in the Marine Barracks and the rifle range area south of Sumi." There was also a gun emplacement on the beach, "which enfiladed the approach over the reef and knocked out several boats."

The first assault wave had barely cleared the first low ridge when Shepherd's amtrac lumbered out of the water. He and his small forward CP group climbed over the gunwales, dropped to the beach, and scrambled for cover. They set up in a coconut grove about two hundred yards southeast of Gaan Point, where minutes earlier, tanks had knocked out a particularly troublesome blockhouse. The sand-covered concrete emplacement, with a four-foot-thick roof, was built into the nose of the Point. It remained undetected until the assault elements of the 22nd Marines approached the beach. The two Japanese guns (a 75mm and a 37mm) opened fire, knocking out two dozen amtracs before Marine tanks knocked it out with their main guns.

By early afternoon, Shepherd's command post was up and running and he assumed control of all the troops in his zone of action. "I have always been an advocate of a commander getting ashore as soon as practicable. You can't sit back on a ship and just read messages. Nobody's going to say that they're doing badly because nobody wants to admit that." Shepherd pushed his commanders to get off the beach. "Many of the casualties in the first waves were caused by machine gun nests along the shore line. Once we broke through the initial beach defenses, we just coasted. When I say coasted, I mean that our plan of attack was to drive right straight through to Mount Alifan." Shapley's 4th Marines on the right flank ran into heavy enemy resistance. Shepherd noted that "A support position consisting of well defended caves connected by tunnels was found on the western slopes of Alifan Massif between Mt. Alifan and Mt. Tanae."

Shepherd ordered Shapley to continue the attack. "I felt that if we had that piece of high ground we would be all right. My plan of attack worked out very successfully." By late afternoon, the 4th Marines dug in for the night on the western slopes of their objective. Shepherd sent a short status report to General Geiger. "Own casualties about 350. Enemy [losses] unknown. Critical shortages fuel and ammunition all types. Think we can handle it. Will continue as planned tomorrow." In mid-afternoon, Shepherd ordered the army's 305th Regiment to land. Communication problems plagued their landing and the last elements did not get ashore until the following morning. Meanwhile, Geiger ordered the 306th Regiment to land by noon on the 23rd and the 307th Regiment the next day, which gave Major General Bruce his entire command. After four days of heavy combat, the brigade had cut off the Orote Peninsula, but it had not been without cost. There were one thousand Marine casualties, of whom 188 were killed in action.

By the 25th, the brigade stretched across the neck of the heavily defended, eight-square-mile Orote Peninsula—4th Marines on the left, 22nd Marines on the right. Shepherd gave them one day to get into position. They were now ready for the assault. After four days of continuous fighting, however, the troops were greatly fatigued. Facing them were more than 2,500 members of the well-trained Special Naval Landing Force, sometimes referred to as Japanese Marines, from the 54th Keibitai Guard Force, remnants of the 38th Infantry Regiment, and various support units, under the command of Commander Asaichi Tamai. During the early evening, Marines in the front lines knew that something was up. "The Japanese were screaming, surging, laughing, capering—they were smashing empty bottles against the big mangroves and clanging bayonets against rifle barrels." Platoon Sergeant Hank Bauer waited for the attack.

"Then, this one old Jap, he could speak English, yells out, ' 'Merican Maline, you die tonight! 'Merican Maline, you die tonight!' Well, we had this real tough guy from Texas, and he yells out, 'Tojo eats shit, yuh slant-eyed son of a bitch!' "

Just a few minutes before midnight, a Japanese officer staggered out of the mangroves, a saber in one hand and a flare in the other. Behind him stumbled a *saki*-mad battalion of the 18th Regiment. They struck the center of the 22nd Marines, who quickly overwhelmed the frenzied attack. According to historian Harry Gailey: "Before most of the desperate, drunken, would-be suicides reached the Marine[s] in their holes they were caught in the open by brigade and 77th Division artillery supplemented by Corps' 155s." Bauer was on the firing line. "It was the craziest thing you ever saw. Hell, some of them were falling-down drunk. They were laughing and cursing in this hysterical tone. We literally shot the shit out of those poor bastards. I'm sure many of them were dead before they really knew what was happening."

A second attack met the same results. A Marine historian described the scene: "At its height, flares revealed an out-of-this-world picture of Nipponese drunks reeling about in our forward positions, falling into foxholes, tossing aimless grenades here and there, yelling such English phrases as they managed to pick up, and laughing crazily." A platoon from the 4th Marines caught the Japanese in the flank, killing more than 250 without suffering a single casualty. One of their numbers wrote that "The enemy dead laid [sic] two or three deep in front of our lines." One lieutenant reported, "Arms and legs flew like snowflakes. Japs ran amuck. They screamed in terror until they died." Early the following morning, Shepherd visited the front lines. "At daylight over 400 enemy dead lay in front of our lines. I personally counted them (as best I could) myself. Within the lines there were many instances when I observed Japanese and Marines lying side by side, which was mute evidence of the violence of the last assault."

Promptly at seven o'clock the next morning, Shepherd ordered the brigade to attack. The two regiments jumped off, after a heavy fifteen-minute artillery preparation—one artillery battalion fired a thousand rounds in support—and didn't stop until the Orote Peninsula was secured four days later.

Bodyguards
Eddie Craig

Two Marines often accompanied Craig as bodyguards on his tours of the front lines. "I have always been most fortunate in picking drivers and runners. They were both fearless and outstanding Marines." One, Private First Class Arthur Highsaw, always positioned himself in front of Craig, using his body as a shield. "Highsaw was standing by me when he suddenly dropped his automatic rifle and spun around. He had been hit in the upper arm by a Jap sniper. As he was carried away, he said, 'I'm sorry I crapped out on you like this, colonel." Highsaw was evacuated to a hospital ship and Craig did not expect to see him again. "However, the next morning, he appeared with his automatic rifle ready to accompany me on my rounds of the units. He had escaped from the hospital ship. He looked white and drawn and, as I spoke to him, he fell over in a dead faint." Highsaw was evacuated for a second time, and that was the last time Craig saw him.

Craig was down to one man, Corporal Walter Lamka, his runner. "Lamka and I were on our way from the company CP towards one of the platoons. Suddenly a machine gun opened up on us and we both hit the ground and rolled into a shallow depression. Every time we moved, the machine gun would fire at us, and the bullets were just grazing us. I felt we would never get out of it." A Marine patrol happened by and attacked the Japanese position from another angle. "We rolled, got up, and ran into the jungle. We jumped into a Japanese gun pit that was surrounded by dead bodies. We landed right on top of them—and when the firing stopped, we got quickly out of the mess."

The 77th Infantry Division was deployed on the 9th Marines' right flank. Craig was anxious to ensure that his troops were in the right position, so he went forward on a personal reconnaissance. "I started out in a jeep with Corporal Lamka and proceeded over a fairly good carabao cart trial to the northwest. We had just entered a broad valley and were driving along over smooth ground when I happened to look down and just ahead of the jeep. . . [and] I saw many low mounds. I suddenly realized that they were land mines and yelled at the top of my voice, 'STOP!' " Lamka slammed on the brakes and the two looked around. They had driven into the middle of a mine field. "There was nothing to do but back out over our own tire tracks. We were lucky to get out alive."

After extricating themselves, the two drove on until reaching a former Japanese first aid site. "We ran across some twenty-five dead Japanese soldiers on litters. Most of them had a big hole in their chests, indicating they had blown themselves up with hand grenades, even though wounded." Craig had seen other examples of the Japanese penchant for suicide rather than surrender. "It was hard to believe that men in a wounded condition would choose death to capture." He did not feel sorry for them, however. "I was shown a group of Guamanian Chamorros which one of the patrols had overrun. Every man had been beheaded by the Japs. . . . They lay in the jungle with their hands tightly bound behind their backs, flies crawling over them and their heads lying about among the bodies. This had been a cold-blooded massacre without reason. . . ."

The Japanese did not intend to release captured Guamanians. Lieutenant Wilcie O'Bannon related, "It appeared that the Japanese had practiced their samurai sword action, just chopped across the body horizontally."

Perils of Command

Craig learned that his right flank was being held up and went forward to see what he could do. "I always felt that a commander should be where his troops are held up and cannot advance. Being there he can take any required action on the spot and his presence sometimes steadies the situation." He caught up with the right flank platoon and was advancing with it when "we received intense machine gun fire from Asan ridge, which was then to our right rear. Taking cover, we located the position, a concrete machine gun emplacement not over twenty-five yards away, and took it out."

After watching the unit take its objective, Craig started back to his CP. "As I was walking along the road . . . with Captain George Percy and a runner, I was surprised to look to my left and see a couple of Japanese soldiers who had just come out of a cave. One of them raised a square package in his hand and threw it at me. It landed some distance away and exploded with a terrific roar, knocking me off the road into a ditch filled with sharp stones." Craig's companions were farther from the explosion and did not get its full effect. Several Marines came to the rescue, including a crew with a jeep-mounted antitank gun, which blasted the cave, killing the inhabitants. Craig was unhurt but "was severely bruised from the concussion, which really made my teeth chatter for a while."

The regimental CP moved with the advance, often setting up just behind the front lines. "It was sometimes more secure and safe than further back." Craig personally selected many of the command post sites, usually in a location that placed him in a position to control the movement of his Marines. On one occasion, the CP was set up in the thick jungle at the intersection of several trails and road junctions. "Shortly after I had picked the place as a CP site . . . a Japanese officer wandered into the middle of things and was shot as he started to pull his pistol. Later, a Japanese private was also shot . . . at this important road junction." Shortly afterward, he went forward to check on the advance. "About three hundred yards up the trail, I noted a well worn path leading to a knoll. Steps had been carved in the steep slope." Craig stopped the jeep and got out to look it over. "I changed my mind and decided to get back in and continue to the front. Stopping a messenger, I told him to tell Major Lips (operations officer) to have a patrol investigate this area, and drove on to the front."

Upon returning from the front, Craig was surprised to hear the sounds of a small battle. The patrol he had ordered to investigate the knoll was heavily engaged with a large Japanese force and had suffered several casualties. An army battalion happened to be in the area. "I quickly explained the situation to the commanding officer and he immediately organized a full scale attack. Quite a battle ensued and the army suffered many casualties before the place was overrun. It was found that the main position was a huge concrete underground bunker with steel doors. Inside was a complete headquarters with communications. The place was so large that trucks were parked inside. It appeared that this was the secondary command post for the Japanese command on Guam. How thankful I was that I had changed my mind and decided not to investigate this interesting looking knoll."

The knoll, officially known as Mount Mataguac, was attacked by infantrymen of the U.S. Army's 1st Battalion, 306th Regiment. After a spirited assault using flamethrowers, white phosphorous grenades, and massive charges of TNT, they overran the headquarters. The body of Lieutenant General Hideyoshi Obata, commander of the 31st Army, was found inside the elaborate command post. Obata just happened to be on an inspection tour at the time of the invasion and was caught on the island. After writing a last message to the emperor, he committed suicide, just before the Americans sealed the entrance.

Tanks, Tanks, and More Tanks

The 9th Marines advanced more than six thousand yards and seized a critical road junction. Craig followed closely behind. As his jeep headed down a small valley, "We heard the sound of motors starting. Before we could locate the position of the noise, two enemy tanks rolled out of cleverly camouflaged positions on the side of the hill to our right and headed toward us firing machine guns and small caliber cannon. They were not over one hundred feet away and I had visions of losing all my men who were in the immediate vicinity. A bazooka man . . . and his assistant went into action immediately. With a calmness that was uncanny, they proceeded to knock out the two tanks in quick succession!" A couple of gutsy Marines jumped on the tanks, forced open a hatch, and dropped hand grenades inside, finishing off the crews. "We later found two well-camouflaged, unmanned tanks dug into the side of a hill, just a short distance away."

During the advance toward the northern end of the island, Craig went forward to Tiyan Airfield, which had just been captured. "As I reached the southern end of the airfield, a Japanese tank suddenly appeared and cut right across my bow. It turned and started down the road towards the 2nd Battalion assembly area. I had my driver follow it, and was not over one hundred and fifty feet behind it. As it reached the battalion position, the top of the turret flew open and a Japanese officer started wildly firing his automatic pistol. The Marines were so surprised, that the tank drove right through them and they did not fire a shot. The Jap tank continued on towards a jungle area and stopped. Three Japs jumped out and fled. It was one of those incredible Japanese actions for which there is never an explanation."

Fancy Meeting You Here

As the 3rd Division's right flank unit, the 9th Marines were tasked to make contact with Shepherd's brigade working its way north on the Orote

Peninsula. Craig was anticipating making contact on July 26. "I was in great hopes of pushing ahead and making contact with the brigade by nightfall." Instead, he received an order to fall back by the assistant division commander. "I tried to argue against such a move . . . however, I didn't get very far." Instead, he sent a patrol to make contact. "I was most happy when at 20:00 that night the patrol returned with a personal message from General Shepherd." The two finally made contact a few days later. "It was evening when General Shepherd . . . came over to visit me. He had just arrived when a number of artillery shells started to land in the very near vicinity of my CP. We both ducked behind a cement wall and continued our conversation while sitting on the ground." Just two old friends quietly reminiscing in the midst of a shelling!

"To the Colors"
Lem Shepherd

The 4th Marines ran into a buzz saw early on the 28th when they ran into one of the strongest defensive lines on the peninsula. General Shepherd just happened to be on one of his daily frontline visits and observed the action. He immediately ordered up two platoons of medium tanks to support the attack. In a fine display of tank-infantry coordination, the strongpoints were destroyed and the surviving Japanese put to rout. At dawn, Shepherd ordered one of the heaviest bombardments since the initial landing pounded the enemy's position. He remarked that "Artillery was the most effective weapon employed during the operation. Reports from prisoners of war indicate that artillery fire has a great demoralizing effect on their troops."

The 4th Marines pressed forward, completing the reduction of the Orote Peninsula. That afternoon, with artillery booming in the background and the occasional snap of small arms fire, a group of high-ranking Marine officers, including Generals Geiger, Shepherd, and Smith, gathered on the grounds of the destroyed Marine Barracks. Geiger snapped an order and a Marine bugler sounded "To the Colors," as a U.S. flag was run up the flagpole. Shepherd's comments reflected the emotional moment. "On this hallowed ground, you officers and men of the 1st Marine Brigade have avenged the loss of our comrades. . . ." Howlin' Mad summed up the brigade's achievement: "The capture of the Orote Peninsula was, in some respects, the outstanding accomplishment of the Guam campaign." It was not without cost, however: 115 Marines of the brigade died and more than 700 were wounded. Japanese losses on the peninsula totaled 2,500.

Tragic Ending
Eddie Craig

By August 10, the end was in sight—one more push. Craig ordered a company to clear Peti Point and went along with them. "Nearing the point, we ran into a small group of enemy, and in the short skirmish, one of my men was killed and one wounded. It was a sad sight because the buddy of the man shot through the head went temporarily insane. He had just had too much and it was more than he could take. He ran screaming and hysterical into the jungle and it was some days before he was eventually found." Geiger declared Guam secure on August 11, although Japanese stragglers hid out for months in the thick jungles and caves of the island. In 1949, when Eddie Craig commanded the 1st Provisional Marine Brigade on Guam, his men captured two Japanese soldiers. They surrendered after seeing a photograph of Emperor Hirohito with two American MPs standing near him. They had clean, well-patched uniforms and lived in a well-stocked cave near the officer's mess.

CHAPTER SEVENTEEN

OPERATION STALEMATE

Major General William H. Rupertus, commanding general, 1st Marine Division, briefed his officers just three days before the landing on Peleliu. "We're going to have some casualties, but let me assure you this is going to be a short one, a quickie. Rough but fast. We'll be through in three days. It might only take two." Five days later, Lewis Puller's 1st Marine Regiment had fought itself out, suffering 56 percent casualties, 1,749 killed and wounded. A sergeant remarked, "This ain't a regiment. We're just survivors." The remnants of Puller's regiment were pulled out of the battle and evacuated back to the Russell Islands by LST (landing ship, tank). A bedraggled Marine wearily dragged himself over to the side of the transport; a clean, close-shaven, starched young navy officer asked him if he had any souvenirs. "The Marine stood examining him in silence. He patted his behind. 'I brought my ass outta there, swabbie,' he said. 'That's the only souvenir I wanted.' "

Volunteer
Ray Davis

In the spring of 1943, Davis was in command of a special weapons battalion, which was being farmed out to various infantry units, leaving him with little to do. One day while walking on the beach, he ran into "Chesty" Puller, who had just taken command of the 1st Marines. Davis "complained to the pugnacious officer that all my units were being doled out and I was being left behind. Puller replied in his characteristic fashion, 'It's a hell of a note when a man wants to go to war and no one will let him. I'll tell you, Old Man, get in that ship there, and tell them I said to take you!' Puller hired me on the spot to be his first battalion commander." Davis high-tailed it to the ship, sans written orders or baggage, and sailed to Pavuvu as first battalion's volunteer commander.

Pavuvu, a small island in the Russells, was picked by Geiger as a training area for the 1st Division after the Cape Gloucester campaign. Unfortunately, it turned out to be a bad choice. The camp was located in a six-hundred-acre coconut grove that reeked of rotting coconuts and palm fronds. The stench permeated everything, clothing, equipment and even food. There was inadequate drainage, and the area soon turned into a sea of mud. "Instead of getting a chance to relax, the battle-weary Marines found themselves turned to constructing a livable camp area." Private First Class Eugene B. Sledge, who had the misfortune to experience the island firsthand, recalled that "Most of the work parties I went on . . . were pick-and-shovel details to improve drainage and pave walkways with crushed coral, just to get us out of the water . . . on Pavuvu, simply living was difficult."

Despite the terrible living conditions, Davis immediately started small-unit training. "We employed mortars overhead with live ammo, plus rockets and flame throwers in assault teams . . . totally realistic. It was dangerous, but we were going into a very dangerous situation." He pushed his troops hard because captured documents described the heavy fortifications they would face on Peleliu. "We built Japanese-style bunkers, then assigned a squad of Marines, with satchel charges, flame throwers, rockets/bazookas the task of taking the bunker."

Halfway through training, a senior lieutenant colonel was given command of the battalion, bumping Davis to the number-two slot. On his first day in command, Davis took him on a tour of the training area. "He walked up on it and started yelling, 'Stop it, stop it, somebody is going to get killed.' He had just come from teaching tactics in Quantico, with extensive safety rules, but he finally saw that this was the way it had to be out here." It turned out that realistic training was not his only failing. "Just two days later, he took a small boat over to another island to check on supplies—and never came back." Davis found out that there was a navy hospital on the island staffed with nurses. "Our commander had joined up with the Nurse Corps." Puller found out and threw a fit, reducing the lieutenant colonel to his permanent grade of first lieutenant. Davis was restored to command, just in time to lead the battalion on Peleliu.

Breakwater of the Pacific

Brigadier General Merwin Silverthorn, Geiger's chief of staff, remarked after the battle that "everything about Peleliu left a bad taste in my mouth. The fighting, the casualties, the difficulties at Peleliu were never properly explained." Ray Davis thought it was "the most hotly contested and brutal campaign of World War II." First Lieutenant William Sellers wrote, "Japs, Japs, Japs, and . . . trying to stay alive in all that confusion, but we did manage to stop 'em. My God, though, so many of our men paid a dreadful price." The ten thousand Japanese defenders expected to make Peleliu the "breakwater of the Pacific" for the invaders.

Barely six miles long, with a maximum width of slightly more than two miles, the claw-shaped island was a defender's dream. Silverthorn described the terrain as abominable, the worst he had ever encountered. "It was as though several submerged reefs had been forced up out of the water with their jagged edges and made several ridges that were up to two hundred to three hundred feet coming to a sharp ridge just like the ridge of a house." The dominant terrain feature was the 550-foot Umurbrogol Mountain, nicknamed "Bloody Nose Ridge" by the Marines. A Leatherneck wounded in the fighting described the ridge: "It was a place that might have been designed by a maniacal artist given to painting mathematical abstractions—all slants, jaggeds, straights, steeps, and sheers with no curve to soften or relieve. The Umurbrogol was a monster Swiss cheese of hard coral limestone pocked beyond imagining with caves and crevices. They were to be found at every level, in every size—crevices small enough for a lonely sniper, eerie caverns big enough to station a battalion among its stalactites and stalagmites."

The Japanese defenders created a nightmare of mutually supporting concrete blockhouses, machine gun emplacements, entrenchments, and individual riflemen's positions. Davis commented that "The Japs were in deep caves, had small holes for fixed machine gun fire, etc. Consequently, we were being hit from all sides with no way to get at them." "The Island had been mined for many years for phosphate deposits," Silverthorn wrote. "So, the situation actually existed where the Marines would capture the ground and be in possession of the ground, and the Japanese would be underneath. There would be no way to get at them, and they would come out at night . . . sometimes with swords, and attack the Marines with these medieval weapons—very sharp swords capable of cutting a man's body in two."

Because of American successes at Saipan, Bougainville, and Guam, the Japanese changed their tactics. Instead of attempting to annihilate invaders at the water's edge, they constructed a defense in depth for a war of attrition (*jikyusen*) to play for time and bleed the invaders dry. Peleliu was organized into four defensive sectors that utilized the rugged terrain to construct mutually supporting positions. The main line of resistance was prepared far enough inland to minimize the effectiveness of the pre-invasion bombardment. This was backed up by defense in depth to wear down the American attackers combined with the hoarding of sufficient reserves to mount counterattacks. Davis noted that "Lieutenant General Sadae Inoue ordered his troops to fortify the island, no more suicide attacks; stay in their positions; kill the enemy until they themselves die for the Emperor!"

Same Old Navy Story
Roy Geiger

Geiger and key members of his staff left Guam on the morning of August 12 to begin planning for the Peleliu operation. They flew to the Russell Islands to confer with Rear Admiral George H. Fort, the task force commander. Silverthorn's reception warned of bad things to come. "The very first thing that Admiral Fort told us was that, 'You're not going to get all the gunfire support here that you got on Guam. I don't have the ships, and we don't have the ammunition.' It was the same old navy story." The navy announced there would be two days of preliminary bombardment. Geiger found this unacceptable and argued forcefully for at least one more day, which was grudgingly accepted. Fort remarked acidly that "The idea which some people seem to have of just firing at an island is an inexcusable waste of ammunition." Rear Admiral Jesse B. Oldendorf, commander of the Fire Support Group—five battleships, eight cruisers, and fourteen destroyers—ended the bombardment early, saying, "We have run out of targets."

Soon after arriving, Geiger learned that the division commander was laid up with a severely broken ankle and unable to supervise effectively the division's final preparations. Brigadier General O. P. Smith, the assistant division commander, assured Geiger that "in the remaining two weeks before the landing I felt that General Rupertus's ankle would mend sufficiently to permit him to carry on." A gravely concerned Geiger simply replied, "If I had known I'd have relieved him!" Rupertus had fallen during a landing exercise and fractured his ankle. In his biography of O. P. Smith, *The Gentle Warrior*, Clifton La Bree wrote that "It was common knowledge that many of the men in the division had a very low opinion of Rupertus, especially for his poor performance on Guadalcanal." La Bree cited a battalion commander who claimed, "He (Rupertus) just sat on his duff in a bunker and let others do the dirty work."

Rupertus' prediction of a quick operation infected the troops with a cockiness that did not survive the ride to the beach. Japanese anti-boat guns opened up with a vengeance as the amtracs bumped over the fringing reef. O. P. Smith remembered, "The Japanese fought back from the beginning. As the leading waves of amphibian tractors approached the edge of the reef they came under Japanese mortar fire . . . casualties were severe from the fire of large caliber automatic weapons located on the headlands north and south of the beach. The enfilade fire from these weapons caused heavy casualties among the amphibian tractors." Sergeant James Moll described the experience: "As we got closer to the beach, we could see the enemy's shells dropping and some of our landing craft being hit. I could hear machine gun bullets hitting the armor plate in front of me. As we got closer, my heart was beating like a jackhammer." E. B. Sledge's amtrac headed for Orange Beach 1. "Suddenly a large shell exploded with a terrific concussion, and a huge geyser rose up just to our right front. It barely missed us. The front of the tractor lurched to the left and bumped hard against the rear of another amtrac that was either stalled or hit. Japanese shells were screaming into the area and exploding all around us." An aerial observer reported excitedly, "There are amtracs burning on the reef. Repeat: There are amtracs burning on the reef."

On the Job Training
Ray Davis

Ray Davis peered over the side of the lurching amtrac and saw a scene of utter destruction. Oily black smoke rose into the sky, marking the funeral pyre of more than twenty burning tractors off White Beach 1 and 2. The bright flashes of exploding mortar and artillery fire marked the landing beaches that were wreathed in a heavy pall of dust and smoke. Japanese anti-boat obstacles, posts strung with barbed wire, formed irregular patterns in the shallow water. Small flags marked artillery and mortar registration points.

Davis was knocked off his feet when the heavy vehicle slammed into the edge of the fringing reef. The driver gunned the engine, and the powerful machine easily lifted itself up and over the coral. Splashes from Japanese artillery or mortar fire erupted to the right and left. The craft ground to a stop, the ramp aft came down fast, and Davis scrambled out into the maelstrom. Combat artist Tom Lea described the scene: "I fell flat on my face just as I heard the *whishhh* of a mortar I knew was too close. About fifteen yards away, on the upper edge of the beach it smashed down four men from our boat. I saw a wounded man near me, staggering in the direction of the LVTs. His face was half-bloody pulp, and the mangled shreds of what was left of an arm hung down like a stick, as he bent over in his stumbling, shock-crazy walk. He fell behind me, in a red puddle on the white sand."

Davis was scheduled to land an hour after the initial landing. "My battalion landed in reserve, which was meaningless, because the Japanese defenses were so thick and so sturdy that when I got off the amphibian tractor on the beach, my run for cover was not quick enough, and I got a fragment from a mortar shell through my left knee. It wasn't serious—I just put tape over it and got to work." Sledge described the pandemonium. "Up and down the beach and out on the reef, a number of amtracs and DUKWs [amphibious trucks] were burning. Japanese machine-gun bursts made long splashes on the water as though flaying it with some giant whip. The geysers belched up relentlessly where the mortar and artillery shells hit. I caught a fleeting glimpse of a group of Marines leaving a smoking amtrac on the reef. Some fell as bullets and fragments splashed among them. Their buddies tried to help them as they struggled in the knee-deep water."

Davis' men had to fight their way off the beach. They suffered heavy casualties from the murderous Japanese fire. "The enemy had tunneled back under the coral ridge lines, sometimes 100 to 200 feet, and they would lay a machine gun to shoot out of a distant hole, with deadly crossfire from well dug-in and fight-to-the-death defensive positions."

O. P. Smith described the terrain: "Particularly back of the northern end of the beach, the ground was rugged and well wooded. About 200 yards inland from the beach was a 30 foot coral ridge. Eight hundred to 1,000 yards inland from White 1 were the southern noses of the high rugged ground in the central part of the island. This high ground dominated the beaches and the airfield."

Tom Lea remembered, "Turning my head seaward I saw a direct center hit on an LVT. Pieces of iron and men seemed to sail slow-motion into the air. As I looked over my shoulder a burst smashed into a file of marines wading toward our beach from a smoking LVT. Jap machine guns lashed into the reef while lines and marines fell with bloody splashes into the green water. The survivors seemed so slow and small and patient coming in, out there."

Lead from the Front
Roy Geiger

Conditions ashore were chaotic. Japanese fire had decimated unit leaders, disrupting the normal flow of information up the chain of command. Those still alive were trying to get the decimated assault units off the beach and to stay alive in the hurricane of fire. Reporting information was not a priority. Puller rode in with the first wave and, as it grounded, "went up and over that side as fast as I could scramble and ran like hell at least twenty-five yards before I hit the beach, flat down . . ." What few reports that got through were sketchy and did not present a clear picture of conditions on the beach. O. P. Smith established a temporary CP in a deep antitank ditch about one hundred yards off the beach. Heavy Japanese fire pinned him down behind a sand berm, unable to report accurately the condition of the three assault regiments. A shortage of landing craft and his bad ankle kept Rupertus aboard his floating headquarters, the converted APA troop transport USS *DuPage*, where he monitored progress from a folding canvas chair on the deck. Fragments of the chaotic conditions ashore came across the command radios, which were scattered around him.

Geiger waited impatiently aboard the flagship, *Mount McKinley*, for a more complete picture of the landing. All he knew was that all hell had broken loose. Fanatic Japanese resistance had caused heavy casualties. There was little progress and the attack seemed to be stalled. By mid-afternoon, he could not stand the inactivity and decided to go for a firsthand look. "Descending to the foot of the ship's accommodation ladder, he hailed a passing landing craft and prevailed on its coxswain to give him a lift ashore." The landing craft weaved through the jumbled mass of burning amtracs, dodging Japanese mortar and anti-boat fire, to land Geiger near O. P. Smith's CP. Smith, who was crouched in a ditch when Geiger slid over the bank, related that Geiger "came up to me, and I said, 'Look, general, according to the book you're not supposed to be here at this time.' He said, 'Well, I wanted to see why those Amtracs were burning.' And he found out. There were thirty-eight of them that were burned."

Geiger was not content and asked Smith where the airport was located. "I said, 'That's simple, all you have to do is just climb up this bank and there it is. About that time, the Japs put over . . . rockets; they made a horrible screech and it sounded like they were just clearing your head." Startled, Geiger hastily slid down the bank, having seen all the runway that he wanted to see. Later, despite the Japanese fire, he left the comparative safety of Smith's CP and made his way to visit both the 5th and 7th Marines. When he returned, he asked Smith to point out the 1st Marines' position. "He wanted to see Lewie [Puller], but I said, 'Now look, general, there is a gap of eight hundred yards above here, and we don't know who's in there, and you just shouldn't go up there.' I had to do quite a bit of talking to talk him out of that." Smith put together a rough estimate of Marine casualties. They came up with 250 casualties, which was well short of the official count of more than 1,200, most in the 1st Regiment's zone of action.

Before returning to the ship, Geiger and his aide, both in khaki and fore and aft caps, walked up to some prone Marines on a rocky ridge. They were firing at Japanese on the next ridge only one to two hundred yards away. One of the Marines looked at Geiger and shouted, "Get down, you old fool! Do you want to get us all killed?" Geiger said, "Sorry son," turned, and walked away.

Interestingly, Geiger was ashore getting a firsthand look at the situation well before the division commander, Rupertus, made it to the battlefield. Geiger came ashore the afternoon of the first day, while Rupertus did not land until the second day. F. P. Henderson, a corps artillery officer at Peleliu, remembered that Geiger "was not a corps commander who conducted his battle only from his CP. He spent much of his time roving the battlefield so he could have a personal knowledge of the terrain, the action and the condition and morale of his men. It's amazing that guy got out alive. I thought he was going to get creamed or something. He was going to catch one on Peleliu. He'd go out and go climbing up the mountains, up on the hills, right up at the front, and talk to the guys. And if you got your head around a rock, the chances were at this time that you'd get plugged between the eyes. Marines were getting killed daily like that. But he'd go out there and do it, and we worried ourselves to death about him. We didn't want any corps commander getting shot, particularly him."

Ray Davis

Davis committed two companies, A and B, to close a gap on the regiment's left flank, when a company of the 3rd Battalion was cut off and surrounded. They were stopped cold and pinned down by the heavy Japanese fire. Davis rallied his men and partially closed the gap. In the meantime, Puller gathered a scratch force and built up a second line behind the north flank. Early in the afternoon, Davis threw in C Company, his last fresh infantry, against a thirty-foot coral ridge two hundred yards inland from the beach. In a vicious, no-holds-barred slugfest, his Marines captured the ridge and made contact with the isolated company. Utterly spent, the battalion dug in for the night.

The 1st Marine Regiment now had all three battalions in line. Assistant division commander O. P. Smith reported, "Their casualties had reached the 1,000 mark. It was a heavy price to pay for a beachhead only 300 yards in depth, but the capture of a fortified beach is never cheap."

As darkness fell, exhausted Marines peered out into a nightmarish no-man's-land of shattered trees and blasted coral rock. Parachute flares turned this broken landscape into an eerie patchwork of green light and shadow. Japanese infiltrators skillfully exploited the cover to advance toward the American positions. Suddenly, the Marine lines were blanketed with grenades and mortar fire. Japanese infantry rose out of the darkness. With screaming battle cries, they ran forward—to be met by the concentrated fire of B Company's automatic weapons and small arms fire. The fighting became hand-to-hand, but the Japanese attack faltered, beaten back by superior firepower. The few survivors scuttled back to their caves.

The second day ashore, Davis' battalion was ordered to attack, straight into the teeth of the enemy defenses. "Our mission the next morning was to go through the lead battalion to seize the regimental objective, some coral ridges." Historian George McMillan wrote, "The 1st Battalion (Lieutenant Colonel R. G. Davis) started out fine, moved with surprising ease for about an hour, but then was brought up sharp by fire from a concrete blockhouse the size of a small office building which stood directly in its path. Its reinforced walls were four feet thick, and as if that were not enough protection it was also supported by twelve pillboxes all connected by a maze of tunnels." E. B. Sledge was glad his battalion did not have the mission. "We pitied the 1st Marines attacking the ridges. They were suffering heavy casualties." Admiral Oldendorf had been badly mistaken. There were plenty of targets! The bunker and pillboxes were not even scratched. Tom Lea observed the action. "Looking up at the head of the trail I could see the big Jap blockhouse that commanded the height. The thing was now a jagged lump of concrete, smoking. It was a smoking heap of rubble. . . . There were dead Japs on the ground where they had been hit. . . . I saw some of the bodies were nothing more than red raw meat and blood mixed with the gravelly dust of concrete and splintered logs."

"I took twenty-five casualties, including three dead," Davis recalled, "trying to take that objective." He pulled the troops back and directed First Lieutenant N. R. K. Stanford, his naval gunfire forward observer, to knock it out. "I was lying in the coral rubble of the shattered bunker in front of the blockhouse with the Nambu fire going high to my left and the Jap mortars bursting in the ripped and twisted coconut grove behind me." The outline of the emplacement was blurred by the haze of coral dust, which hung in the air from muzzle blasts and mortar fire. "I set up my

SCR-284 (radio) nearly at the top of an abandoned Jap bunker and crawled through the loose coral to look over a broken timber revetment at the top of the bunker." His radio operator handed him the handset and he established contact with "Ironsides," the code name for the battleship USS *Mississippi*. "Ironsides, this is Charlie Nine. Target at . . . reinforced concrete blockhouse . . . AP (armor piercing) one round. Main battery . . . commence firing."

The 14-inch shell passed low over his head with a heart-stopping crack and landed beyond the target. He requested an adjustment. "Down 200, one salvo." The salvo roared past, smashing into the bunker. "I was numbed from the concussion and it took my eyes a few seconds to focus, but I could see that the camouflage had been stripped away and the shape of the blockhouse altered." An eyewitness reported, "The blockhouse began disintegrating, the big armor-piercing and high-capacity shells crumbled the walls, and their terrific concussion killed those Japanese missed by fragmentation." Davis stopped to reorganize prior to assaulting the high ground. Heavy Japanese mortar and artillery fire pounded the exposed Marines. Casualties mounted. Davis quickly reformed his unit and launched them in an assault against the coral bluffs to the east and west of the coast road.

As the attack continued toward the Umurbrogol's outpost hills, "The Japanese turned their fire on it," McMillan recorded, "cutting our exposed front lines to ribbons under perfect observation. The 1st was forced to push on, to seek desperately for some of that high ground to storm the Japanese out of their emplacements on the bluff." Infantry could not do the job alone. Davis called up Sherman tanks, which fired point-blank into the mouths of caves, while his riflemen inched forward in the 112-degree heat. According to O. P. Smith, "For the assault, eighteen medium tanks were assigned to the 1st Marines. Of these, seventeen were hit by HE shells either while en route to the beach or on the beach. Three were knocked out before they reached the beach. The depth of water off the beach saved others from serious damage by absorbing the shock of the explosion. Within a few hours, six tanks were knocked out in addition to those lost on the beach. These tanks, although absorbing a lot of punishment, did considerable damage to the Japanese."

Men clawed upward. McMillan noted, "The pock-marked surface offered no secure footing even in the few level places. It was impossible to dig in; the best the men could do was pile a little coral or wood debris around their positions. The jagged rocks slashed their shoes and clothes, and tore their bodies every time they hit the deck for safety." O. P. Smith wrote, "Men could not dig in; the best they could do was to pile rubble around themselves. Many men were wounded by rock fragments thrown up by the blast of the Japanese mortar and artillery shells."

Davis watched as men fought and died along faint paths that ended abruptly in sheer cliffs. They had to turn around and backtrack. George McMillan explained that "Each blast hurled chunks of coral in all directions, multiplying many times the fragmentation effect of every shell." E. B. Sledge was told by survivors that the 1st Marines "not only received heavy shelling from enemy caves there but deadly accurate small-arms fire as well. . . . The enemy fired on them from mutually supporting positions, pinning them down and inflicting heavy losses." O. P. Smith remembered, "There were dozens of caves and pillboxes worked into the noses of the ridges and up the ravines. It was very difficult to find blind spots as the caves and pillboxes were mutually supporting. We found out later that some of the caves consisted of galleries of more than one level with several exits."

By late afternoon, Davis' men gained the forward slopes but at a huge cost: 250 Marine casualties. A company commander reported, "We're up here, but we're knee-deep in Purple Hearts." The battalion had established itself firmly on the forward slopes of the first series of hills. Thirty-five caves had been captured.

The Japanese, however, were not the only enemy the Marines had to face. O. P. Smith noted, "Beginning with the second day the troops had to contend with an additional enemy, the extreme heat. The thermometer went up to 105 degrees. In the intense fighting over rugged ground, the men soon exhausted their canteens. Resupply was difficult. We began to have a good many cases of heat exhaustion."

Above and Beyond
By the 19th, Davis' battalion had all but disappeared. "I lost all my platoon leaders and our casualties amounted to about 70 percent in ten days."

Sledge passed by the shattered unit. "As we walked along one side of a narrow road, the 1st Marines filed along the other side. . . . The three decimated battalions trudged past us, but I was shocked at the absence of so many others whom I knew in the regiment. . . . The men in the 1st Marines had so many [casualties] it was appalling."

Despite the heavy losses, C Company was attached to the 2nd Battalion and ordered to seize Hill 100, a vital piece of terrain that in Marine hands would allow them to attack Bloody Nose Ridge from the rear. Davis recounted that company's struggle to capture the height. "The deepest penetration the 1st Marines made on the 19th was achieved by C Company commanded by a twenty-five-year-old Massachusetts native, Captain Everett Pope. Already reduced by casualties to just ninety men . . . the Marines approached Hill 100. Enemy fire . . . took a heavy toll of the attacking Marines. As twilight fell, the Marines took [any] cover they could among the jumbled rocks. The Japanese went for Pope's men after dark, and they kept coming . . . two Japanese suddenly materialized near the position defended by Lieutenant Francis Burke . . . and Sergeant James P. McAlarnis. One of the Japanese ran a bayonet into Burke's leg. Burke tore into his attacker beating him senseless with his fists. McAlarnis, meanwhile, went to work on the second Japanese with his rifle butt. They tossed the bodies over the precipice."

The fighting became hand-to-hand, and as dawn approached, Pope's company was down to about a dozen men and they were running out of ammunition. "Pope received orders to withdraw," Davis continued. "The order came just as the last Japanese assault began to sweep the survivors off the ridge. Those who could scrambled down the slope as fast as they could. Of the dozen or so men Pope had brought up the hill, only nine made it down safely. . . . Many were wounded, including Pope himself. Sometime during the fighting, he had taken a spray of shrapnel in the legs and thighs." Pope gathered the survivors together just as he received orders to attack again. "He contacted regiment and reported that he had only fifteen men and two officers able to attack. The order was rescinded."

C Company's heroic fight marked the end of the battle for Davis' command. After 197.5 hours of combat, his battalion had suffered 71 percent casualties and was virtually destroyed. Everett Pope was the only company commander to walk off the island. Of the nine infantry platoons in the 1st Battalion, not one platoon commander survived the battle—and only seventy-four Marines reported for duty. Private Russell Davis, a rifleman in the 1st Marines, put it more succinctly: "The whole motley outfit—a fighting outfit only in the minds of a few officers in the 1st Regiment and in the 1st Division—started up the hill. I have never understood why. Not one of them refused. They were the hard core—the men who couldn't or wouldn't quit. They would go up a thousand blazing hills and through a hundred blasted valleys, as long as their legs would carry them. They were Marine riflemen."

O. P. Smith reported a truly staggering butcher's bill: "In this six-day assault against the high ground north of the airfield the 1st Marines engaged in one of the bitterest fights in the Pacific War. Out of a strength of approximately 3,000 men, the regiment had suffered 1,737 casualties (299 killed in action and 1,438 wounded in action). It had killed an estimated 3,700 Japanese in the eight days it had been in the lines. Losses in the rifle units had been so heavy, particularly among the officers and noncommissioned officers, that the units were no longer effective."

Roy Geiger

Geiger visited Puller's command post to get a feel for the situation on the ground. Puller, with characteristic bravado, said he was "doing all right with what he had," but he looked "very tired" and was not able to give a clear account of the situation. In an interview with the author, Ray Davis said that Puller was carried around on a stretcher because of an old wound from Guadalcanal. Davis thought that was the only reason Puller had not been killed, because he could not go as far forward as he normally did.

Geiger proceeded to division, where he reviewed the 1st Regiment's casualty reports. He found that more than half of Puller's regiment were casualties. "General Rupertus, realizing that the 1st Marines was spent, was in a state of despair. He had no more replacements to give to the fight for the ridges. Regardless, he refused to request assistance and strongly argued against bringing in army troops. Puller had lost all touch with reality in his frenzied determination to fight the Japanese to the last man, if necessary." Geiger told Rupertus, "The 1st Marines were finished," and, over the division commander's strenuous objections, ordered it relieved by the army's 321st Infantry. A reporter asked them as they came out of the line, "You the 1st Marines?" One of the survivors wearily replied, "There ain't no more 1st Marines."

At high noon on October 30, D-day plus thirty-five, Geiger turned over responsibility of the campaign to the army's 81st Division. He left the island immediately afterward. One of his staff reported him as saying, "I'm glad it's finally over and the Marines can leave." Rupertus, who had predicted a "rough but fast" campaign, simply acknowledged the comment with "I am too." Later, Geiger commented, "The only difference between Iwo Jima and Peleliu was that at Iwo Jima, there were twice as many Japs on an island twice as large, and they had three Marine divisions to take it, while we had one Marine division to take Peleliu." Ray Davis commented, "We could have saved a lot of lives by not trying to take the whole island. After we secured the airfield, we should have pulled back, got into a siege stage, got our guns up, and just pounded the place."

CHAPTER EIGHTEEN

SINO-AMERICAN COOPERATIVE ORGANIZATION

Bob Barrow

Barrow learned that Admiral Milton E. Miles expected everyone to live with the Chinese, sharing what little food, clothing, and shelter they had. Lieutenant General James Masters remembered, "We were told when we went out there, never to eat any fresh vegetables or fresh fruit . . . to boil all water thirty minutes, and always drink it while it was still hot. He [Miles] required everybody who served out there never to eat with a knife and fork, but to eat with chopsticks." Lieutenant Milton A. "Peanut" Hull, USMCR, a SACO veteran, considered that "The type of American for this duty must be a combination of Marine Raider and quartermaster. He must be able to live off the land in winter and summer, to use the facilities and equipment at hand. His attention to duty must be unquestioned, and he must be willing to take chances. He must have and can place complete confidence in the Chinese guerrilla." Living conditions in the field were rough, to say the least. Marine First Lieutenant Ted Gwai Tai "Liberal Heart" Cathey, Barrow's field commander, reported, "Living conditions are of the poorest. Americans live off the land, having two meals each day, which is adequate when accustomed to it." The trick was to get used to the diet of rice with a few vegetables mixed in—no meat—eaten with chopsticks. Barrow said that "Rice for this Louisiana boy was like giving candy to a child." The average American in the field lost thirty to forty pounds and inches off his waistline.

Barrow was constantly on the move via shanks mare. Walking twenty to thirty miles a day was not uncommon. A Guadalcanal veteran, Marine Major Ed Dupras, rashly informed Miles, "I'm fresh from the field, no trouble at all." Three months later he reported, "Marines don't know the first thing about walking until they come to China." Barrow described a typical move. "Everything we had was transported by local village coolies, who were hired for the day. Everything we had was broken down into loads up to fifty pounds and packed into woven bamboo baskets eighteen inches wide at the top and about two feet deep. Two baskets fit over each other, making a very secure load that could be waterproofed with treated paper. The baskets were hung from the ends of a yo-yo pole, a flat piece of flexible bamboo that was carried over the shoulder. The coolies assumed a gait, which caused the pole to flex up and down so that the weight wasn't always bearing down." Barrow estimated that one hundred coolies could transport five tons of material twenty-five to thirty miles in ten hours. "The Chinese coolie could move vast amounts of supplies." Barrow tried using the yo-yo pole but could not do it, much to the amusement of the Chinese.

At night, Barrow's party stayed with Chinese peasant families, sharing space in one-room farmhouses. Occasionally they found more spacious quarters in a school or other public building. He found it a great experience. "We were totally dependent on the Chinese. Most had never seen a westerner, which made us curiosities wherever we went. I never received such hospitality and acquired such good feelings as I did for those Chinese. I gained a high respect for the peasant to live with adversity. Nothing shaped my life more than living with them." Barrow never traveled with a large contingent of guerrillas. They remained scattered over a large area to avoid creating a hardship on the local peasants, as well as to keep from attracting unwanted attention. They moved often, responding to intelligence reports that were provided by the local peasants, who hated the brutal Japanese.

U.S. Naval Unit 5

Barrow was lucky to be assigned to Naval Unit 5 located in Nanning, described as one of the finest towns in free China. The headquarters was located in an old French mission, a solid masonry building three stories high. Food was plentiful and even "Americanized." Pop's Lucky Café specialized in hamburgers a la Stateside. For a lucky few, there was liberty, although it expired at 11:00 p.m. Barrow did not have time to enjoy the relative comforts of the city, for the seventeen-man cadre's immediate concern was to train and equip a force of more than one thousand Chinese guerrillas. The intensive training included day and night firing of infantry weapons, Thompson submachine guns, carbines, .45 pistols, .38 revolvers, as well as practice in demolitions, aircraft identification, ambushes, street fighting, and tactical indoctrination. Barrow reflected that "We trained, but in some respects, we were trained by the Chinese in field craft and how to get along in a guerrilla environment." After six weeks, the force "graduated" and Barrow left his relatively comfortable surroundings for the Spartan existence of a guerrilla in the field. He shed his Marine uniform for the nondescript cotton garment of the Chinese peasant. He hoped it would help him blend in, but at six foot three inches, it was hard to conceal his western heritage. The padded uniform kept him warm in dry, cold weather but soaked up water like a sponge when it rained.

Barrow's unit was constantly on the move, "swimming" among small bands of guerrillas, who lived in the villages and were intimately familiar with the territory. They had complete cooperation of the population, who hated the Japanese and were happy to provide support for the guerrillas despite the threat of retaliation. "The Japanese engaged in food gathering expeditions," Barrow noted. "They took all the rice and created hatred among the locals." Lieutenant Milton A. Hull cited an example of Chinese sacrifice. "The mayor of Anwha village was summoned. We asked him at what time the troop train was scheduled to pass the point of our demolition. He gave us this answer immediately: 'Yes, I will tell you when the train is coming. I will be killed tomorrow for doing it but after I am dead the new mayor who takes my place will help you in any way he can.' The Japanese hold each civilian leader responsible for his area; for any sabotage in that area, the Chinese official is executed."

Dividing the guerrillas into small detachments made it easier for the Chinese to conceal their presence and avoid retaliation from Japanese counter-guerrilla forces. It also made it possible to slip through Japanese lines. Barrow noted that "The Japanese were scattered around.

They controlled the major cities, railroad junctions, and major routes of communication, but they weren't all over the country. We could move between their strong points, almost at will." Their mission, once in enemy territory, was "to continually harass the Japanese units and prevent their freedom of movement." The guerrillas employed hit-and-run tactics, ambushes, sniping, nighttime raids, and assassinations.

4th Column, Chinese Commando Army

Ted Cathey's 4th Column operated in the important Hankow-Changsha area, a rail and water terminal for shipping troops and supplies to French Indochina, Malaya, and all through South China. Barrow joined the column in the fall of 1944 "for a couple of interesting operations." On one mission, Barrow had a memorable experience. "I remember one operation with two hundred guerrillas against a village under Japanese control. Our target was to kill or capture the Chinese puppets they had left in charge. We walked all day and half the night, until we got to the outskirts. It was freezing cold, snow on [the] ground and slippery as hell on top of the rice paddy dike. Suddenly my feet went out from under me and I fell into a sealed-off area, about as big as a large tub, where they put their night soil [human excrement]. I went completely in, one of the most ghastly experiences of my life. I smelled to high heaven!" Barrow made his way to a peasant hut. "I took off all my clothes and stripped completely down. They pulled out a large wooden tub, heated water, and I scrubbed down." A couple of steadfast women washed his reeking clothes and dried them by the fire. "If something had happened, I would have been in a hell'va fix!"

Barrow's next foray was an attack on the Japanese garrison at Ningshan and Siangtan, a three-day walk in the dead of winter. On the morning of February 11, the 4th Column set out for Taomachchow, a temporary headquarters near the objective. Weather conditions were abysmal. Heavy snow and mud-covered trails hampered movement. Freezing temperatures drained energy, making the hike a test of character. Frostbite was a constant danger. Upon reaching Taomachchow, the group divided into two attack elements. Barrow's group, under Lieutenant W. L. Morris, walked through the night and rested during the day, to avoid being detected by the Japanese garrison. That evening, Morris and Barrow accompanied the guerrilla leader to his forward command post. At a pre-arranged signal, the guerrillas swept forward, overcoming heavy Japanese resistance. The assault force killed more than a hundred Japanese soldiers, including the entire staff of the garrison. They also destroyed a *godown* (warehouse), a barracks, and three bridges before withdrawing. Following the action, the Americans pulled out and hiked back to Taomachchow, the rally point. Upon arrival of the second group, both units returned to head-quarters. Major E. P. Dupras, USMC, wrote a citation for their success: "The entire group of Americans conducted themselves in an exemplary manner while operating in Japanese territory. . . . The group walked a distance of about 375 Chinese *li*, roughly about 125 miles, during a period when all civilian activity within the area had ceased due to weather and deplorable conditions of the road."

2nd Column, Chinese Commando Group

A month later, Barrow was ordered to join the 2nd Column. "I was put in charge of a four-man team to work with the Chinese against the Japanese-held Canton-Hankow corridor. This was a most interesting experience for a young Marine lieutenant. I had two CPOs (chief petty officers) who were much older than I was. They were demolition experts, one from Texas and one from Chicago—one blew up buildings and the other oil wells. I had a radio operator, who was a former carpenter from Missouri—but I had no radio. He became the armorer because he could fix anything. Barney Riever, a schoolteacher, from Pennsylvania, was the corpsman. He was the most valuable, well trained, smart, and had a fine supply of medicine." Barrow received the broadest possible guidance. "My orders were to work against the Japanese—to make it difficult for the Japs to supply their troops—no other instructions. I did not have a radio, nor did my Chinese counterparts, so there was no way to report my actions. For a young officer, conducting independent operations, with little guidance, contributed greatly to my development as a Marine officer."

CHAPTER NINETEEN

SULPHUR ISLAND

In October 1944, the Joint Chiefs of Staff directed Fleet Admiral Chester W. Nimitz, CinCPac, to seize the strategic Japanese-held island of Iwo Jima, 660 nautical miles southeast of Tokyo. The tiny volcanic island, barely eight square miles in area, was one of the most heavily fortified islands in the Pacific—and by far the toughest "nut" Marines would have to seize. Intelligence reports indicated the island was honeycombed with multistoried blockhouses, camouflaged pillboxes, and thousands of yards of concrete-lined interconnecting caves and tunnels. Hundreds of artillery pieces, mortars, antitank and machine guns were sited to cover every square inch of ground. The formidable Lieutenant General Tadamichi Kuribayashi, onetime leader of the emperor's elite Imperial Guard, commanded more than twenty thousand combat veterans.

Kuribayashi, in a break with the traditional Japanese all-out counter-attack against the beachhead, adopted a policy of attrition. There would be no massive banzai attack to stop the invaders at the water's edge. Instead, he divided the island into five defense sectors and ordered his men to defend these positions to the death. He planned to slow the invaders with small infantry units supported by automatic weapons, while relying on artillery, mortars, and rockets emplaced to the north and south to enfilade the beaches and make them untenable.

Mount Suribachi, the major terrain feature in the south, was a 550-foot extinct volcano, which loomed over the landing beaches. It bristled with weapons of all types, ranging from casemated coast-defense guns and artillery to automatic weapons emplaced in mutually supporting pillboxes. Many of these emplacements were constructed of reinforced concrete with walls four feet thick and cleverly camouflaged to blend in with the terrain. The entire island was honeycombed with these defensive fortifications. Many had several levels that were connected by tunnels and had multiple entrances, which allowed the defenders to move throughout the system without being exposed to direct fire. Kuribayashi issued a last message two days before the landing: "I pray for a heroic fight."

Major General Harry Schmidt commanded the veteran V Amphibious Corps (VAC). The fifty-eight year old was a veteran of two Pacific campaigns—Roi-Namur and Saipan. VAC comprised three Marine divisions: the battle-hardened 3rd and 4th Divisions and the 5th Division, which was organized around a considerable number of combat-experienced troops. VAC was the largest force of U.S. Marines ever committed to a single operation—eighty thousand men, more than half of whom were combat veterans. In the opinion of historian Colonel Joseph H. Alexander, "The troops assaulting Iwo Jima were arguably the most proficient amphibious forces the world had seen."

Eddie Craig

Shortly after the end of the Guam Campaign, Craig relinquished his command of the 9th Marines and reported to the V Amphibious Corps as the G-3 (operations officer). He was immediately immersed in planning for the Iwo Jima operation, code-named Detachment. "I was given a one-page directive which had come from Fleet Marine Force Headquarters in Honolulu to prepare orders for a landing on Iwo Jima. The 4th and 5th Divisions were the assault force for the landing . . . and the 3rd Division, which was still on Guam, was to be brought in as reserve or as needed." To facilitate planning, Schmidt and his key staff officers flew to Hawaii where the bulk of his force was in training. Craig immediately began the task of preparing a concept of operations. "My main difficulty in preparing the orders in Hawaii for this operation was getting in contact with [the] many units which were scattered all over [the] Hawaiian area and in Guam."

Craig quickly roughed out a concept of operations. "During my time in Honolulu preparing these orders with a very competent staff, we prepared for the initial landing with one alternate plan. The plan was never carried out, of course, and the original landing order was never changed from the one that we made in the rough a few days after arriving in Honolulu."

A Tough Proposition

Craig found that terrain dictated the landing plan and subsequent scheme of maneuver. "Selection of the landing beaches was a simple matter, there being only two available beach areas large enough to support a landing. Both were good beaches equally well defended, with the southeastern one perhaps better from the standpoint of fewer natural obstacles immediately inland. Because the prevailing wind was indicated being from the north and west in February, the southeastern or lee beaches were selected." However, Mt. Suribachi loomed over the entire southern end of the island, completely dominating either landing beach. In addition, the steep cliffs of the Rock Quarry overshadowed the right flank, sandwiching the landing beach between the two high grounds. The terrain north of the beaches compounded Craig's tactical dilemma. The land rose unevenly onto the Motoyama Plateau, falling off sharply along the coasts into steep cliffs and canyons. The broken, convoluted, cave-dotted landscape represented a defenders' dream and an attackers' nightmare.

The final plan, issued on December 23, 1944, called for the simultaneous landing of four reinforced regiments, nine thousand men, in forty-five minutes. The landing was to be preceded by three days of naval gunfire and aerial bombardment. Craig argued for a ten-day bombardment, but was overruled, much to the disgust of the naval gunfire expert Lieutenant Colonel Donald M. Weller, USMC. "The issue was not the weight of shells, nor their caliber, but rather time. Destruction of heavily fortified enemy targets took deliberate, pinpoint firing from close ranges. Iwo Jima's 700 hard targets would require time to knock out, a lot of time." Holland Smith gloomily predicted heavy casualties, possibly as many as 15,000. Secretary of the Navy James V. Forrestal, on board the flagship said, "Iwo Jima, like Tarawa, leaves very little to choice, except to take if by force of arms, by character and courage."

Into Harm's Way

The requirement for naval shipping to support MacArthur's campaign in the Philippines forced two postponements of Operation Detachment.

Finally, in early December, VAC was notified that D-day was set for February 19, 1945. Loading started almost immediately. Corps troops and the 4th Division embarked from Maui, while the 5th Division loaded from Hawaii, "the big island." The landing force rendezvoused off Maalaea Bay, Maui, to conduct a week of rehearsal exercises. Craig emphasized their importance. "This rehearsal was conducted in every possible detail in accordance with the preferred (southeastern beach) plan of attack against Iwo Jima."

The residents of the sleepy little Hawaiian island of Maui woke to find an armada of ships at their doorstep. Thousands of men swarmed ashore, tearing up the pristine beaches and quiet backcountry and completely shattering the pastoral setting. Distant explosions marked the detonation of naval gunfire and aircraft ordnance on Kahoolawe's live fire range. The seven-day exercise was closely monitored by the commanders and key staff of the landing force. They gathered aboard the command ship USS *Auburn* (AGC-10) for a critique of the exercise. Craig was generally satisfied with the results, although the absence of several assault organizations detracted from their overall value.

The men were granted one last liberty on Oahu before sailing for the objective area. Historian Howard M. Conner explained that "One-quarter of the troops had regular liberty ashore each day and another fourth could go ashore in organized liberty parties to playing fields and beaches near Pearl Harbor and at Kaneohe Bay." There was some concern that, with the number of men ashore, word would somehow leak out about their destination. Counterintelligence officers spread the rumor in Honolulu's bars and hotels that Formosa was the next target.

With twenty-three days remaining before D-day, the immense convoy sailed for Saipan, the forward staging and final rehearsal area. Craig noted that the staff used the time to hone its skills: "While enroute to the forward area, an extensive command post exercise, coordinated with naval forces, was conducted on board the *Auburn*." Upon reaching Saipan, additional rehearsals were held. "Assault waves were boated and dispatched from the line of departure but were not landed. The sea was rough and several Marines were hurt as landing craft bounced up and raked them as they hung on the debarkation nets."

Late on the afternoon of February 16, Navy Transport Squadrons 15 and 16, carrying the assault forces, left the Saipan anchorage. They were scheduled to arrive on station off Iwo Jima prior to dawn on the 19th. Reveille for Captain James G. Headley, Lima Company, 3rd Battalion, 25th Marines, came early. "We arose at 05:00 to find the sea calm and the promise of a clear day. Iwo lay low on the horizon and about all we could see were the huge flashes as the many battleships let go with their main batteries." Craig was up before dawn, restless with anxiety. He went up on deck, but it was still too dark to see anything except the continuous flash of the ship's gunfire. He went below to the joint operations spaces, where his staff followed the action by monitoring the radio frequencies.

Land the Landing Force

Dawn of D-day found the weather clear, with visibility virtually unlimited, temperature about 68 degrees, wind eight to twelve knots from the north, surf conditions good. Admiral Turner's flagship broadcast: "Very light swells. Boating: excellent. Visibility: excellent." H-hour was set at 9:00 a.m. At 8:30, sixty-eight armored, cannon-firing amphibious tractors [LVT(A)s], followed by more than four hundred of their troop-carrying brethren, crossed the line of departure. Combat correspondent Technical Sergeant Henry A. Weaver wrote, "There were the faintest grins on the faces of the Marines as they crouched in the landing craft that was bouncing toward the beach of Iwo Jima. It was D-day and this was one of the initial assault waves. On the inside of the ramp, the coxswain had painted with bold letters and heavy brush: 'TOO LATE TO WORRY.' " Naval gunfire thundered overhead, in a massive bombardment of the landing beaches. The assault waves hit the beach within two minutes of H-hour and advanced inland, against furious resistance. Jim Headley was in the assault wave. "Woody's company [Captain Elyn W. Woods, commanding Company I, was wounded in action by a gunshot in his left side] was the first to hit the beach and I heard him report by radio that they had received no fire. Tom [Captain Thomas S. Witherspoon, commanding Company K, was wounded in action by shrapnel in neck], who was next to hit, reported that they were starting to receive mortar and small arms fire. L Company followed and then all hell broke lose. By the time four or five waves had hit, the entire beach and the Japs, apparently waiting for the most opportune target, let go with everything they had." Hundreds of Marines hugged the black volcanic sand, pinned down by the relentless shelling. Casualties were heavy.

Headley had several narrow escapes. "A bullet went through one side of the top of my shoe and out the other without even breaking the skin. A tank hit a mine about twenty feet away from me and the concussion knocked me right on my pratt. Things looked pretty bad and I began wondering if we were going to be able to stay on the beach. . . . Officer casualties were high so that the men were without leadership."

The beach resembled a junk yard. Disabled and broached landing craft, mired vehicles, abandoned equipment, and bodies littered the sandy terraces. Japanese artillery mercilessly pounded the wreckage into impenetrable rubble, jamming the beach approaches. Coast Guard Coxswain Marvin J. Perrett steered an LCVP (Boat number 21 from the USS *Bayfield*, APA-33) toward an opening. Wreckage prevented it from beaching properly. A motor mech dropped the ramp and the load of troops splashed ashore. One man fell beneath the ramp. Perrett applied full power to back away. Water poured over the stern and killed the motor. Plunging waves crashed over the sides. Number 21 joined dozens of other landing craft beneath the water.

Eddie Craig

The Corps headquarters came ashore on D+5. A landing craft, mechanized (LCM) came alongside *Auburn*. Craig and his staff climbed into the boat for the run to the beach. As the small boat neared the island's northwestern beaches, he could plainly see the flag atop Mount Suribachi. The coxswain carefully maneuvered through the heavy boat traffic to bring the craft's bow against the beach. The ramp dropped and Craig stepped ashore. He immediately sank up to his ankles in the coarse volcanic ash. "I was immediately struck by how difficult it was to move through the black sand. There wasn't any traction, each step was an effort." A guide appeared and led him to the command post, a "little northwest of Mount Suribachi" at map coordinates TA 147 R.

The CP was crammed into the narrow southern end of the island, between artillery positions, first aid stations, supply dumps, and subordinate unit command posts. It was a lucrative target for Japanese gunners. "The Japs were shelling the area we were in with guns and spigot mortars. In addition, they had a form of rocket made from five-inch naval shells, which would periodically go over our CP. Most of these rockets dropped into the sea at the south end of the island however."

Craig selected a site for his operation. "The small CP tent where I had my G-3 Section was placed in a slight defilade behind a small sand hill, but this, of course, did not protect against high-angle fire, and many shells fell around it." The Japanese had every inch of the area zeroed in and began a merciless shelling. "We were all congregated in this tent the first night ashore when suddenly the Japs opened up with everything they had. Shells were landing and exploding all around us. Rank was forgotten as well as dignity when all of the officers and men in the tent hit the deck in a pile three or four high. There we lay as the shells thumped and exploded around us. We fully expected that the entire G-3 Section would become casualties [in] one fell swoop. The shelling stopped as suddenly as it had begun, and we unscrambled from the pile and went back to work."

The heavy Japanese fire added impetus to the construction of shelters. Craig and his assistant, Lieutenant Colonel Joe Stewart, took time out to get underground. "The two of us decided to construct a double foxhole. We dug into the loose black sand and shored the sides up with whatever we could find but mostly sand bags . . . [and] empty cardboard tubes the 105 shells came in filled with sand, and [with] some pieces of lumber, we covered the foxhole, leaving only a very small entrance at one side." Craig developed claustrophobia in the small space. "I will never forget the terror-filled moments in that hole when the Jap shells would be landing all around us. Joe and I would lie with our faces in the sand and pray that nothing landed on us as the explosions shook the sand down on us." Headley wrote that "The ground around us geysered as their big mortars and rockets fell like rain. Their biggest weapon was a rocket that had a one-thousand-pound war head, shot out of a concealed position in the ground, and when that baby hit the whole island would shake."

Craig's G-3 Section prepared daily written orders for each division. "These orders usually got out and to the units by about four o'clock in the afternoon, so the division naturally had to rush to get their orders out to the various units down to the companies by the following morning. However, due to the short distance involved and the density of the troops on the island, this was not too difficult a situation as it might seem. The lines of communication were very short and could be handled by runners or verbally over the telephone in many cases."

The corps headquarters remained in the same location throughout the campaign, but Craig refused to wait for information. "I found that it was impossible for me to sit back at the corps CP and have a clear conception of what was actually taking place at the front. I had capable assistants . . . and therefore had no qualms about leaving the CP . . . and [making] trips to the front. This resulted in a number of important tactical changes which were incorporated in the daily operations orders." Craig also expected his subordinates to go to the front. "It was my policy as G-3 to require that at least one of my assistants go to the front each day and see for himself what the situation was and advise me on his return. I believe our Operations Section was always well informed as a result."

On one occasion, Craig was by himself, on the way to a battalion headquarters. "I noticed a dead Marine with most of his lower body blown off lying nearby, and in an instant realized that he had stepped on a land mine. I stopped in my tracks, looked at the ground, and found that I was in the middle of a mined area . . . so I carefully retraced my steps and got out without further incident." Craig worked his way forward to a company command post. While he was talking to the company commander, "a Marine crouching nearby yelled, 'Look out, there's a Jap right there,' and pointed to a crevice in the rock almost beside me. Sure enough, there was a spider hole, as we called them, and tightly wedged in it, with a grenade in his hand, was a Jap soldier. A Marine covered him with an automatic rifle, and the company commander tried to induce him to come out by offering cigarettes and C-rations. The man was near enough to touch but would not let go of the grenade or move. Water was finally offered him and he still refused to move. A burst of fire finally settled the question and the war went on."

Prophetic Prediction

By the second week of the campaign, Holland Smith's shocking prediction had come true. VAC had suffered thirteen thousand casualties, three thousand of whom were killed in action. Assault elements of the three divisions were exhausted, and the end was not yet in sight. Craig personally observed the blooding. "I was watching a small advance of Marines over ground that was defiladed. A squad in rather close formation started to cross a knoll on which a number of dead Marines were lying. I heard someone shouting a warning to the squad to keep off the knoll. They had reached the dead Marines and some of them had bent over to examine one of them who was apparently only wounded. A sharp burst of fire from an unseen place mowed down seven of the squad. Others were wounded but managed to roll down out of the danger area. I had never seen so many Marines shot down at once before, and it made me feel very depressed."

Iwo was not a place to visit. "Looking toward the knoll on my right hand," continued Craig, "I noticed a huge figure of a man dressed in a new camouflage uniform lying dead on a litter where he had been abandoned by carriers. As none of our personnel were dressed in camouflage, I noticed him particularly and wondered who he was. He must have been over six feet four and built like a giant. The front of his jacket was red with blood. I never did find out who this casualty was, and surmised at the time that he must have been an observer sent ashore from some ship."

Death Valley

By D+25, depleted regiments of the 5th Division had reached the Japanese commander's final command center, an eight-hundred-yard pocket of incredibly broken country, which the troops dubbed "Death Valley." Craig went forward to check on the situation. "This area had been held by some six or seven hundred Jap troops and was their last stronghold on the island. The Gorge was a jumble of rocks surrounding an area some seven hundred yards by three hundred yards. It had steep sides and the Japs were concealed in the crevices and caves along these sides. It was almost impossible to locate where defensive fires came from due to excellent concealment, and the smokeless and flashless powder that the enemy was using." The Marines pressed forward in cave-by-cave assaults with flamethrowers and demolitions. Casualties were heavy. According to historian Joseph H. Alexander, the 5th Division "reported that the average battalion, which had landed with 36 officers and 885 men on D-day, now mustered 16 officers and 300 men, including hundreds of replacements funneled in during the fighting."

As Craig approached the Gorge, he "passed long lines of dead Marines laid out on the ground . . . covered with ponchos, their booted feet sticking out." He found a young platoon commander, who commenced to brief him on the situation. "In the middle of the briefing, a barrage of phosphorus shells fell around us. I thought that the end had come, and we lay crouched down in the hole with our faces in the dirt for a long time, it seemed, before the barrage stopped. Phosphorus shells are most terrifying when they are landing almost on you." Inching forward, Craig watched a squad cautiously move among the rocks. "I saw a Marine fall, shot directly through the head at very close range. He never saw the enemy. Another was wounded and then a third shot through the head from the rear. Others were wounded while I still watched as though from a seat in the audience at a theatre." One of Headley's Marines expressed a similar frustration: "How the hell can you fight something you can't see?" Headley wrote, "The thing that made it so tough was the Japs were completely concealed in caves, pillboxes carved out of the rock, or crevasses and there were so many of them you could never tell where the next shot came from."

The men that Craig watched were new replacements, brought up from the rear and hastily thrown into the attack. "It looked like murder to me. These men did not know war; they did not even know the squad leader in some cases." Craig made a strong recommendation to land the veteran 3rd Marine Regiment, the corps reserve. His request fell on deaf ears, as Holland Smith refused to send them in, with the comment, "You got enough Marines on the island now; there are too damn many here." The problem was not with the number of Marines, but the fact that the replacements lacked experience. "The new men . . . were not only new to combat, but they also were new to each other, an assortment of strangers lacking the life-saving bonds of unit integrity." Craig "returned to the corps CP sick at heart, knowing that this slaughter would probably go on till the Gorge was secured."

Work Through the Pain

The pressures on Craig were tremendous—little sleep, poor, inadequate food, and the constant threat of death or injury took its toll. "Towards the end of the Iwo Jima Campaign, I noticed an increasing symptom of stomach trouble. I could not eat much and many times threw up what I had eaten. Pains in my stomach made it almost impossible to sleep at night. I threw up and noticed some blood was in the residue." He refused to turn himself in to sickbay as long as the battle lasted. Finally, the corps headquarters evacuated the island and returned to Hawaii, where he turned himself in to the hospital. The doctors diagnosed his symptoms as an ulcer, and he spent a month recuperating.

Butcher's Bill

The battle for Iwo Jima far exceeded even Holland Smith's grim prophecy. One-third of the assault force became a casualty—24,053 Marines and navy personnel, of which 6,140 died. Japanese losses were more than 22,000 dead. Military historian Dr. Norman Cooper said, "Nearly seven hundred Americans gave their lives for every square mile. For every plot of ground the size of a football field, an average of more than one American and five Japanese were killed and five Americans wounded."

CHAPTER 20

ASSAULT ON THE GREAT
LEW CHEW

On the evening before the landing, Ernie Pyle, the celebrated war correspondent, made his way through the crowded troop compartments. "We were carrying Marines. They were a rough, unshaven, competent bunch of Americans. We were nervous. Anybody with any sense is nervous on the night before D-day. . . . We would take Okinawa—nobody had any doubt about that. But we would have to pay for it. Some on the ship would not be alive in twenty-four hours." Hours later, a predawn Reveille ushered in April Fool's Day, 1945— Love-day, the landing on Okinawa, or Lew Chew (ancient Chinese navigator Shukan had thought the Ryukyu Islands resembled "floating globes" or "precious stone balls": Liuchiu). Private E. B. Sledge was in the 5th Marines, scheduled to land over Yellow Beach 2. "Tension mounted on the eve of D-day. We received final orders to move in off the beach as fast as possible. We were also reminded that although we were in regimental reserve, we would probably 'get the hell kicked out of us' coming on the beach. We were all tense, particularly with the intelligence estimate that we could expect 80–85 percent casualties."

Multicolored pennants fluttered from the masts of the wave control boats. Promptly at 8:00 a.m., they were hauled down, the signal for wave after wave of troop-carrying LVTs to make the four-thousand-yard swim to the beach. Naval gunfire and air support bombarded the landing areas in a carefully choreographed ballet of explosives designed to keep the enemy's heads down until the last moment. Eight assault battalions—eight thousand Marines of III Phib Corps—churned toward the four color-coded beaches. A Japanese observer reported on the landing: "At 8:00 a.m. the enemy infantry disembarks from the thousand-odd landing craft, thrusting onto the shore. The sweep of the ordered military formation is impressive. It is as if the sea itself were advancing with a great roar." The assault troops boiled out of the amphibious vehicles and surged inland. Sledge was positioned in a Higgins boat headed toward the transfer point. A nervous buddy exclaimed, "The first wave's goin' in now. Stand by for a ram." The man next to him sighed, "Yeah, the stuff's gonna hit the fan now."

Sledge's boat pulled up to an amtrac. "The landing is unopposed," a Marine shouted. "It's straight dope. I ain't seen no casualties. Most of the Nips must have hauled ass." The word was passed to Lem Shepherd aboard the command ship. "We had made plans for every contingency but we certainly didn't have any idea that we were going in there standing up. We just couldn't believe it." Ernie Pyle heaved a sigh of relief. "I had dreaded the sight of the beach littered with mangled bodies, and my first look up and down the beach was a reluctant one. Then like a man in the movies who looks away and then suddenly looks back unbelieving, I realized there were no bodies anywhere—and no wounded. What a wonderful feeling." Shepherd commented that "There was a lot of glory on Iwo, but I'll take it this way." Colonel Yahara watched confidently: "Contrary to their expectations, the enemy meets no resistance from Japanese troops. They will complete their landing unchallenged. Advancing with such ease, they must be thinking gleefully that they have passed through a breach in the Japanese defense. They will be wrong. . . . The Japanese army has withdrawn and concealed itself . . . with plans to draw the Americans into a trap."

Operation Iceberg

The Okinawa invasion force was huge. Its sheer size dwarfed any previous amphibious operation in the Pacific. Silverthorn commented on the size of the operation. "Technically, Okinawa was the largest amphibious operation in the history of warfare, larger than the Normandy landings. I say technically because the Okinawa operation had four divisions in the assault—two Marine and two army—and each division had two regiments in the assault.

But, on the Normandy operation . . . they had Omaha Beach, and then you had Utah Beach, and then you had an airdrop of one or more divisions. Now, you take all of those together, and they are larger than Okinawa. But you take any one of them for a landing operation in its technical, strict, limited sense—just landing against opposition or landing on a hostile beach in one particular place: the number of assault regiments at Okinawa exceeded the number of assault regiments at either Omaha Beach or Utah Beach. So that's why I say technically it's the largest one."

The assault forces, designated the Tenth Army, commanded by Lieutenant General Simon Bolivar Buckner, Jr., USA, consisted of two corps, one army and one Marine—180,000 combat troops. Geiger's III Phib Corps totaled almost 90,000 Marines. Silverthorn described the embarkation as a tremendous accomplishment. "The III Phib Corps mounted out with 87,000 troops. These troops were embarked in 175 troop and cargo carrying vessels, and they were loaded out at Oahu [and] Kauai in the Hawaiian Islands; Saipan, Tinian, and Guam in the Mariana Islands; Kwajalein in the Marshalls; the Russell Islands; Guadalcanal; and Espíritu Santo, which is down four hundred or five hundred miles south. That is nine different loading places, widely separated—87,000 troops. In addition to that, we had 2,859 troops embarked with us that were members of the 1st Garrison Eechelon that were going to come in and be part of the Island Command. And so we had a grand total of 89,850 officers and men. Now, we had 113,775 short tons of cargo and equipment of the assault force, and we had another 12,000 short tons of garrison shipping with us for a total of 125,000 tons of equipment. So when we arrived in the transport area off Okinawa with that force of troops . . . I say it was a major accomplishment."

The navy supported the operation with almost 1,500 ships, everything from battleships and aircraft carriers to specialized landing craft. Facing this mighty force were 100,000 diehard Japanese of the 32nd Army, with orders to fight to the last man—and a new weapon, suicide pilots of the Japanese navy's Special Attack Corps—Kamikaze (Divine Wind) Corps.

Roy Geiger

Geiger and his key staff flew to Hawaii to meet their army counterparts and begin operational planning. Silverthorn recalled the initial meeting. "We all reported in at Schofield Barracks on the 10th of December. We sort of felt on our toes. We'd conducted two landing operations and been the overall commander [for] Guam and Peleliu, and we felt we knew the way things should be done and what we wanted." This time, however, III Phib Corps was subordinate to the army. "We would be one-half of the combat activities of the Tenth Army. The other half was the XXIV Corps. So there was a sort of a feeling of being on your toes to create the very best impression." Tenth Army assigned III Phib Corps its mission and then stood back to evaluate the results. Silverthorn noted that "The corps went to work and came up with its solution, which was a very normal solution; we were to land on the left of the Tenth Army, and we decided that we were to go right straight across the island, cut the island in two, and then be prepared to operate either north or south. It was quite a simple tactical solution."

Geiger presented the plan (Plan Fox) himself, which was out of the ordinary, as the chief of staff normally gave the briefing. Silverthorn thought Geiger handled it well. "With his [Geiger's] academic background at Leavenworth and the War College, then the Naval War College also, he was perfectly competent to make the presentation himself." Geiger proposed the simultaneous landing of the assault regiments, eight battalions—eight thousand men—of two divisions. He planned to employ the 6th Marine Division on the corps' left flank, with the 1st Marine Division on its right, adjoining the Army XXIV Corps' 7th Division. The 2nd Marine Division was slated to make a diversionary landing on the southeast coast on L-day and then revert to Tenth Corps reserve. Following the initial landing, the two Marine divisions were to attack eastward, cutting the island in two. The 6th Marine Division would then reorient its attack, swing north, and secure the upper two-thirds of the island. The 1st Marine Division was to revert to army reserve.

Buckner accepted the plan (OpPlan 1-45), and both staffs returned to Guadalcanal, where he got the opportunity to observe III Phib Corps "in the field." Silverthorn remarked, "They looked us over pretty carefully for three or four days. And I feel that they departed there, after seeing us in our offices doing our planning and seeing us in the field with our own equipment and our troops, with a feeling of respect for the professional competency of the Marines."

The two general officers had forged a close personal friendship while attending the army's Command and Staff School in the early 1920s and had maintained contact through the years. In fact, Benis M. Frank, chief Marine Corps historian, noted that "General Buckner felt that he should designate an alternate commander in case anything happened to him. Evidently, based on what he saw in General Geiger, he recommended General Geiger to be his alternate if something happened." O. P. Smith discussed the issue with Buckner. "Now the senior army officer in the Tenth Army, General Wallace . . . was a major general and he was next senior to General Buckner. But General Buckner didn't feel he was qualified to command an army in the field, and he did feel that General Geiger was so qualified." The selection was not without rancor. Buckner submitted his recommendation through army channels, but it was "shot down." Once Tenth Army came under the command of Admiral Nimitz as a naval task force, Buckner resubmitted the recommendation and it was approved.

Striking Sixth
Lem Shepherd

Lem Shepherd's 6th Marine Division was the youngest of the Corps' wartime divisions, although more than half the strength of its three infantry regiments were combat veterans. The division was formed around the 1st Marine Brigade's two veteran infantry regiments, the 4th and 22nd. Bringing it up to strength were the 29th Regiment, which had been blooded on Saipan; a regiment of artillery; a tank battalion; engineers; a reconnaissance company; and a host of combat support units. John C. McQueen, the division's chief of staff, noted, "It [6th Division] was built up to be a very heavily reinforced division. I think we landed on Okinawa as the strongest Marine division in history. As I remember, we had over twenty-two thousand people." Marine Brigadier General O. P. Smith said that "The 6th was 'more flashy' than the 1st Marine Division, which was 'more of a plugging division' than the 6th Division." In his mind, the 6th Marine Division was "a little more cocky than the 1st Marine Division." In a word, the division had, "style."

Russell E. Honsowetz, who had commanded 2nd Battalion, 1st Marines, at Peleliu and was the 1st Marine Division's G-3 on Okinawa said there was a great rivalry between the two Marine divisions. "We used to look for the 6th Division periodic report, the daily report, like today you look for the Sunday funnies, because it was . . . well, it was something. One day they came out . . . and it said, 'Today the 6th Division is locked in mortal combat in the precipices of Motobu Peninsula with the Okinawan Home Guard. The ferocity and tenacity of the Japanese is surpassed only by the Okinawan Home Guard.' They were trying to make a war up there and all the dammed Okinawans had were some pointed sticks. I don't think they even had rifles!" Honsowetz described another incident between the two divisions: "Then on another day, they [6th Division] said they'd killed . . . they had bodies stacked up like cord-wood; they had really slaughtered them. So General del Valle [commanding general 1st Marine Division] said, 'I want to go see that,' so we went over. General Geiger was going to see it too, so we all went and never could find any bodies stacked up like cord-wood. Finally we found one emaciated looking body and we looked at it. Then we went around Motobu Peninsula and came up on the other side and here was one body. But Pedro wasn't about to buy that. He said, 'Goddammit, Lem, I think you drug that one over the hill and he was the one we just saw on the other side of the hill."

In a sense, the 6th Marine Division was Lem Shepherd's creation. He organized it, hand-selected its leaders, supervised its training, and took it into its only combat operation. "I was very fortunate in having a very able staff, able officers—my G-3 was [Victor] Krulak, and other officers who I had gotten assigned to my staff were very well versed in tactics." Robert Sherrod, the veteran combat correspondent, observed, "Shepherd had chosen his staff carefully, and he had built up one of the best I saw in the war against Japan." Brigadier General Ed Simmons, a World War II and Korean War combat veteran who served as director of Marine Corps History and Museums for twenty-five years, remembered General Shepherd as "a brave, non-theatrical officer, who built his units around a strong staff. It is difficult to separate his persona from his staff." Shepherd was known as a "schools man" from his days as an instructor of tactics. For five and a half months in the Tassafaronga area of Guadalcanal, he instituted and supervised tough, realistic combat training. "We had a program that started with a squad and went through a platoon, company, battalion, and regiment exercises. That was when the development of tank-infantry doctrine was perfected."

Shepherd pushed the division hard, training for an entirely different type of warfare. "Previously the operations . . . had been on small islands that you overran in a day . . . just a frontal advance and that was it. There wasn't a need for tactical maneuvers. But I have always believed there should be a scheme of maneuver in every attack. You just can't frontal attack and go through. There must always be a flanking movement, to encircle or at least bring pressure against the flank of an enemy position, and we worked on this during our period of training before Okinawa." Shepherd admonished his commanders, "Don't try to out slug the Jap; out-flank him." However, he required his commanders to press the attack. "We will attack and attack vigorously, and we will continue to attack until the enemy is annihilated." Silverthorn noted that "General Shepherd was very alert to be around the training program, which was a very active one . . . very severe, long hours spent there until all the units were tired." Shepherd himself commented that "When we went into Okinawa, the 6th Marine Division was the best trained organization the Marine Corps ever had, in my opinion."

Love-day

Easter Sunday dawned bright and clear. The temperature was a comfortable 75 degrees. Seas were calm, much to the relief of the Marines with weak stomachs. A light offshore breeze kept the smoke away from the land, allowing the men in the landing craft to see the beaches. Ernie Pyle watched through binoculars. "There wasn't a dead or wounded man in our sector. . . . There wasn't a single burning vehicle. Nor a single boat lying wrecked on the reef or shoreline. Medical corpsmen were sitting among their sacks of bandages and plasma and stretchers, with nothing to do." Colonel John McQueen, Shepherd's chief of staff, remembered that there was "no resistance at the beach line. Our reconnaissance teams had been in there and verified that there were no Japs, no Japanese beach defenses that amounted to anything." Colonel Yahara watched the landing. "Since early dawn, the silhouettes of enemy troopships have darkened the coastline. Ten battleships and ten cruisers form the core of the attack force: some two

hundred lesser ships line up offshore . . . [along] a seven- to eight-kilome-
ter-long coast zone. Smoke and debris from the explosions and fires rise up
to the sky. The enemy aircraft . . . conceal themselves in the convenient
smoke screen before carrying out their bombing operations."

Roy Geiger

Buckner, pleased with III Phib Corps' exploits ashore, signaled Geiger: "I
congratulate you and your command on a splendidly executed landing and
substantial gains in enemy territory. I have full confidence that your fighting
Marines will meet every requirement of this campaign with characteristic
courage, spirit, and efficiency."

Geiger, as usual, went ashore early to observe the action. He and
Silverthorn arrived at the newly captured Yontan airfield just as two
American planes attempted to land. "All of the navy shipping in the harbor opened up, particularly the 20 and 40 millimeter guns on LSTs, and
shot down those two American planes, who attempted to fly over the fleet
and show they were American but didn't stand a chance. It's a very sorry
spectacle to see your own airplanes shot down by your own men. Now, it
affected us in that as they would sweep over toward those planes, our entire
camp was just riddled with 20 and 40 millimeter bullets. It went through
field desks; it went through tubes of paste. General Geiger and I were out
there watching it behind one tree, and one of those 40 millimeters hit the
tree we were standing behind."

The Drive North

The 6th Division swept north on both coasts, two regiments abreast. Tanks
loaded with infantry pushed forward, unimpeded but for occasional snipers
or clumsy roadblocks, which bulldozers or the tanks themselves could
knock aside. Here and there the Marines would observe what were obviously freshly planted mines, which the tanks were easily able to avoid.
Silverthorn remembered, "As we advanced on course, resistance began to
stiffen: the Japs were in there. However, someone in the division had
dubbed it the 'Striking Sixth,' because we moved pretty fast, and we didn't
have the bulk of the Japanese in front of us." On April 8, however, they
came up against the main Japanese northern defenses—two thousand

seasoned troops of the 44th Independent Mixed Brigade—on the Motobu Peninsula. They were holed up in a well-fortified maze of caves and manmade fortifications on the 1,500-foot Mount Yaetake. Shepherd maneuvered two regiments—4th and 29th—to attack the Japanese in a pincers movement. As the Marines jumped off, word swept through the ranks of President Roosevelt's death. E. B. Sledge noted, "Not the least bit interested in politics while we were fighting for our lives, we were saddened nevertheless by the loss of our president."

The two regiments fought slowly through the Japanese defenses in a slow, deadly slugging match. Colonel Victor Krulak, the division operations officer, described the die-hard defense. "They were just there—they weren't going anywhere—they were going to fight to the death." The defenses were formidable—foxholes, dugouts, camouflaged emplacements, machine gun nests, all cunningly integrated to provide interlocking fields of fire. Shepherd pushed his commanders hard. One of them did not measure up to his "attack, attack vigorously" expectations and was relieved. Five days later, Marines from the 4th Regiment burst into the Japanese commander's headquarters. Shepherd looked over the defensive positions on the mountain and said, "The Japanese positions were extraordinarily well prepared and organized. The enemy's tactical disposition and employment of his troops were more intelligently conducted than in any previous operation I have observed."

O. P. Smith was proud of Shepherd's division. "The campaign in the north should dispel the belief held by some that Marines are beach-bound and are not capable of rapid movement. Troops moved rapidly over rugged terrain, repaired roads and bridges, successfully opened new unloading points, and reached the northern tip of the island, some fifty-five miles from the original landing beaches, in fourteen days."

Roy Geiger

Geiger continued his habit of visiting the front lines every day. He also expected his staff to make personal contact with their opposite numbers at the division level. Silverthorn remembered that "Every night after dinner we had a staff conference that would run as long as it was necessary to report, in which the Gs and special staff officers, if they had something special to report about, would report to the commanding general the action of their own specific department. And in that way, the general by personal inspection and visit and then by these staff conferences was absolutely up to the minute on what was going on. . . . One night an officer reported that the Japanese were committing suicide by jumping over a cliff. Geiger growled, 'I hope it's a high cliff.' "

During the fighting on the Motobu Peninsula, General Geiger got a little too close to the action. Geiger biographer Roger Willock (*Unaccustomed to Fear*) wrote, "On at least one occasion the corps commander was forced to take cover in a ditch from low flying Corsairs whose pilots seemingly were inclined to engage anything on the ground that moved, be it friend or foe."

When the corps was ordered to the southern end of the island, Geiger found it was taking too long to travel from his headquarters to the front lines. He directed Silverthorn to find another location. "You go down and pick a forward CP for the corps and have it well forward." Silverthorn found a site in the city of Naha, which was still being "liberated." He found a building occupied by the headquarters of one of Shepherd's reserve battalions. "I told the battalion commander that I was moving the corps headquarters in there the next day, and he would have to find himself another place. He looked at me with surprise and pointed out that the Japanese front lines were exactly 1,000 meters away by map distance and that I was under small arms fire from the Japanese there."

Silverthorn was undeterred and sent a detail to put up a few tents. "There was a concrete tunnel there which would take care of any shelling, and when those tents were put up I got a telephone call which said: 'The Japs just shot the pole out of the tent that you're supposed to go into.' My jacket was hanging on that pole, and they shot both arms off the jacket!" Geiger ignored the threat and occupied the exposed position—under direct Japanese small-arms fire. He directed Silverthorn to displace the rest of the staff, including its communications van. Silverthorn dragged his feet because the loss of the vehicle would have been catastrophic. "So I manufactured excuses and I stayed up there at Futema maybe two or three days until the Japanese got driven off the heights . . . to the impatience of General Geiger. He never did understand why it took me so long to get down there."

The forward location of Geiger's CP caused something of a flap because it was several miles in advance of the two division headquarters. Silverthorn remarked lightheartedly, "No self-respecting division commander could have his quarters in rear of his corps commander—so without saying a word, General Geiger's action required the division commanders to move their headquarters well up, which they did." Geiger's advance CP marked the first time that the corps had been in a building—even though it was pretty well shot up. Silverthorn described the structure: "There were many shell holes in the tile roof of this building. There were so many that when the rains came, we erected tents inside. I was proud to be under shelter at last. We were a field outfit that had been living out in the woods, and now we had a building to ourselves."

The Abyss

A little more than a week after the landing, XXIV Corps ran into trouble. The Japanese had constructed three successive defense lines and concentrated the bulk of the 32nd Army, tens of thousands of its best troops, in the southern third of the island. They dug in, taking maximum advantage of the terrain; high ground was riddled with tunnels, caves, and weapons positions; artillery and mortars were registered to cover every square foot of ground. Silverthorn described Okinawa as "the most ideal terrain for defense that I've ever seen. It's cut up with a lot of gullies and ravines, and these in turn are terraced, forming good stable platforms for small bases of fire; and each one protecting the other." It was truly a killing ground, and the army advance stalled. Ian Gow, in his book *Okinawa, 1945: Gateway to Japan,* wrote, "The Japanese [in Okinawa's south] were in extremely well-thought-out, well-prepared positions, in terrain superbly suited for defense units. They were determined to . . . [make] American infantry and its support units pay dearly for every advance, and advances would usually be measured in yards rather than miles."

Geiger's III Phib Corps was ordered south. Silverthorn recalled, "As May approached, we had the northern half of the island secured, and we were informed by Tenth Army that we would then take a position in the lines, which we eventually did soon after the 1st of May and took a regular sector with two divisions abreast and stayed that way until the island was secured about the 21st of June." Silverthorn believed the Marines were at a disadvantage because "We had two divisions in the line and kept them in the line all the time from about the 7th of May. The army had three divisions, 27th, 77th, and the 96th. So, they could have one division out of the lines recuperating and receiving replacements, but the III Phib Corps couldn't do that . . . we had to keep our two divisions in the line. That made it more of a hardship on the Marines than the army."

Shepherd learned of the new assignment and during a visit by the army commander, took advantage of the opportunity to discuss another option. "I tried to persuade General Buckner to land the 2nd Marine Division, which was being held in army reserve, on the southeast coast of the island. In my opinion this would have forced the withdrawal of Japanese troops from Shuri to defend the beachhead established by 2nd Division, thereby weakening the strongly defended enemy line, which extended from Conical Hill on the east coast to Sugar Loaf Hill on the west coast. But Buckner did not agree with my concept on the premise that the division could not be supplied. I told General Buckner that a Marine division always carried with it a thirty-day supply of food, ammunition, etc., and once their transports were unloaded, the division could take care of itself. But like so many army officers, General Buckner did not cotton to amphibious operations and failed to see the versatility inherent in a Marine task force, which is capable of landing at any point on an enemy coastline where the beaches are suitable for landing operations and sustaining itself for a limited period of time."

Buckner was concerned that a southern landing would turn into another Anzio. He believed that with III Phib Corps' fresh troops and massed firepower the Japanese defenders could be quickly forced out of their stronghold. Buckner's refusal to consider the end run guaranteed that American infantry would assault straight into the teeth of the Japanese defenses.

Weather also played a factor in the fighting. In April, during the move south and the initial contact with the Japanese, temperatures were extremely high. Silverthorn remarked, "It was so hot and dusty that the MPs had to control the traffic with a gas mask. It was so dusty that actually the dust was six to eight inches thick on the road. During the heat, the men weren't allowed to do any bathing in local streams on account of the flukes.

They never understood passing a nice stream . . . and not being able to even wash in that stream." A month later, Silverthorn's jeep sank radiator deep in the mud on the main road.

On May 21, the rains began, a ten-day torrential downpour, creating a hell on earth for the waterlogged infantry. Sledge, like thousands of others, barely existed in the appalling conditions. "The weather was chilly and mud, mud, mud was everywhere. . . . The mud was knee deep in places, probably deeper in others if one dared venture there. For several feet around every corpse, maggots crawled about in the muck and then were washed away by the runoff of the rain. The scene was nothing but mud; shell fire, flooded craters with their silent, pathetic, rotting occupants; knocked out tanks and amtracs; and discarded equipment—utter desolation. Men struggled and fought and bled in an environment so degrading I believed we had been flung into hell's own cesspool."

While the infantry slugged it out on the ground, Japanese suicide planes, called Kamikazes, were savaging the navy. Silverthorn was saddened by the losses. "During that time the navy was suffering tremendous casualties . . . over four thousand men killed." Admiral Nimitz urged General Buckner to speed up the campaign: "I'm losing a ship and a half a day, so if this line isn't moving within five days, we'll get someone here to move it so we can all get out from under these damn air attacks." The Japanese had other plans.

Lem Shepherd

During the planning for the move south, Shepherd asked that his division go into line along the coast, on the extreme west of the corps' zone of action. He figured this position would allow him to make maximum use of naval gunfire in his attack up the coast. "Let me take the zone of action along the west coast. We'll push right on down until we out-flank Shuri Castle." Geiger agreed, but when the order arrived, it tied his division to the advance of the 1st Marine Division, negating his freedom of maneuver. Shepherd approached Geiger again. "General, I want to make my main effort along the coast so that I can get around behind Shuri Castle and get into the southern end of the island." Geiger saw the sense in the request and ordered his operations officer to change the plan.

McQueen remembered, "By the time we reached the northern end of Okinawa, we got orders that the division was to take over the right flank in the southern area of Okinawa, relieving a pretty depleted army division there." As the division trucked south, it passed convoys of army troops headed away from the fighting. Flushed with victory from their swift triumph in the north, they were contemptuous of the dispirited army troopers, particularly the 27th Division because of their poor performance under Marine control on Saipan. Private First Class W. R. Lightfoot, as quoted by James H. Hallas in his book *Killing Ground on Okinawa: The Battle for Sugar Loaf Hill*, spoke for most Marines: "We heard the army was having trouble. . . . We figured we could handle it—kick a little ass and that would be it. . . . Others expressed their contempt with oaths, calling the soldiers doggies and barking, as well as more overt action. They pelted the army convoy with rocks, C-ration cans—anything we could throw at them." In his book *Tennozan: The Battle for Okinawa and the Atomic Bomb*, George Feifer recounted army retaliation, writing, "A few soldiers pretended to film Marines, mocking their supposed hunger for glory and publicity. 'Go ahead and bark,' some shouted at the Leathernecks, 'You bastards live like dogs anyway.' " There was no love lost between the two units.

Shepherd was not among those who thought they would have a cake walk. He briefed his officers that "Southern Okinawa is different from anything this division has encountered in the operation so far." He then reminded them, "Don't try to out-slug the Jap; outflank him, keep driving—your enemy can't think as fast as you can and he is no match for a determined, aggressive Marine who has confidence in himself and his weapon." Shepherd's first test came during the capture of the Oroku Peninsula and its airfield. "The initial plan . . . was to make a river crossing of the Kokuba Estuary. . . . My staff and I decided that this was exactly what the Japanese thought we would do and had planned their defenses to resist such an attack." He proposed an amphibious landing on the northwest coast of the peninsula in an envelopment. "Geiger approved of my proposal, which was to land the 4th Marines in assault just north of the Naha Airfield, supported by two companies of tanks and followed by the 29th Marines." McQueen worked hard to make it happen. "We got busy, and during some of the time he [Silverthorn] said he was a little bit doubtful whether we would get the boats, and I said, 'General, then we'll have to swim across, because General Shepherd wants to do it this way!' "

The navy came through, and the division executed a surprise landing. McQueen commented that "The Japs were expecting an attack on the other side—the land side—and they never dreamed we were coming in back of the airfield. Initially it wasn't too bad there . . . but then the terrain became very rugged, and the Japs were very dug in, and most of them were naval troops. They were well armed and pretty well trained, and the admiral [Ota] in command there, as I remember, rather than surrender took his own life." The 22nd Regiment established a blocking position across the neck of the peninsula, while the 4th Marines pushed the Japanese into them. Shepherd recounted that "Since the defenders were unable to escape across the Kakuba Estuary, they were all either killed or taken prisoners in the final assault of our troops. . . ."

Shepherd witnessed an incident of Japanese fanaticism. "My chief of staff, Colonel Johnny McQueen, and I watched the final assault from a bluff overlooking the Kokuba Estuary near Naha. An interesting incident occurred in the last stage of the battle. Several Japanese officers committed hari-kari on the beach opposite to where we were observing the final assault. We saw one Japanese officer take off his sword, lay it on top of a rock, and blow himself up with a grenade. McQueen said to me, 'I want that sword' and left immediately to cross over the estuary by a bridge we had erected near Naha. By the time Johnny arrived at the spot where the Japanese officer had placed his sword on a rock, the sword had disappeared, apparently taken by one of the men of the attacking troops. The next day McQueen sent out a memorandum to the infantry regiments participating in the attack stating that he would give the man who found the sword $100 for it. The Marine who found the sword turned it in a few days later and received Johnny's reward of $100."

The two watched another wounded Japanese officer leaning against a seawall in the estuary. McQueen observed that "You could see the Marines there with rifles pointed at him begging him to come out and give up, but he said no, and finally I saw his body crumple and sink, falling into the water." Another incident that McQueen vividly recalled with some amusement was a visit to a POW compound. "When I went to the prisoner of war enclosure, a very snappy little Japanese—a sergeant or a corporal—got up, saluted smartly, and said in perfect English, 'Good morning, colonel, I just want to let you know that we have no trouble here.' I said, 'You speak perfect English.' He said, 'My name is Frank, and I went to the University of Chicago. I wish to hell I was back there now!'" Taken aback, McQueen asked him how he got to Okinawa. "Like a fool my relatives and friends were writing me and told me to come home, and I went home from Chicago, and here I am."

An Unprepossessing Little Hill

Captain Owen Stebbens, George Company, 22nd Marines, took a long look at his company's objective, "an oddly shaped mound of dirt rising from the flat terrain. The objective . . . was a stark hill, barren except for a few scrubby trees. . . . It looked no more ominous to us than other draws, ravines, or steep inclines faced in previous combat actions." The hill was so small that it did not even show up on a standard military map. Stebbens would not last the day—wounded and evacuated—and his company would spend itself trying to take the "unprepossessing little hill." One survivor of the battle said, "It wasn't a mountain. It wasn't even a hill. It was a piece of shit!"

Stebbens' battalion commander, Lieutenant Colonel H. C. Woodhouse, took one quick look at the hill's odd shape and said it reminded him of a sugar loaf. The name stuck—and became synonymous with the 6th Division's Okinawa sacrifice. According to Shepherd, the insignificant hill, fifty feet high and three hundred yards long, "was the western anchor of the Naha-Shuri line. . . . Sugar Loaf covered the western flank of the central defensive position at Shuri Castle." Elements of the Japanese 15th Independent Mixed Regiment and the 6th Special Regiment waited patiently for the Marine advance—secure in the knowledge that the terrain favored their defense. There was no cover on the bare approaches, tunnels and galleries allowed the safe movement of Japanese troops, and the entire area was open to fire from machine guns, mortars, and artillery.

Sugar Loaf was the apex of three strategically located pieces of high ground. Shepherd described the complex: "Sugar Loaf was supported by two hills, which we called Horseshoe and Half-Moon, and these mutually supporting positions were what caused us heavy losses. We'd get on top of the hill and then we'd get fire from Half-Moon on the one side and Horseshoe from the other, which made it almost impossible to stay on the slopes of Sugar Loaf." Colonel Yahara thought the fortifications on Hill 51.2 (Sugar Loaf) were "ideal." "Our stronghold on the escarpment was located within deep depressions which led to a network of caves and tunnels. Our soldiers jumped out of their caves as soon as the enemy tanks passed, crawled forward, and engaged in hand-to-hand combat with enemy soldiers."

Captain Stebbens' company found out the hard way that Sugar Loaf was anything but a piece of cake. They started the attack on the morning of May 12 with 215 men. By nightfall, only seventy-five Marines remained. G Company earned the nickname, "Shot-to-Shit Company." Private First Class Jack Houston remarked that "We'd been shot up so bad that the 3rd Platoon no longer existed, and our squads and fire teams were gone because the company was so short of people." The history of the 6th Marine Division described Sugar Loaf's defenses: "In many cases the original caves had been developed by networks of tunnels with exits on both forward and reverse slopes of the hills as well as the flanks. Each hill was thus a fortress . . . machine-gun positions were built into small compartments radiating from the tunnels, and rifle slits were dug into the hills themselves . . . outside, octopus-type foxholes protected the mouths of caves. If a unit had as many as five automatic weapons, at least two would be emplaced with intersecting fields of fire, while the others covered weak points in the defense or were emplaced for use against targets of opportunity."

Lem Shepherd

"The Japs had positions behind Sugar Loaf Hill where they had burrowed. They had built dugouts of concrete on the opposite side of the hill, and they would wait till we got some men up on top and then they'd swarm over from the reverse side in large numbers and overrun our Marines—a tremendous reverse slope defense." Company after company attacked the complex, only to be shot to pieces. McQueen remarked years later, "Sugar Loaf was a tough nut to crack. I personally felt that we initially didn't put enough force in there. I felt, and told General Shepherd, that I thought if we would put a battalion size in there, and take the losses, it would have been cheaper in the long run." Shepherd was just as succinct: "We fought hard for that hill and we lost a great many people." E. B. Sledge aptly described the infantryman's anxiety going into the attack: "I found it more difficult to go back each time . . . into the zone of terror. With each step toward that hellish region where fear and horror tortured us like a cat tormenting a mouse, I experienced a greater and greater dread. I felt the sickening dread of fear itself and the revulsion at the ghastly scenes of pain and suffering among comrades that a survivor must witness."

The 22nd Marines' attack on Sugar Loaf stalled. Shepherd replaced its commander "when he faltered" with a more aggressive officer. "I think Colonel [Merlin F. "Red"] Schneider had the feeling that this operation might be his last. So he became over-cautious and spent most of his time in his regimental command post established in an Okinawan tomb. I couldn't get him to go up front to see what the hell was going on. It comes to what I have just been saying, a troop commander must feel the pulse of his advance units, and to do so he must go forward, which Schneider failed to do. I gave him the devil about it two or three times. Finally, I said, 'You've got to visit your battalions. I've been up to each battalion and some of their companies. You're a regimental commander. You don't even know where they are.' " Shepherd sent Silverthorn to look over the situation. "I was sent down to interview, to find out what was wrong in Schneider's outfit. General Shepherd said, 'Go down there and find out what's wrong.' I took the division surgeon with me. I suspected what was wrong, because I knew "Red" Schneider pretty well, and he was taking to the bottle too much. I remember we arrived maybe at 9 o'clock or 9:30 one morning, and Red looked as if he was just about all in. And the division surgeon looked him over very carefully, so when we went back, we recommended to General Shepherd that someone else be put in there . . . obviously he was in no physical condition to continue."

Shepherd reassigned Lieutenant Colonel Bob Roberts from his staff to take over the regiment. He thought it "was a great lesson in psychology, true leadership, which immediately reestablished the morale of his faltering troops." Roberts told Shepherd that "They need somebody to get them out of their foxholes, get them to move forward." Roberts' regiment continued the attack, supported by a battalion of the 29th Marines and heavy supporting arms. Sortie after sortie of aircraft dropped one-hundred- and five-hundred-pound bombs, while artillery and naval gunfire pounded the hill. The infantry assault was stopped cold by heavy automatic weapons fire, artillery, and mortar fire. A Marine observation post took a direct hit, killing six and wounding three, including the battalion commander and four company commanders. The survivors pulled back braving heavy fire to evacuate the wounded. Sledge lay behind cover and "watched helplessly as the four stretcher bearers struggled across the muddy field with bullets flailing all around them. It was one of those terribly pathetic, heartrending sights that seemed to rule in combat: men struggling to save a wounded comrade, the enemy firing at them as fast as they could, and the rest of us utterly powerless to give any aid. To witness such a scene was worse than personal danger. It was absolute agony." The dead lay where they had fallen.

Attack followed attack. The 6th Marine Division suffered staggering losses. Sledge peered out from his waterlogged position on a scene of utter devastation. "It was the most ghastly corner of hell I had ever witnessed. As far as I could see, an area that previously had been a low grassy valley with a picturesque stream meandering through it was a muddy, repulsive, open sore on the land. The place was choked with the putrefaction of death, decay, and destruction. In a shallow defilade to our right . . . lay about twenty dead Marines, each on a stretcher and covered to his ankles with a poncho. . . . The whole area was pocked with shell craters and churned up explosions. Every crater was half-full of water, and many of them held a Marine corpse. The bodies lay pathetically just as they had been killed, half submerged in muck and water, rusting weapons still in hand. Swarms of big flies hovered over them. . . . Everywhere lay Japanese corpses killed in the heavy fighting. Infantry equipment of every type, U.S. and Japanese, was scattered about. . . . The mud was knee deep in several places. . . . The stench of death was overpowering."

During one of his daily visits to the front lines, Shepherd and his operations officer, Colonel Victor Krulak, discussed a new plan of attack with the 29th Regiment's commanding officer, Colonel William J. Whaling. They decided to send the entire regiment in column, with each battalion taking one of the hills. The 2nd Battalion, Lieutenant Colonel William G. Robb, drew Sugar Loaf. Silverthorn remembered the officer. "Robb said, 'I can take care of the hill. Give me my battalion and I'll take it.' And Robb took it, and he ended up with the Navy Cross."

Tanks played a key role in the final victory. Shepherd remarked that "Tanks were effectively used in the final seizure of that Sugar Loaf Hill. It wasn't until we organized the tank-infantry attack that swung around behind Horseshoe and Half-Moon and came in from the flank that we were finally able to overcome this position. . . . The tank-infantry attack came in from the east and around behind, as we went up from the other side."

The ten-day battle for Sugar Loaf Hill cost the division 2,662 men killed and wounded and an additional 1,289 nonbattle casualties since the start of the attack. Roberts bluntly stated, "It was a hell of price to pay, but we took the damn thing!"

Death of an Army Commander
Roy Geiger

Early in the morning on June 18, Geiger and his aide left the CP for the front lines. Just after lunch, he received word that General Buckner had been wounded while visiting the observation post (OP) of the 8th Marines. The OP was located on a rock shelf on the south side of Mezado ridge, within view of the Japanese positions. Geiger's aide noted in his log that "At about 1340, word was received at Corps Headquarters that General Buckner had been badly hit while at OP of 8th Marines, and later, that he was dead. Five Japanese shells struck the coral outcrop near Buckner, sending a lethal splinter into his chest. He fell into the arms of Major William Chamberlin and was carried off the hill on a poncho and taken to an aid station, where he lay dying." "A Marine private held his hand and kept repeating, 'You are going home, General; you are homeward bound." (*Seven Stars: The Okinawa Battle Diaries of Simon Bolivar Buckner, Jr., and Joseph Stilwell*, edited by Nicholas Evan Sarantakes) Geiger's aide accompanied the body to the III Amphibious Corps Hospital, while a high-level conference convened to determine his successor. Silverthorn attended. "I well remember the conference. . . . General Hodges [John R. Hodge], the commanding general of the XXIV Corps, General Geiger, and the Island Commander, Major General [Fred C.] Wallace, met down at Tenth Army headquarters to talk over who was going to be in command of the Tenth Army."

Wallace was the senior general and cited a publication, *Joint Action of the Army and Navy,* as authority to assume command. Silverthorn noted, however, "It had been entirely superseded by amphibious doctrine developed in the '30s and implemented in World War II. His reference fell on deaf ears as far as Generals Geiger and [Hodge] were concerned. Well, he persisted in it. Finally, General Geiger sort of with a note of impatience said, 'The hell with *Joint Action of the Army and Navy . . .*' Geiger was senior to [Hodge], so it was perfectly agreeable to [Hodge] that General Geiger should command the Tenth Army. So, it was really General [Hodge] and General Geiger who decided . . . and overruled him [Wallace]." Admiral Nimitz confirmed the decision with a dispatch directing Geiger to assume immediate command of Expeditionary Troops (TF-56) and Ryukyus Forces (TF-99). Geiger was immediately given a third star and became the only Marine— and the only aviator of any service—to command a field army. Four days later, he declared that organized resistance on Okinawa had ceased.

Senior army commanders were not happy with the decision. Silverthorn recalled how they scrambled to bring in a more senior officer. "Well, the Army got hold of General [Joseph W.] Stilwell, who was over in the Burma-China theater and flew him over to Okinawa." Stilwell arrived on June 23 and was invited to join Geiger and Silverthorn for lunch at III Phib Corps headquarters. Silverthorn recollected that Stillwell "was wearing his campaign hat, which he took off and threw on the floor. There weren't any places to hang it. He wanted to know if he could pull up a chair and join us, and of course, we had already invited him. The informality of that meeting was most impressive. He was a field soldier who knew that he was dealing with a field soldier in the person of General Geiger, and immediately there was a rapport that was established that was good to see. So, General Stilwell assumed command."

Lem Shepherd

On the afternoon of Buckner's death, Shepherd was on his way to the front when he received word of the army commander's demise. "He was in my territory and I wanted to be there with him . . . and I hot-footed it up there to join him." Shepherd was too late; Buckner died before he could get there. "I continued on to observe the advance of the 22nd Marines. Before

I got up there, I heard Bob Roberts had been killed. It was a terrible shock to me." Shepherd was "very close" to Roberts and had cautioned him to be careful. "Shortly after Roberts took command, the 22nd Marines resumed its forward advance in the attack on Naha and on the southern tip of Okinawa. I will always recall my last conversation with Colonel Roberts. We were down at the southern tip of Okinawa on Medazo Ridge and only had a little way to go to complete the seizure of the island in the 6th Division zone of action. I had gone forward in the late afternoon to issue orders to Roberts for the next day's attack. I said to Bob, 'If everything goes well, we should capture that last ridge of organized Jap resistance. The end is in sight. We have the Japs licked. You just push them down into this lower packet there, where they can't do anything but surrender or be killed.' I further said, 'Now, Bob, for God's sake, don't expose yourself unnecessarily. I know you always want to be up there leading your troops in the front line. You've gotten through this war safely so far. Why, you've gotten two Navy Crosses already. For God's sake use a little discretion, and don't try to lead the leading wave.' "

Roberts ignored Shepherd's warning and was in the front line when a Japanese sniper shot him. Roberts' orderly went berserk, according to Shepherd. "He was so mad he took his Tommy gun and he went right into this nest of snipers and killed half a dozen of them. Miraculously he wasn't killed himself." The young Marine was in tears. "I'd known the boy. He was always with Roberts. He said to me, 'He was the finest man I have ever known. You know, general, why he got killed? He didn't wax his moustache this morning!' The orderly continued, 'The night before, he was working late preparing the order for the attack, and the colonel didn't have a chance to wax his moustache. And that's why he was killed.' "

Okinawa proved to be a blood bath. More than 100,000 Japanese soldiers lost their lives and as many as 150,000 native Okinawans died in the fighting. The Tenth Army sustained almost 70,000 casualties, including 7,000 dead. Marine losses—ground, air, ship's detachments— amounted to 20,000, of whom 3,445 were killed in action. III Phib Corps infantry units had been decimated. Sledge survived the battle. "We each received two fresh oranges with the compliments of Admiral Nimitz. So I ate mine, smoked my pipe, and looked out over the beautiful blue sea. The sun danced on the water. After eighty-two days and nights, I couldn't believe Okinawa had finally ended."

After the battle Geiger wrote a letter to Alexander Vandegrift, his comrade from Guadalcanal who was the incumbent Commandant of the Marine Corps: "This has been a hard campaign. The officers and men have simply been marvelous. They have carried on day and night, mud and battle, without a murmur and could have continued had it been necessary. They have carried out every mission assigned by the Tenth Army and have broken through every position of the Japanese defenses which stood in their way in a minimum of time. The Marine Corps can ever be proud of the two divisions, which fought on this island. The cost has been high, but the time element was essential and I am sure you will be happy to know that the Marines required no urging to attack, attack, and again attack, until the Japs were completely annihilated."

Between the Wars
Lem Shepherd

At forty-nine, Lem Shepherd was at the top of his game. His command of the 6th Division during the bloody fighting on Okinawa proved him to be a tough, highly competent combat leader. He was slated for an additional combat command when the war ended. After accepting the surrender of Japanese forces in Tsingtao, China, Shepherd returned to the United States and was assigned as chief of staff at Headquarters Marine Corps, Washington, D.C. Two years later, he returned to Quantico as the commandant, Marine Corps Schools. In June 1950, he was promoted to lieutenant general and given command of Fleet Marine Force, Pacific, with headquarters at Pearl Harbor.

Roy Geiger

At war's end, Geiger returned to a hero's welcome. Pensacola proclaimed "Geiger Day," and honored him with a parade and banquet. The Pensacola News-Journal described the homecoming as "resembling a Wall Street ticker-tape ovation." Geiger returned to Hawaii, where he served as the commanding general, Fleet Marine Force, Pacific, a position he held until mid-November 1946. Noticeably sick, he returned to the Naval Medical Center at Bethesda for a medical examination. On January 23, 1947, Lieutenant General Roy Geiger passed away from lung cancer. He was buried at Arlington National Cemetery. The News-Journal described the ceremony: "The flag-draped casket bearing his body was pulled by a caisson pulled by white horses and followed by a single riderless horse with the general's boots reversed in the stirrups and his sword hung backwards in the saddle. As the body was laid to its final resting place . . . a squadron of Corsairs made three passes tipping their wings over the grave. A place at the head of the squadron was left open in honor of the Corps' dead hero."

By special act of Congress, June 30, 1947, Roy Stanley Geiger was posthumously elevated to the rank of full general.

Eddie Craig

In 1946, after a series of assignments in the United States, Craig was promoted to brigadier general and assumed duties as assistant division commander, 1st Marine Division, Tientsin, China. A year later, the division was withdrawn from China and a provisional brigade was activated on Guam, with Craig as its commander. He returned to Camp Pendleton upon completion of the assignment and resumed duties as assistant division commander, 1st Marine Division. In the summer of 1950, he was acting division commander.

Ray Davis

Davis returned home after Peleliu and served successively as tactical instructor, Marine Corps Schools, and chief of the Infantry Section, Marine Air-Infantry School. In 1947, Davis joined Craig on Guam, serving as his G-3 (Operations and Training) and G-4 (Logistics). Upon completion of the two-year tour, he received orders to Chicago, Illinois, as the inspector instructor, 9th Marine Corps Reserve Infantry Battalion. In the summer of 1950, the battalion completed their two weeks of training at Camp Lejeune.

Bob Barrow

Barrow remained in China for a year after the war. Upon his return, he was assigned as the aide-de-camp to the commanding general, Fleet Marine Force, Atlantic, until 1948. After completion of Amphibious Warfare School, he received orders to Camp Lejeune, North Carolina. In June 1950, he commanded Company A, 1st Battalion, 2nd Marines.

General Lemuel C. Shepherd Jr.

General Roy S. Geiger

Lieutenant General Edward A. Craig

General Raymond G. Davis

General Robert H. Barrow

Major General Raymond G. Davis, Commanding General 3rd Marine Division, 1969. At the time of his assignment, Davis had received every personal decoration for bravery (except a low level award)—Medal of Honor, Navy Cross, Legion of Merit, Silver Star, Bronze Star, and Purple Heart, plus numerous campaign awards.

Major General Raymond G. Davis talking with a captain company commander in the 9th Marines, just prior to a helicopter assault. The captain was due to rotate home within one week. (The author is standing with his back to the camera.)

Major General Lemuel C. Shepherd, Commanding General 6th Marine Division, handing a flag to Lieutenant General Roy S. Geiger. General Shepherd went on to become the Commandant of the Marine Corps.

Lieutenant General Holland M. "Howlin' Mad" Smith, General Alexander A. Vandegrift, and Lieutenant General Roy S. Geiger (left to right) in the Commandant's Officer Headquarters Marine Corps, Washington, D.C.

Lieutenant General Roy S. Geiger, just after taking command of 10th Army on Okinawa to replace Lieutenant General Buckner, killed in action. *Courtesy of Colonel Edward C. Kicklighter, USMC (ret.)*

Lieutenant General Roy S. Geiger and unknown Marines at a front line observation post, Okinawa. General Geiger was known as a fearless officer who constantly visited the front lines. *Courtesy of Colonel Edward C. Kicklighter, USMC (ret.)*

First Lieutenant Robert H. Barrow of the Sino-American Cooperative Organization (SACO), somewhere in China. *Courtesy of General Robert Barrow, USMC*

First Lieutenant Robert H. Barrow, SACO—note Chinese uniform. Barrow went on to become the Commandant of the Marine Corps. *Courtesy of General Robert Barrow, USMC*

Rear Admiral L. F. Reifsnider, USN, and Major General Roy S. Geiger aboard the USS Cincinnati, en route to Saipan and Okinawa. *Courtesy of Colonel Roy S. Geiger, USMC (ret.)*

Lieutenant General Roy S. Geiger and Major General Hal Turnage after the war. *Courtesy of Colonel Roy S. Geiger, USMC (ret.)*

Official photo, Major General Lewis B. Puller. The legendary "Chesty" Puller received five Navy Crosses for bravery in combat.

Lieutenant Roy S. Geiger, circa 1918. *Courtesy of Colonel Roy S. Geiger, USMC (ret.)*

Geiger's aircraft with his aide, Lieutenant Edward C. Kicklighter, looking out the window. *Courtesy of Colonel Edward C. Kicklighter, USMC (ret.)*

Marines embarking on the USS *Nitro* headed for Nicaragua, 1929. Note the World War I packs and .03 rifles. *Author's collection*

Marines clamber ashore from Landing Craft Vehicle Personnel (LCVP) during training at New River, North Carolina, in 1942. *Author's collection*

Marine machine gun position overlooking Naha, Okinawa, 1945.

A direct hit during American bombardment destroyed the Japanese airplane in this concrete revetment on Okinawa. Marines use it as an antitank gun position, 1945.

Marine tank crew, somewhere in the Pacific.

Marine bathing on Guadalcanal.

Recaptured American flag, Guam, 1944. Flag held by Sergeant Donald C. Bushnell (left) and Captain Louis Wilson, who later became the Commandant. *Author's collection*

Marine anti-aircraft gun crew, somewhere in the Pacific.

Marine tanks and infantry of the 6th Division enter Naha, capitol of Okinawa.

Marine command post established near the ruins of a tomb in Okinawa. The mausoleum was destroyed during pre-invasion shelling.

Marines load landing boats in preparation for leaving Okinawa.

Marines moving through heavy snow during Chosin Reservoir campaign.

Lieutenant Baldomero Lopez over the seawall in Inchon. The Lieutenant was killed minutes later and received the Medal of Honor.

Marines join their tanks and deploy to take out an enemy position in Korea.

Marines watching a napalm strike near the Chosin Reservoir, 1950.

Lieutenant General Simon Buckner, Commanding General 10th Army (left), Major General Lemuel C. Shepherd, Commanding General 6th Marine Division (center), and Brigadier General William T. Clement, Assistant Division Commander, Okinawa.

Brigadier General Edward A. Craig, Commanding General 1st Marines Brigade, saluting flag at Bean Patch, Korea.
Courtesy of Major Jack Buck, USMC (ret.)

Landing beach under heavy naval gunfire as amtracs head in, Peleliu.

Lieutenant General Geiger's command post. Admiral William F. Halsey turns his back to the camera to walk away after making a humorous remark.

Marines of the 1st Engineer Battalion in position on Peleliu.

Machine gun action against Suicide Ridge, Peleliu.

Wounded Marine being given water by a buddy while waiting for stretcher bearers, Peleliu.

Disembarking from amtrac under fire, Guam.

Marines moving to the front lines through the bombed-out, otherworldly terrain of Peleliu.

Assault against Japanese positions along a ridge on Peleliu.

Enemy sniper fire pins down Marines behind gravestones on Cemetery Ridge, Okinawa.

A Marine throws a Molotov cocktail, Suicide Ridge, Peleliu.

Major General Commandant, George Barnett, World War I. *Historical Division Archives, Quantico*

Marines search abandoned house, Korea, 1950.

Remains of an amphibious truck destroyed by a landmine on the Iwo Jima beachhead. Mt. Suribachi is visible in left background.

Pinned down on the beach of Iwo Jima, with Mt. Suribachi in background. The loose volcanic sand was difficult to move through for men and machine alike.

Marines of the 28th Regiment, 5th Division, raised the flag atop Mt. Suribachi on February 23, 1945, after over twenty-two hours of intense fighting up the slopes.

Air strike on Iwo Jima.

Captured Japanese souvenirs—Nipponese gas masks and the Japanese marine emblem—displayed by Private Frank Massaro, Guadalcanal.

Marines struggling to move their 105mm howitzer by hand, Okinawa. The man riding keeps the gun balanced, which makes it easier to move.

Gullwing Corsairs of the "Death Rattlers" fighter squadron over Okinawa.

Author with Lieutenant General Edward A. Craig, USMC (ret.), San Diego, 1985.
Author's collection

Lieutenants Craig and Sturgis on top of an armored car, 1918.

Topographic table, World War I—like Shepherd used in France.
Author's collection

First Lieutenant Harold G. Schrier's patrol taking the flag up Mt. Suribachi.

First Lieutenant Harold G. Schrier's patrol making their way up the slopes of Mt. Suribachi.

General Douglas MacArthur congratulating Brigadier General Craig for defense of the Pusan Perimeter.
Courtesy of Major Jack Buck, USMC (ret.)

Plane crash, Quantico, Virginia, 1925. Amazingly, no one was hurt.
Author's collection

Private First Class Harry Kizierian, relieved from the front lines after twelve days of fighting, Okinawa.

PART FOUR

KOREAN WAR

CHAPTER TWENTY ONE

POLICE ACTION

The predawn darkness was broken by the sharp flash and crump of exploding mortar and artillery fire. The detonations spewed jagged metal in a lethal arc of death and destruction. This deadly orchestration began in the early morning hours of Sunday, June 25, 1950 (5:00 p.m., June 24, in Washington, D.C.). Seven Russian-trained infantry divisions and an armored brigade of thirty-five-ton Russian-made T-34 medium tanks of the North Korean People's Army (NKPA) stormed across the 38th Parallel. The main attack, two divisions and most of the tank brigade, struck south, through the Uijongbu Corridor, the historic invasion route that led straight to the South Korean capitol of Seoul. (Soviet records indicate that in January 1950 Kim Il Sung visited Moscow to argue his case for invading South Korea. Immediately after the visit, Russia provided military advisers and huge amounts of weapons and supplies.)

In a coast-to-coast coordinated attack, the *In Min Gun* (North Korean army) brushed aside the ineffective resistance of the Republic of Korea (ROK) frontier force. Within three days the invaders seized Seoul, the capital, thirty-five miles south of the 38th Parallel, forcing the government to flee and turning its citizens into fugitives desperate to escape the fighting. The North Korean army was executing its operational plan, which called for advances of fifteen to twenty kilometers a day with main military operations completed within twenty-two to twenty-seven days.

In that summer of 1950, North Korea fielded an army of more than one hundred thousand men. Almost one-third were seasoned veterans who had served in the Chinese Communist Eighth Route Army in

World War II and in the civil war against Chiang Kai-Shek's Nationalists. Three of the front-line divisions were almost entirely composed of veterans. The technical branches were largely staffed by Koreans who had served in the Soviet armies or had received a military education in the Soviet Union. All political officers and lower-level cadres were Soviet-trained. The senior commanders were graduates of the Whampoa Military Academy, China's West Point, and many had held commissions in the Soviet army during World War II.

Facing them were four poorly trained ROK divisions, armed primarily with light infantry weapons. They did not have any tanks, medium artillery, or effective antitank weapons. Most of their equipment was cast-off American World War II material. Their senior leadership was not professionally qualified. Many were political appointees, with little military experience. Junior officer and NCO leadership left a great deal to be desired, although many were tough and courageous, as would be seen in the first weeks of the war. Unfortunately, bravery alone could not stand up against the well-trained, ruthless *In Min Gun*.

Call for Help

Captain Joseph Darrigo U.S. Army, of the Korean Military Aid Group (KMAG), and the only American near the onslaught, barely managed to escape the advancing North Koreans. Awakened by the massive shelling, he struggled into shirt and trousers and raced for his jeep. Small-arms fire chipped stone from the outside walls of his house. After a harrowing nighttime drive through darkened streets filled with *In Min Gun* troops, Darrigo reached the ROK 1st Division headquarters at Munsan just minutes before it was overrun. He spread the alarm up the chain of command. The U.S. Ambassador, John J. Muccio, received Darrigo's sketchy report and cabled the State Department with a priority night dispatch: "According to Korean Army reports, which are partly confirmed by [a] KMAG field adviser report, North Korean Forces invaded ROK territory at several points this morning. It would appear from the nature of the attack and the manner in which it was launched that it constitutes an all-out offensive against the ROK."

A United Press correspondent, Jack James, sniffed out the story and beat Muccio by wiring it to New York as an urgent news flash.

"Fragmentary reports indicate North Koreans launched Sunday morning attacks generally along entire border. Headquarters ROK's 1st Division fell 9:00 a.m. Tanks supposed [to have been] brought into use Chunchon fifty mile northeast Seoul." James scooped his buddies; they were still sleeping off a late-night drinking binge.

Muccio's encrypted cable arrived at the State Department's communication room at 9:26 p.m., where it was decoded. Secretary of State Dean Acheson held the communiqué up for several hours trying to verify its contents before calling President Harry Truman at his vacation home in Independence, Missouri. Truman had just finished dinner and settled down in the living room to read when the security phone rang. It was Acheson: "Mr. President, I have serious news, the North Koreans are attacking across the thirty-eighth parallel."

As the North Koreans approached the capital, harried embassy staffers threw boxes of classified papers and documents on a bonfire in the parking lot. They piled suitcases, boxes of clothing, and personal effects in the building's hallways. Muccio was eating lunch with Colonel Sterling Wright, chief of the KMAG, when two North Korean Yaks strafed the building. The two jumped into a vehicle and took off, starting a mass exodus of employees.

The ambassador, his staff, and the Marine Embassy Guard crossed the Han River Bridge, just hours before it was blown up by panic-stricken ROK engineers. Thousands of Korean troops were trapped on the outskirts of Seoul, along with all their heavy equipment and rolling stock. Hundreds more were killed when the span tumbled into the river. The engineer commander was summarily executed for cowardice.

Trygve Lie, Secretary General of the United Nations, called the Security Council into emergency session and declared North Korean aggression a breach of the peace and demanded their immediate cease-fire and withdrawal. Two days later, after hearing nothing from the North Koreans, the Security Council passed another resolution, calling upon UN members to provide economic and military assistance to embattled South Korea. The United Nations was in the fight. Fortuitously, the Russian delegation was absent when the vote was taken or certainly they would have vetoed the resolutions. Documents from the Soviet archives suggest that

Stalin supported the North Korean invasion because he didn't think the United States would get involved. U.S. Secretary of State Dean Acheson may have inadvertently given the Soviet leader that idea at a press conference in mid-January 1950 in which he described the American sphere of interest in the Pacific and did not explicitly mention Korea.

Acting quickly, President Harry S. Truman ordered American naval, air, and ground forces into action. The first contingents to arrive were hastily assembled occupation troops from Japan. They were understrength, soft from occupation duty, and short on heavy weapons and equipment. Lem Shepherd considered, "In retrospect the army had a couple of 'makee-learnee' divisions in Japan. It was during the Occupation period. The men were living in the lap of luxury in Japan. They weren't worrying about any war. A lot of them had come in after World War II, and had no combat experience—and there were very few veterans there."

The American formations were immediately thrown in to battle the North Korean advance. They were chewed up by the tougher, Soviet-trained and -equipped NKPA, who totally outfought the unprepared and ill-equipped Americans. They retreated in the face of the North Korean onslaught, trading space for time in an effort to regroup and establish a sustainable defensive perimeter. Even with the arrival of additional reinforcements, American forces were pushed farther and farther south, toward the vital seaport of Pusan. Shepherd felt there was a definite quality difference in the opposing forces. "They [U.S. forces] were not trained soldiers. All of a sudden they were thrown into battle against a strong enemy. These North Koreans were fighters and had successfully overrun South Korea. I can't blame or criticize the army too much—they just were not prepared for combat against a determined enemy."

Send in the Marines

General Clifton B. Cates, Commandant of the Marine Corps, was closely following events in Korea. He pushed for the deployment of the Fleet Marine Force but was stymied by the inaction of the Joint Chiefs of Staff (JCS). General Cates could not even discuss the issue directly with them, as the Corps was not a regular member, only sitting in when invited. Exasperated, the commandant prodded Admiral Forrest P. Sherman, Chief of Naval Operations, into sending a "back channel" message to General Douglas MacArthur, Commander in Chief, Far East (CINCFE), and supreme commander of UN forces in Korea, asking if he wanted the use of a Marine brigade with supporting air. "Forrest, it looks like the Army's 24th Division is in a pretty bad spot over there. We can furnish a brigade by draining our two divisions. Why doesn't MacArthur ask for Marines?" Sherman asked. "How soon could you have them ready?" "We can have them ready as quickly as the navy gets the ships," Cates replied. "Leave it to me," Sherman assured him. "I'll send a 'blue flag' [a private message between senior navy commanders] to Joy [Vice Admiral C. Turner Joy] and tell him that he can inform MacArthur that the Marines can send a brigade and an air group."

General MacArthur, with his back to the wall in Korea, fired off a message to the JCS: "Request immediate dispatch of a Marine Regimental Combat Team and supporting Air Group for duty this command—MacArthur." In the meantime, General Cates sent the 1st Marine Division at Camp Pendleton, California, a "be prepared to deploy" warning order. He continued the pressure on the joint chiefs by showing up uninvited when they met to discuss and finally approve MacArthur's request. Cates dairy entry for July 3 noted: "Orders for employment of FMF approved."

Lem Shepherd

Lem Shepherd was worn out. Except for a few days here and there, he had not had an extended period of leave since returning from the Pacific in 1946. He was determined to take some time off before reporting to his new command as Commanding General Fleet Marine Forces, Pacific (FMF-PAC) located at Pearl Harbor. He planned a leisurely automobile trip cross-country with his wife, visiting friends and indulging in one of his favorite pastimes, fly-fishing. The chief of fisheries in Washington had authorized him to fish in Yellowstone Park's Lake Pearl, which was closed to the general public.

On June 25, the Shepherds reached Colorado Springs, where they spent the night. At breakfast the next morning, Lem picked up a local paper and learned of the North Korean attack. "Well, that's MacArthur's bailiwick; I won't worry about that one," he remarked to his wife. "The war was in Korea and we didn't have any Marines there, so I continued my trip on up to Yellowstone with my family."

Shepherd was wrong, however. Twenty Marines of the Seoul Embassy Guard were scrambling to evacuate the ambassador and his staff. In his book *The New Breed: The Story of the U.S. Marines in Korea,* Andrew Geer described the embassy guard standing on the dock at Pusan when their buddies in the 1st Marine Brigade arrived. "What'n hell took you so long? This is the end of the line for us."

By the time Shepherd reached the park, the war was heating up, so he sent a telegram to his boss, Admiral Arthur W. Radford, Commander in Chief, Pacific Fleet (CinCPacFlt): "I am proceeding according to my itinerary, but if you wish me to cut short my leave, I will do so. If you need me, I will come by air rather than sea."

Early the next morning, Shepherd checked the local telegraph office. Finding nothing, he and his aide rented a boat and started on the long-awaited fishing excursion. "Well, we'd just gotten about 100 yards off-shore when a little girl came down to the beach waving a telegram. It was from Admiral Radford, 'Prefer that you come by air rather than by transport and take the rest of your leave some other time.' " Shepherd canceled the remainder of his leave, packed his bags, and left for Salt Lake City, the nearest airport. A Marine plane took him and his aide to San Francisco, where he caught another plane for Honolulu.

"When I got off the plane the next morning at eight o'clock, I was handed a dispatch by the [Fleet Marine Force Pacific] chief of staff [Colonel Gregon Williams], which had just been received directing me to send the 1st Marine Brigade to Korea." Colonel Williams was a hard-bitten, no-nonsense Marine, who pushed the small FMFPAC staff to complete the mounting out orders. Shepherd remembered: "It took an awful amount of work to get that order out, as the staff was not organized in those days. We had no plan for the emergency confronting us and only a small staff with whom I had never worked."

Eddie Craig

General Cates' warning order reached Camp Pendleton, California, home of the 1st Marine Division, and was delivered to the assistant division commander, Brigadier General Edward A. "Eddie" Craig, in the early morning hours of July 3. "My wife and I had spent a very pleasant weekend at Pine Valley (in the eastern San Diego County mountains) and were returning to Camp Pendleton when we heard on our car radio the news that the North Koreans had invaded South Korea. I remarked to my wife, 'Well this is it again and it looks like another war for the Marines.' " Shortly afterward, he received a phone call from the assistant commandant, Major General Oliver P. Smith, ordering him to take command of the 1st Provisional Marine Brigade and "have it ready to move out at the earliest possible date." Shepherd's ciphered activation order reached the division communication section four days later. "Take whatever is required and available in troops and equipment from the 1st Marine Division and 1st Marine Aircraft Wing, plus what Marine Corps Headquarters provides from other sources, make a provisional brigade consisting of the 5th Marine Regiment Reinforced and Marine Aircraft Group 33, both at reduced strength, embark them in ships the navy will provide, and set sail for the Far East."

Craig had his work cut out for him. The division was seriously undermanned because of cuts imposed upon the Corps by Secretary of Defense Johnson after World War II. Lem Shepherd noted that "Louis Johnson hadn't helped us along, and the Marine Corps was just about to go out of existence. We had only about sixty thousand to seventy thousand Marines at the time. To form the brigade took a great deal of effort just to get out the initial orders." Craig was able to field one understrength infantry regiment, the 5th Marines, commanded by Lieutenant Colonel Raymond L. Murray. "To bring the brigade up to strength I had to strip the division, and being in command of the base and the division at the time [Major General Graves B. Erskine, the division commander was on a classified assignment to Vietnam, leaving Craig in command], I had the choice of taking anybody I wanted," Craig said. "Naturally, I took the best I could find."

Even with these efforts, the brigade had serious shortages of personnel. "We were on a peacetime strength basis, and the 5th Marines consisted of three infantry battalions with only two rifle companies; and those two companies had only two platoons each." A third platoon was added to each company just prior to shipping out. However, the brigade did not get a third company for each battalion until the Inchon landing. The artillery battalion had four 105mm howitzers per battery rather than the normal six. "I immediately, of course, made requests that the 3rd company be put into each battalion and that the 3rd platoon be furnished. I also requested additional guns for the artillery battalion." Craig felt that with two-company infantry battalions commanders were at a tactical disadvantage in every engagement. Without a third maneuver element they lacked flexibility in the attack. When defending, they had to scrape up whatever they could to have a reserve. This situation became critical during the first battle of the Naktong.

A few miles up the road at Marine Corps Air Station, El Toro, the 1st Marine Aircraft Wing was doing the same thing. Brigadier General Thomas J. Cushman formed Marine Aircraft Group (MAG) 33, consisting of four squadrons: Marine Fighter Squadron (VMF) 214, VMF-323, VMF (Night-fighter)-513, and VMO-6, an observation squadron, which included four HO3S1 helicopters and four OH light observation aircraft. A naval aviator for more than thirty years, Cushman, like Craig, served in the "Banana Wars" and saw action as a wing commander during World War II. Designated as deputy brigade commander, Cushman brought a wealth of aviation experience, which complemented Craig's ground expertise. Together, they formed an extremely effective air-ground command team.

The Marine Corps Supply Center at Barstow, California, was ordered to equip the brigade with rolling stock—tanks, trucks, jeeps, and amphibian vehicles. At the end of World War II, the Marine Corps established a stockpile of war reserves. Code-named "Operation Roll-Up," everything that could be shipped back from the Pacific was repaired and squirreled away in this desert center, including "abandoned" army equipment that could be rehabilitated. Nobody looked closely at unit designations, and after a new paint job and serial numbers, the equipment certainly looked Marine! The center went into high gear. Reconditioned rolling stock jammed the highways between the two bases. According to Andrew Geer, "There were more veterans of Iwo [Jima] and Okinawa among the vehicles than there was [sic] among the men who would drive them."

To make up some of this personnel shortfall, Marines from all over the United States were ordered to "get to Camp Pendleton NOW." By train, plane, and bus, dozens of former recruiters and guard company troops poured into the base. Captain "Ike" Fenton remembered, "These men were shipped from the posts and stations by air, most of them arriving with just a handbag. Their seabags were to be forwarded at a later date. They didn't have dog tags and had no health records to tell us how many shots they needed. Their clothing consisted of khaki only, although a few had greens. They had no weapons and their 782 gear [web equipment] was incomplete. We had a problem of trying to organize these men into a platoon and getting them squared away before our departure date." Fortunately, most were veterans and needed only a short "snapping in" period to bring them up to speed, much of which was done on the transports at sea.

Among the newcomers was the brigade chief of staff, Colonel Edward W. Snedeker, who was returning to the States from overseas when the war broke out. "Upon arrival in San Francisco with my family, on the 5th of July, I had orders waiting to report immediately to Camp Pendleton. I called General Craig, who gave me enough time to get the car off the ship and to drive down to the base." Snedeker hurriedly loaded a surprised wife and kids into the car and sped off, arriving early on the 7th. He immediately immersed himself in work, leaving his wife to settle the family. Seven utterly hectic days later, he sailed with the brigade, 6,534 Marines, of whom 90 percent of the officers and 65 percent of the staff non-commissioned officers (SNCOs) were combat veterans. However, only 10 percent of the junior enlisted men had seen action. Craig recalled that "All the units of the division were so far understrength, so inadequate for their mission as a division unit that they hardly could fill the duties of a brigade unit; however, such personnel, as we had, were well trained and were in high spirits."

The brigade's final destination remained something of a mystery. Craig was told that it would probably not go directly into combat, but rather stage in Japan and wait for the rest of the division before being committed to Korea. However, Craig believed otherwise: "It was my opinion that being a Marine unit we should be prepared for any eventuality. The chips were down; the Marine Corps was on the spot; it was up to us to put up or shut up. It was a real test of the Marine Corps."

Craig made sure that most of the ships were combat-loaded, just in case they had to make an assault landing in Korea. He was well aware of the 1st Marine Division's fiasco on the New Zealand docks before Guadalcanal. The ships had not been combat-loaded in the United States and had to reconfigured prior to sailing. Contemporary World War II accounts tell of docks awash in soggy pasteboard, mounds of unmarked boxes and containers, and harassed working parties.

As Craig's staff struggled to complete the brigade's movement orders, the navy was trying to find enough amphibious shipping. At the end of World War II, most of the amphibious ships had been sold off, mothballed, or broken up for scrap. A nation that leapfrogged across the Pacific—island by island—from thousands of ships was forced to lease those same vessels from its former enemy. For the Inchon landing, American-built LSTs were chartered from and manned by Japanese merchantmen. Because of this shortage, Craig was forced to leave behind much of the brigade's rolling stock, some one hundred and fifty to two hundred vehicles, and had to depend on the army's largesse for transport. "It was necessary for me on arrival there [Korea] to go to the army and get an extra truck company. The army was very good about this, and they not only furnished the trucks, but many jeeps for our reconnaissance company. They were completely equipped, even with .50-caliber machine guns."

Lem Shepherd

A few days after Shepherd arrived in Hawaii, Admiral Radford suggested that he fly to Japan for a conference with General MacArthur. "I think you had better go out to Korea and see General MacArthur and find out what all this thing's about. We're getting a lot of dispatches here which are rather confused. I want somebody to tell me what the situation is out there." Shepherd knew MacArthur from World War II. He had been the assistant division commander in the 1st Marine Division under MacArthur in the Cape Gloucester campaign. In addition, MacArthur's chief of staff, Major General Edward M. "Ned" Almond, and several others in the Far East Headquarters were fellow "ring-knockers" from VMI. "I did have a number of army friends in the Far Eastern Headquarters. During my two years' experience overseas with the army in World War I, I met a lot of Army people, and I didn't have the antagonism towards them that a lot of Marines did." Shepherd respected the army general. "[MacArthur] had a keen mind . . .

[was] a great leader . . . a fearless, courageous man. I believed, as all of us did during World War II, that MacArthur was a political general—everybody was calling him 'Dugout Doug.' I don't want to hear that about General MacArthur again—I'm telling you, he had the guts!"

MacArthur, always the gracious host, welcomed Shepherd as an old comrade-in-arms. "We had a lengthy conversation in his office. You know, he always wanted to talk. My God, talk, talk, talk, forty minutes, telling me all his experiences. We talked about Korea, we talked about this and that, and as we got up to go, he very courteously—he was always very courteous—he got up and went to the door of his office." A large map of Korea hung next to the door. MacArthur put his hand on Shepherd's shoulder and pointed, with his everpresent pipe stem, to a spot on the map adjacent to Seoul on the west coast of the peninsula. "Lem, if I had that 1st Marine Division as I had at Cape Gloucester, I'd land here at Inchon and cut the North Korean lines of communication." Shepherd was not taken aback, he had been thinking about the commitment of Marines a great deal. "[If] We have only a Marine brigade in Korea, its identity will be lost among all those army divisions. On the other hand, if we could get a Marine division ordered to Korea, it would be a unit of sufficient size to take care of itself independently. With a major general in command, he would not permit his division to be pushed around."

Shepherd had made up his mind to push for the commitment of the 1st Marine Division if the opportunity presented itself—and here was the opening he needed. "General, why don't you ask for them? They're under my command, as part of FMFPAC, but I can't order them from the West Coast to the Far East without the Joint Chiefs of Staff approval." Shepherd had received a report from an aide that President Truman was going to call up the reserves. "It was on this promise that I based my decision, because I knew that we had expended everybody on the West Coast to get the brigade going, but with the reserves being called up, we would be able to mount out a full division."

MacArthur, not batting an eye, said, "That's the kind of talk I like to hear," and immediately asked Shepherd to write the message for him. "Sit down at my desk and write a dispatch to the Joint Chiefs of Staff, requesting that the 1st Marine Division be sent out to my theatre of command."

Shepherd took one look at MacArthur's huge desk, four times the size of his own, and knowing that MacArthur would scrutinize every word, he was terribly disconcerted. After all, the Far East commander had five stars and Shepherd was a junior three star. MacArthur had an aura, a presence that was almost larger than life. "It really shook me, so I said, 'Well, General, I will go out to the office of your chief of staff [Major General Almond] to draft this message and bring it in to you for approval." Shepherd scrounged a message pad and jotted down his thoughts. It took him three drafts before he got the delicately worded message in a form that he thought was suitable. "I finally came up with a draft that I believed suitable. It was a delicate dispatch to compose. Here I was, recommending that a Marine division be sent to Korea, and the Commandant [of the Marine Corps, General Cates] didn't know anything about what I was doing. It was a hell of a spot to be in, but the ball had been dropped in my hands and I felt I must run with it." MacArthur approved the request without change, but the joint chiefs turned it down— and three more—before finally approving the fifth message.

Shepherd's next task was to convince the commandant, General Cates, that it was the right thing to do. Cates had recently committed the 2nd Marine Division to a NATO mission, which did not leave enough men to form the 1st Division. They met in San Diego to wish the brigade good luck as it shipped out. Cates was somewhat put out with Shepherd for committing his Marines without consulting him. Fortunately, the two officers were friends of long standing, or it could have turned out badly. Shepherd pleaded his case: "Clifton, you can't let me down. I have recommended the commitment of a Marine division to MacArthur for Korea. Please back me up." Cates responded, "We haven't got the men, we haven't got the men." But Shepherd won the day with, "Clifton, we're fighting a hot war over there in Korea. NATO is something they're just forming on paper. We belong in the Pacific. The Western Pacific is our theatre." Cates finally gave the commitment his full backing. Victor Krulak, Shepherd's G-3, described the meeting: "I remember there was a pretty spirited dialogue at Camp Pendleton between General Cates and General Shepherd . . . about what we could or couldn't do. Neither General Shepherd nor I was very popular at that time because we had obviously overextended. We did exactly the right thing. We marched to the sound of the guns. . . ."

Eddie Craig

The brigade had just seven days to get organized. No one slept during that final hectic week, working around the clock under the watchful eye of the brigade commander. Craig recounted, "During this time I was busy with a thousand details of the organization and move." Craig was everywhere, encouraging, cajoling, and sometimes just plain "kicking ass," when and where it was needed, in his own quiet but forceful manner. "Before the Brigade left for Korea, we worked from 7:00 a.m. u[ntil] 2:00 or 3:00 in the morning every day." One day, 1st Sergeant John Farritor was working in the [artillery] storeroom at 2:00 a.m. and General Craig walked in. "I was a little surprised. He said he just wanted to know how things were going. He was a hands-on general." Having shipped out more times than he could count—Haiti, Nicaragua, China, Guadalcanal, Bougainville, Guam, Iwo Jima—Craig knew what had to be done, and how to do it. Craig, however, was not a micro-manager. He provided guidance to his staff and commanders and then stood back to let them carry it out. "I learned early in my career to rely on my non-commissioned officers, and they never let me down. When I became commander of a unit and had staff officers, I gave them full rein and trusted them, and they, too, never fell down on me. I believe that what success I had in the Marine Corps was the result of the work of those officers and men."

As the deadline for embarkation approached, the pressure became even more intense, but Craig's steady hand brought a sense of organized urgency out of mad confusion. As usual, most of the grunt work fell on the shoulders of the small unit leaders—the junior officers, staff, and non-commissioned officers—who had to organize hundreds of newcomers into fire teams, squads, platoons, companies, and battalions. Conflicting priorities—working parties, administrative processing, weapons and equipment issue, inspections, and a hundred and one other details—were enough to make a grown man cry. In fact, one detail brought even the strongest to their knees; according to Lieutenant Jack Buck, "Inoculations had to be given. In my case, I recall receiving seven shots at the same time. It was still the era of 'heavy needles.' After a number of penetrations of muscular biceps, it came close to feeling like a heavy punch." Yet somehow, the brigade shaped up, as the old salts knew it would. However, it was still a great sense of relief that embarkation day had finally arrived. The brigade surgeon, Captain "Doc" Herring, USN, "Went on board USS *Clymer* to count noses. Drunk or sober, they're all here and that's phenomenal."

Craig told them where they were going just before embarking. David Douglas Duncan, the famed war photographer, was there to record their reaction. "The men were dead-panned, for they already had seen pictures and read reports of soldiers who had been caught wounded by the Communists on the field of battle. Craig reminded them of the Marines' historic role in meeting their country's emergencies. They were still expressionless. Then Craig, with his brigade surgeon standing at his side, told his men that 'As long as there were any Marines alive in Korea who could still fire a rifle, or toss a grenade, no other Marine would be left behind upon the battlefield, either wounded or dead.' Over four thousand men shouted in unison as his Leathernecks gleefully slugged each other in the ribs, grinned happily, and wanted to know when the hell they were going aboard ship."

The docks were crowded with family and friends, as well as the curious and a host of well-wishers. A large contingent of press was also on hand to record the occasion for posterity. "There is nothing like the atmosphere of a Marine unit sailing to war. It is ribald, loud, and raucous. Even the families on the dock, for the most part, hide their fears and grief and respond to the carnival spirit." The division band livened things up with John Philip Sousa marches. The bandsmen, caught up in the spirit of the occasion, played their collective hearts out, knowing that their turn would come soon enough. Suddenly they sounded "ruffles and flourishes," the general officer's call, and General Cates came forward to address the formation. "I didn't come here to wave the flag. I came to say good-bye. You boys clean this up in a couple of months, or I'll be over to see you." With the formalities over, the formation broke up and the men filed aboard ship. "The band struck up the 'Marines' Hymn'; lines were slipped, and as the ships slid away, there was a great, gusty roar that drowned out the band."

As the ships of Task Group 53.7 sailed past the breakwater of San Diego harbor, Generals Craig and Cushman, together with a small staff, flew to Pearl Harbor to confer with Lem Shepherd. The two old friends took a few minutes to reminisce and then got down to the serious business of war planning. The brigade needed more men, motor transport, and artillery. Craig stated his case forcefully, and Shepherd promised to work on it. The meeting took on a more somber tone when Craig asked for an eight-hundred-man draft to replace losses. Both officers were well aware of the cost of war, but Craig was particularly affected by casualties. Shepherd knew of his friend's kindly, avuncular attitude toward his men. "I've known Eddie Craig for over thirty years. If he has a weakness, it's the inner torment he suffers when his unit takes casualties." The meeting broke up with Shepherd promising to do all that he could.

The entourage continued on to Japan to confer with senior army and navy commanders. Craig was given an "audience" with General MacArthur, which lasted forty-five minutes. MacArthur, as was his custom, graciously welcomed the Marine brigade commander, and immediately took him into his confidence by outlining the plan for the Inchon landing. He told Craig that he wanted Marines and remarked about his supposed dislike for Leathernecks. In fact, he said, "I have a high respect for them and would like Marines in my command at any time." He went on to say that he had specifically requested Marines because he needed them for the amphibious landing at Inchon. "[The Marines are] going to turn the tide of the war."

In a personal interview with the author thirty years later, Craig enthusiastically recalled the meeting, becoming quite animated in describing MacArthur's "I like Marines" proclamation. On a trip through Tokyo, Commandant Cates asked MacArthur, "why he was so down on Marines." MacArthur replied, "I'm not down on the Marines. The Marines are the best outfit I had in World War II. When I want anything done, I know I can get it done by the Marines."

Craig briefed MacArthur on the peculiarities of the brigade, specifically the close bond between Marine air and infantry. "I told General MacArthur that this brigade, if used as a unit with its air force and with its ground units intact, was a potent unit with great capabilities. He [MacArthur] agreed that any time the Marine brigade was committed that our Marine air force would support us. These instructions were always carried out, and we were never without our Marine air support, which paid dividends in the end by keeping the brigade intact." (The issue of Marine air became a subject of great dispute in Vietnam when the air force pushed for a "single air management" concept—in effect splitting Marine ground from its air.) As the meeting ended, Craig was told to proceed to the Kobe area to find billeting. The brigade was not going to be committed unless the military situation deteriorated further. "I left the office feeling that General MacArthur was behind us in every way. I also had the feeling that I had talked to a great man and a real general. I have always had the highest respect and liking for General MacArthur."

Backs to the Wall

A day later, the orders were abruptly changed. The brigade was to be immediately committed to the defense of the Pusan Perimeter. The situation in Korea had dramatically worsened. The NKPA had broken through the U.S. and South Korea lines, forcing them to retreat toward the vital seaport of Pusan, the last foothold in Korea. Three badly shot-up U.S. and four ROK divisions dug in, forming a ragged, horseshoe-shaped defense line 120 miles long and 60 miles wide, for a last stand. Arrayed against them were eleven well-trained and well-armed NKPA divisions. If the allied force failed to hold, Pusan would fall and, with it, all of Korea.

The Pusan Perimeter was a defensive line in name only. Its American and South Korean defenders were stretched to the breaking point, unable to man the entire line. There were large gaps between units that were exploited by the NKPA to infiltrate small units into the rear areas, sowing confusion and fear. Larger NKPA formations massed to attack, threatening a breakthrough, and there were precious few reserves to stop them. The Marines represented a potent strike force, which was desperately needed to help plug holes and shore up the perimeter.

CHAPTER TWENTY TWO

FIRE BRIGADE

I am heartened that the Marine Brigade will move against the Naktong Salient tomorrow. . . . These Marines have the swagger, confidence, and hardness that must have been in Stonewall Jackson's Army of the Shenandoah. They remind me of the Coldstreams at Dunkirk. Upon this thin line of reasoning, I cling to the hope of victory.

—Unidentified British liaison officer as quoted by Robert Heinl in *Soldiers of the Sea*

Eddie Craig

Craig rushed to Taegu, headquarters of Lieutenant General Walton H. Walker, the Eighth Army's tough blunt commander, for orders. Walker "was very cordial but told me that he did not know exactly where the Marines would be used at that time; that the situation was changing so rapidly that they might be used anywhere on the perimeter; but that probably I would be used on the left flank." Walker's Eighth Army was having a tough time of it. The men were exhausted and demoralized, units were scattered and riddled with casualties, and panic was not too far below the surface. The NKPA seemed invincible. Craig's potent fighting force was desperately needed to stop the North Korean advance. Craig, realizing that his men would be immediately thrown into the fight, sent a message to the brigade, still at sea: "Be prepared to fight!"

There was great concern among the embarked Marine leadership that the brigade might not be able to fight at all. Snedeker, the senior officer afloat, saw one disaster after another strike the small fleet. "One of the transports (USS *Henrico*, APA-45) developed a vibration in its drive shaft and propeller and had to leave the formation and go to San Francisco to get repair work done." A third of the brigade's infantry was aboard, and no one knew how long repairs would take. The Henrico would not rejoin the convoy until the day before the landing at Pusan. The USS *Fort Marion* (LSD-22) accidentally flooded its well deck, immersing all the brigade's M26 tanks in six feet of water. Snedeker recounted that "These were our new type tanks, which had just been received only through a great deal of effort." Their loss was critical. The M26 with its 90mm gun was essential to defeat the NKPA's Russian T-34 tanks, whose 78mm guns were terrorizing ROK and U.S. forces. Crewmembers turned to and were able to fix the tanks, much to Snedeker's relief.

The *Henrico* limped into Oakland Naval Supply Depot, where workmen immediately began repairs. The ship attempted to sail twice but had to turn back each time. Meanwhile, hundreds of embarked Marines could only stare longingly at the beckoning lights of the Bay City, much to the chagrin of the cloistered liberty hounds. They were forbidden to leave the ship because of security concerns. Finally, the third time was the charm, and *Henrico*, now sarcastically nicknamed "Happy Hank," steamed under the Golden Gate Bridge in time to rejoin the convoy on the morning of its arrival at Pusan.

Late in the afternoon of August 2, USS *George Clymer* (APA-27), nicknamed "Greasy George" by the embarked Marines, edged onto the pier. The brigade commander stood impatiently on the dock, looking in vain for signs that his men were ready to fight. Hundreds of rubbernecking Marines lined the rails, as if they didn't have a care in the world. A South Korean band serenaded them with a tinny and slightly off-key rendition of the "Marines' Hymn." Craig spotted his chief of staff. "What battalion is the advance guard?" he shouted. Sensing the look of surprise on Snedeker's face, he asked again, "Did you receive my orders?" They had not; something had gone amiss. "Through some snafu in the Eighth Army channels, my dispatch was never received by the convoy. Consequently, when the brigade arrived, it had no intimation that it would be landed immediately."

While the ships unloaded, Craig conducted a conference to bring his key officers up to speed on the tactical situation. The intelligence officer (G-2), Lieutenant Colonel Ellsworth G. Van Orman, led off the briefing with a grim narrative of the situation, followed by Lieutenant Colonel Joseph L. Stewart, the operations officer (G-3), who sketched in the operations plan. Finally, Craig summed up the meeting: "The situation is serious. We're going into battle against a vicious, well-trained enemy. The Pusan Perimeter is like a weakened dike, and we will be used to plug holes in it as they open. We're a brigade, a fire brigade!"

At 11:00 p.m. that evening, Craig received orders from Walker attaching the brigade to the 25th Infantry Division, commanded by Major General William B. Keane. Craig met the two at their headquarters near Masan. "General Walker told me that he was going to carry out an offensive from Chindong-ni against the Communists. Up to that time the American troops had been retreating or holding the line and had not carried out an offensive. General Walker wrapped up the briefing by stating, "No one is to fall back again to the rear. We are going to stop the enemy where he is and, if necessary, we will fight to the death." It was a rather chilling send-off for commanders who were about to launch the first ground offensive of the war. Craig noted, rather tongue in cheek, "General Walker made these points rather strongly." In fact, Walker's "no retreat" message was akin to Craig's orders to the brigade prior to leaving the States: "You will never receive an order to retreat from me."

Hurrying from the conference, Craig climbed aboard a Sikorsky HO3S-1 three-seat helicopter for a quick flight to brief Lieutenant Colonel Murray on the operation. The pilot, Lieutenant Gus Ludddeke, radioed 5th Marines that Warrior Six—Craig's radio call sign—was inbound. This simple flight represented a tactical innovation—a revolution in the manner in which commanders controlled widely dispersed units—foreshadowing the development of heliborne tactics in the 1960s.

The Pusan docks were a bedlam of noise and organized confusion, as the supplies and equipment for thousands of men were taken from the holds of ships and organized into supply points and vehicle parks. Working parties struggled to unload pallets and break open crates for long lines of Marines forming to draw ammunition, hand grenades, C-rations, and medical supplies. The men worked through the night, and by 6:30 a.m. the first elements were on the move.

As the troops clambered aboard the trucks, rumors were rife. Lieutenant Robert D. Bohn recalled: "The thing I remember most about arriving in Korea is being briefed by some army people who, in retrospect, had obviously never been out of Pusan. These fat lieutenants told us all those horror stories. Although they didn't know what the hell they were talking about, they were very successful in scaring us. We all began to think the North Koreans were about ten feet tall."

The brigade arrived in Changwon late in the afternoon and immediately started digging in on the high ground along the road, preparing for its first night in combat. With the gathering darkness, a phantom army invaded the perimeter and was taken under fire by the inexperienced troops. A single shot was followed by a deadly barrage of automatic weapons fire, as apprehensive Marines blasted bushes and shrubs that, in their minds, had mysteriously turned into North Korean infiltrators. Sometime before dawn, order was restored by veteran NCOs. Craig reinforced the message, making it known, in no uncertain terms, that he would not tolerate a repeat performance. In a personal interview with the author, John A. "Jack" Buck, Craig's aide and longtime friend, related that General Craig came out of his tent that night and ordered Buck to stop the firing. Jack walked to a small hill and had a jeep turn its lights on him. He shouted out for the troops to "knock it off." Fortunately, they did, without ventilating him in the process. "That was the only time it ever took place in the brigade!"

The scheme of maneuver for the attack called for the 5th Regimental Combat team (RCT) to pass through the 27th Infantry and clear the Tosan Road junction west of Chindong-ni. The Marine brigade would then jump off from the junction and attack along the road to Sachon, while the 5th RCT continued to advance along the northern fork to Chinju. The attack was scheduled to commence on August 7, the eighth anniversary of the Marine landing on Guadalcanal.

Crisis at the Crossroads

At first light, after a short air-artillery preparation, the 5th RCT jumped off in the attack only to be stopped dead in their tracks by heavy NKPA automatic weapons and mortar fire from Hill 342, overlooking the road junction. With casualties mounting and the attack stalled, Major General Kean ordered Craig to assume command of all army as well as Marine forces in the Chindong-ni area—making him, in essence, a division commander. Craig went forward on a personal reconnaissance of the road junction. He found it jammed with vehicles and equipment, creating an irresistible target for the NKPA gunners. "Colonel Joe Stewart, my G-3, and I took off at a run and gained cover behind a low stone wall running out from the village but found that we were in the middle of an odorous pile of Korean fertilizer."

David Douglas Duncan, the famed photographer for *Time* and *Life* magazines and a former World War II Marine, happened to spot Craig as he observed the action: "A helicopter came churning over the valley from our rear, then landed out in the nearly dry riverbed below. We both spotted the snow-white head of Marine Brigadier General Edward Craig as he stepped from the plane. With his men scheduled to attack, Craig had moved up, taking personal command of the assault. Watching a slow smile start across his lean, deeply tanned face, while a pair of cool blue eyes swept the nearby hills where his Marines were deepening their foxholes, I knew that this veteran of Iwo Jima and Bougainville could take anything Korea could hand out."

Lieutenant Colonel Harold S. Roise's 2nd Battalion, 5th Marines, was ordered forward to seize Hill 342 and relieve an army battalion and a Marine platoon that was desperately clinging to the crest under heavy pressure. The battalion ran into the same stubborn resistance that stopped the initial advance and was forced to dig in for the night. Lieutenant Colonel Ray Murray was a little slow in reacting. "At one time in the advance we came to a stream with a bridge across it, and one of the tanks broke through and got mired down. I had stopped there and was trying to figure out how to get the tank back on the road. General Craig informed me in no uncertain words that others could figure it out and it was my job to get on down the road. He had a way of telling you to do things that wasn't nasty but you knew you had to get them done. I admired him very much."

Company D had a particularly tough time, losing eight killed and twenty-eight wounded, including the company commander and three lieutenants. Master Sergeant Harold Reeves, the company gunnery sergeant, was awarded the Silver Star for taking command of the leaderless men and holding the position until relieved the next day. Private First Class Doug Koch remembered Reeves had "somewhere over twenty-nine years in the Corps. When he chewed you out, he had the blackest eyes. You could see the sparks flying from them when he really got worked up."

The unexpectedly heavy enemy resistance forced Craig to concentrate his forces against the crossroads, employing the brigade and elements of the 5th RCT and the 27th Infantry. After fifty-four hours of intense infantry action, including hand-to-hand combat, the enemy started withdrawing southwest toward Kosong. They suffered an estimated six hundred casualties. Captured documents revealed that U.S. forces had been opposed by elements of the 13th and 15th regiments of the NKPA's 6th Division. The division was formed by Korean veterans of the Chinese People's Liberation Army (PLA). Early in the war, it was awarded the title of "Guard" because of its fighting spirit.

Two days later, August 11, a Marine artillery barrage flushed a North Korean motorized regiment out of cover, sending it on a frantic dash for safety. As the surviving vehicles fled out of range, carrier-based F4U Corsairs of VMF-323 bombed and strafed the remnants. The "Kosong Turkey Shoot," as it was known, left more than one hundred destroyed or abandoned jeeps, motorcycles, and trucks of the NKPA 83rd Motorcycle Regiment, virtually eliminating it as an effective fighting force. Craig, long a devoted fan of motorcycles, tried to figure out how he could "rescue" one of the undamaged vehicles.

At the height of the action, Master Sergeant Herbert Valentine, flying an OY observation plane, spotted a speeding NKPA jeep with what appeared to be a high-ranking officer in the rear seat. With the Corsairs busy shooting up the convoy, he and his observer, Lieutenant Patrick Sivert, decided to "strafe" the jeep with their .38-caliber pistols. After making several passes without hitting anything—and being shot at by the occupants—they made one last run. The driver took one look too many, missed a turn, and drove off a cliff with the officer still sitting rigidly in the seat. There was a hot debate within the aircrews on whether to paint this "airborne victory" on the nose of the aircraft.

As Craig left the area in his helicopter, the pilot got a call for help from a battle-damaged Corsair that was ditching off the coast. As the helo hovered over the life raft, Craig lowered a line and pulled the pilot into the helicopter. Happy for the rescue, the man slapped Craig on the shoulder. "Thanks for the lift, buddy." They were halfway back to the base before the pilot saw the star on Craig's utility jacket. Craig smiled at the young officer's embarrassment and let him off the hook. "Glad to be of service, lieutenant."

The following day, as Lieutenant Colonel George R. Newton's 1st Battalion, 5th Marines advanced toward the final objective, its lead element, fifteen men of the brigade reconnaissance company, forced the NKPA to prematurely trigger an ambush. In a classic combined-arms/infantry assault, 1/5 broke through the ambush, inflicting heavy casualties. The climax of the attack occurred when Technical Sergeant F. J. Lischeski and a squad of infantrymen sprang their own ambush, killing an entire enemy platoon of thirty-nine men without a single Marine casualty.

As 1/5 fought through the ambush, Craig received orders to send a battalion back toward Chindong-ni, where a reinforced NKPA regiment had infiltrated the perimeter, overrunning two army artillery battalions and cutting the main road. Lieutenant Colonel Robert D. Taplett's 3/5 loaded aboard trucks and rushed twenty-five miles east. After a fifteen-minute artillery preparation, Captain Joseph C. Fegan's Company H jumped off in the attack, little more than three hours after heading out. Taplett related that his lead element ran into a roadblock consisting of two antitank guns, supported by infantry. Craig, who had urged him to move faster, went forward to see for himself. "As he peered around the brick wall a blast of rifle fire . . . and a whining antitank round made him duck back in a hurry." His order, "Get rid of those guns now," had the desired effect, and within minutes Fegan's How Company had eliminated the roadblock.

By the next morning, 3/5 had rectified the situation and forced the enemy to withdraw, but not before the U.S. Army artillery had been destroyed with air strikes to prevent it from falling into the hands of the North Koreans. In a week of hard fighting, the brigade had stopped the NKPA 6th Division cold, just thirty-five miles from Pusan—the high tide of the North Korean advance. The Marine air-ground counterattack inflicted more than 1,900 North Korean casualties, destroyed a motorized regiment's vehicles, and eliminated a major threat to the perimeter. However, the action had not been without cost: 66 Marines were killed in action, 240 wounded, and 9 missing in action. Rifle companies were so depleted by casualties that a call went out for volunteers, which was answered by men from the brigade and regimental staffs, cooks, bakers, and bandsmen—lending credence to the Corps' doctrine that every Marine is a rifleman.

Naktong Bulge

I am going to give you the Marine Brigade. I want this situation cleaned up, and quick.

—Lieutenant General Walton H. Walker, commanding general, Eighth Army, to Major General John H. Church, commanding general, 24th Infantry Division.

The Naktong River, the second largest in Korea, formed a moat, one-quarter to one-half mile wide and six feet deep, almost the entire length of the perimeter. At the confluence of the Naktong and the Nam there is a bulge, four miles east-west and five miles north-south. The U.S. 24th Division, which occupied a series of stongpoints on the high ground east of the river, called it the Naktong Bulge.

At midnight on August 5, elements of the elite North Korean 4th "Seoul" Division forded the stream and advanced toward the American rear, threatening the main supply route (MSR). The seven thousand men were commanded by Major General Lee Kwon Mu, a favorite of Premier Kim Il Sung. His reputation was badly tarnished when he confronted the 1st Provisional Marine Brigade, which was ordered to kick the Seoul Division back across the Naktong. The suddenness of the order caught the brigade strung out, without dependable communication. Lieutenant Colonel Stewart had to resort to penciling a note to Roise: "I wrote on a little piece of brown paper, 'These are your trucks; move to Naktong at once.' " Despite the difficulties, the brigade hit the North Koreans head on, completely destroying them. Stewart observed the action. "As they retreated back across the river, I actually observed for the first time in my life the panic retreat of an enemy force, with our tanks lined up taking pot shots into scores of fleeing enemy troops. Then the air caught the remnants going back across the river, and that division was never heard from again."

Craig was unqualified in praise of his men. "The credit goes to [the] troops," he said. "They displayed a tremendous amount of courage under extremely difficult circumstances. The men were well trained and well led, in most cases by officers and non-commissioned officers who were veterans of World War II."

On August 21, the brigade was pulled out of the line for a much needed rest and refit. They looked like a bunch of rag pickers—rotting uniforms, worn-out shoes, missing equipment—when they arrived at "The Bean Patch," an open field large enough to accommodate the brigade. The men camped out in the open, under the stars, having ditched their shelter halves during the fighting. Eight hundred replacements arrived to fill the badly depleted ranks—Lem Shepherd had lived up to his word. President Syngman Rhee presented Purple Heart medals, but the most important event occurred with the arrival of a beer ration and letters from home. A rumor floated among the men: "We're goin' to join the division and make a landing in th' rear of these bastards." For once, the scuttlebutt was true. The brigade staff was alerted to start planning for the withdrawal from the perimeter. Joe Stewart caught a plane to Japan, but no sooner had he reached the terminal than he received a message, "Return to Korea at once; all hell has broken loose!"

Once More into the Breach

The NKPA launched a massive assault—98,000 men, thirteen divisions—against Walker's thinly deployed forces. They struck five separate points, but their heaviest attack was against the U.S. 2nd Division in the Naktong Bulge. Four North Korean divisions slammed into the Americans, penetrating almost three miles and slicing the division in two. Hundreds of U.S. soldiers were killed, wounded, or missing, and the victorious NKPA were close to a breakthrough. All the ground was lost that the 1st Provisional Marine Brigade had seized at such heavy cost. Walker's forces needed help, so the call went out to the Fire Brigade.

Craig rushed to the 2nd Division CP for a meeting with its commander and the Eighth Army's chief of staff. The two army officers wanted the brigade to attack immediately, despite the fact that one battalion was still on the move and its air-control section had not arrived. Craig refused and the conversation boiled over. "I insisted that the attack be delayed until all my troops arrived and I had my air support properly coordinated." He stood his ground—the brigade would fight as a united air-ground team. Finally, the army backed down. "This was the only heated discussion I had in Korea with the army," Craig related in typical low-key fashion. Shepherd related an example of Craig's graciousness. The army division commander apologized to Craig for losing the ground. "General Craig, I'm horribly embarrassed that you have to do this. My men lost the ground that you took in a severe fight. Eddie, in his very gallant manner, said 'General, it might have happened to me.' " Personally, Shepherd was upset with the army's defeat. "We turned them [the Naktong objectives] over to the army. The next day they lost the ground and Eddie had to go back and recapture the positions. He lost a lot of boys retaking the same damn ground that he'd taken two or three days before. If that had happened to me, I might have been tempted to say to the army commander, 'Well, you damn fool, why couldn't you hold it?'"

On the morning of September 3, the 5th Marines jumped off in the attack with two battalions abreast. A platoon of tanks moved forward to give support, and, as was Craig's style, he moved closer to the action. "I brought up a company of tanks, who fired point-blank into antitank guns manned by the North Koreans. These were knocked out pretty promptly, and our troops made a very good advance through a difficult area." Automatic weapons fire forced Craig and Lieutenant Jack Buck to take cover behind one of the tanks. Buck recalled, "The tank platoon commander, Second Lieutenant Bob Winters, was halfway out of the hatch firing .50-caliber tracers to point out targets for his 90mm cannon." Winters suddenly slumped over the turret, bleeding profusely from a neck wound. Disregarding the enemy fire, Craig and Buck climbed up, pulled the wounded officer off the tank, and dragged him to cover. Craig leaned over the groggy but still conscious officer, giving him words of encouragement. The youngster appreciated his sentiments and according to Buck said, "General, I've got a bottle of whiskey in the hull; you can have it." It was a magnanimous gesture, worth its weight in gold—but it remained in the tank. Craig never ate or drank anything his troops did not have.

Artillery and air strikes supported the attack, pounding the enemy positions. Gull-wing Vought F4U-4B Corsairs doused the NKP with napalm in an almost seamless demonstration of air-ground coordination. Response time averaged seven minutes from air request to run on the target. One army commander reported, "The Marines on our left were a sight to behold. Not only was their equipment superior to ours, but they had squadrons of air in direct support. They used it like artillery. It was, 'Hey, Joe, this is Smitty, knock off the left of that ridge in front of Item Company.' They had it day and night."

The fight continued for three more days before the brigade seized its last objective. One of the highlights of the action occurred when the 1st Battalion overran an enemy division command post. Marines found fully erect tents, a treasure trove of documents, piles of abandoned or destroyed equipment, and two T-34 tanks in perfect operating condition. The area had been saturated with artillery and air strikes. Hundreds of North Korean bodies bore mute testimony to the accuracy of the American firepower.

Among the litter were U.S. Army guns, tanks, mortars, and vehicles belonging to the 2nd Division, captured during the NKPA advance. There was little gloating as it was turned back to its previous owner. Too many Marines had been lost retaking the ground.

Orders were received from Eighth Army for the Marines to proceed to Pusan; they were being relieved by an army regiment that night. The two battalions loaded aboard trucks to follow the rest of the brigade. Numbed by fatigue and icy cold rain, the bent forms huddled together in the cargo vehicles had no regrets as they bade good-bye to the Pusan Perimeter.

This remarkable performance by Warrior Six and the Fire Brigade stabilized the defense of the Pusan Perimeter, gave the defenders a much-needed morale boost, and gained time for MacArthur to plan and execute a "master stroke," the Inchon landing.

Call Up the Reserves
Ray Davis

The windows of Headquarters Marine Corps blazed with light in the late summer evening. Early that afternoon, a grim-faced President Truman had authorized the call-up of the reserves. Now, headquarters staffers were hard at it, preparing mobilization orders for the 33,000 Marines of the Organized Reserve.

In Chicago a sleepy-eyed duty non-commissioned officer (DNCO) slowly responded to the persistent ringing of the entrance bell. He jerked the door open, ready to give "what for" to the wise guy who had just disturbed his sleep. Before he could say anything, the "intruder" thrust a telegram into his hand, apologized for the lateness of the hour, and shoved off. Mumbling obscenities, the by-now wide-awake DNCO ripped open the envelope and glanced at its contents. The military verbiage took him a minute to decipher. He did a double-take. "This is it," he exclaimed, and ran down the passageway to the telephone. Chicago's 9th Marine Corps Reserve Infantry Battalion had just received mobilization orders—it was going to war.

Lieutenant Colonel Ray Davis, inspector-instructor (I&I), was proud of this battalion of reserves. They were a dedicated and hard-working group of citizen soldiers who trained one weekend a month and attended summer camp once a year. "The reserves had great spirit—an esprit, which drove them to be good Marines at night or weekends, after holding down their regular civilian jobs by day or all week long." Many of the men were World War II combat veterans, but most were youngsters just out of high school—a typical reserve unit. When the order for extended active duty arrived, they had just returned from a highly successful training exercise at Camp Lejeune, where they had been classified as "nearly combat ready." Within hours of receiving the notification, the reserve center was a frenzy of activity. Working parties hurried back and forth. Long lines snaked around the passageways—shots, equipment issue, wills and power of attorney, a host of pre-deployment activities. The clock was ticking.

A troop train wound its way from the East Coast across the continent, picking up Marines along the way. The 9th Battalion, in combat gear and carrying weapons, proudly marched down State Street past hundreds of well-wishers to the train station. Wives and sweethearts tearfully waved a last good-bye as the battalion climbed aboard the passenger cars for the three-day trip to Camp Joseph H. Pendleton. Ray Davis watched the train pull away, crestfallen that he wasn't going with them. Orders had arrived, assigning him to the 7th Regiment, then forming at Pendleton's Tent Camp Two, an old World War II encampment fifteen miles from the main base.

Camp John A. Lejeune

The officer-courier strode purposely along the wide corridor, his leather heels clicking noisily on the highly polished tile deck. He pushed open the swinging half-door and entered the richly appointed office. Several senior staff officers stood around black leather chairs and a large mahogany desk, behind which sat the intimidating figure of a major general. Without prelude, the courier handed him a sealed envelope marked "secret," front and back, in heavy red type. The officer slit the envelope with an opener and removed the one-page document. He quickly scanned it and announced, in an incredulous voice, "The division is heading west."

Lem Shepherd's suggestion to MacArthur requesting a Marine division had unintended consequences. In addition to calling up the reserves, Camp Lejeune's 2nd Marine Division was striped of almost seven thousand men, leaving just a headquarters and small cadre on the East Coast. A strategic planner at the Pentagon said, "The only thing left between us and an emergency in Europe are the Schools Troops at Quantico." Camp Lejeune quickly assumed the same frenzied pace as its sister base on the West Coast. Troop trains pulled into Camp Lejeune day and night—hundreds of them—filling the sidings, hurriedly embarking men and equipment as harried staff officers patched together movement schedules.

Bob Barrow

In remarks presented at a 2nd Marine Division ball in 1977, then Lieutenant General Barrow reminisced, "I was a young company commander in the 2nd Marine Division in the spring of 1950. I came to work one morning and didn't get back to my home until over a year later. I was mobilized and deployed in one day." Barrow's company area resembled a madhouse. The brick two-story barracks echoed with the shouts of NCOs gently chiding their flock to "hurry the hell up!" Laggards suffered the full wrath of the frustrated fire team and squad leaders. Men scrambled to empty wall and footlockers, stuffing the contents into impossibly small seabags. The deck was awash with discarded liberty (civilian) clothes. Working parties struggled to crate and load organizational equipment under the baleful eye of the company's senior enlisted man, who despaired of meeting the loading schedule.

Barrow looked on with a studied appreciation of the organized confusion. He knew that "When you go to war, it's always a surprise, and your weapons and gear had best be ready." However, his men were not overburdened with cars, stereos, and wives, and thus it was fairly simple to mount out. "This was a time of paucity of things and people; there was poverty in the armed services in terms of everything but spirit." The men turned to with a will; they were going to war! "It was easy for me also," Barrow remembered. "I didn't have a car, a dog, or a wife, so all I had to do was reach into my wall locker, pull out my pack, and I was ready to go. All I needed to know was where, and how soon." At the end of a very long day, his men moved to the railroad siding, where they were serenaded by the band. The base commander knew Barrow well and, as the train pulled out, he had them play "Dixie," in recognition of Barrow's southern roots.

Camp Joseph H. Pendleton

Colonel Alpha A. Bowser, acting commander of the 1st Marine Division at Camp Pendleton, "was awakened sometime during the middle of the night with a high-priority top secret message, just like there was nothing to it at all. 'The 1st Marine Division would be brought up to full war strength, less the brigade, and would move to the Far East commencing 15 August.' " Bowser sat for a moment, rubbing his eyes, thinking that a clerk had made a mistake in decoding the message. "Well," I thought, "It's a transmission mistake; nobody could send a message like this." At the time of the message, Pendleton was very nearly devoid of Marines.

As the two wide-eyed communicators waited, Bowser dressed and hitched a ride with them to division headquarters. He put a phone call through to Washington and reached the G-3, Major General Al Pollock. The phone line was not secure, so they had to talk without revealing the contents of the message. Bowser said, "I am referring to the message number so-and-so. I just can't help but feel that this has suffered something in the transmission." Pollack, who knew Bowser well, assured him the message was correct. "Well," Bowser replied, "It may be correct, but it's impossible. This is just impossible!" Pollock assured him that it was no mistake and added that, "Tomorrow night at ten o'clock about half of Headquarters Marine Corps will arrive on a United Airlines flight. They have everything that you are going to get: people, supplies from Barstow, supplies from the East Coast, reserves, the works; the entire reserve is being mobilized immediately, the people you've got there will never go home again—they will become part of the division—just keep your shirt on. . . ."

Lem Shepherd

The promised officer augmentation reported and immediately began preparations to mount out. Several days later, Major General Oliver Prince Smith arrived and assumed command of the division. Thousands of men—reservists, 2nd Division augmentees, regulars from posts and stations—poured in at all hours of the day and night. In a one-week period, almost fourteen thousand Marines arrived. Shepherd sent a staff officer to observe preparations. "Colonel Henderson has just returned . . . and has given me a very favorable report on the activities of the 1st Division. I am fully aware of the tremendous task you have to form your division and mount out by the target date. I have every confidence that you will do a good job in accomplishing your mission. I again assure you that I and my staff are most anxious to do all possible to help and support you."

Shepherd sent the promised assistance. "I have ordered my deputy commander, Brigadier General Ivan Miller, to report to you and take over the bulk of his duties in connection with the formation of additional . . . units from the reserves now reporting in . . ." He was concerned about the reserves. "I understand that there are many former veterans among the organized reserve units. . . . I am most anxious to use this material in the formation of the 7th Marines (Reinf) and other units. . . . Otherwise, many . . . may be sent to posts and stations throughout the U.S. Once there, it will be difficult to pry them loose. . . ."

Ray Davis

After an exhausting, nonstop plane and train journey, Davis stood outside the headquarters tent of the regimental commander, Colonel Homer L.

"Litz the Blitz" Litzenberg. He wasn't prepared for the humorless colonel's abrupt welcome-aboard speech. "Litzenberg shook my hand, asked where the hell I had been, and told me that I had just five days to form 1st Battalion, 7th Marines, and take it to war!" Litzenberg failed to mention there were no troops in the battalion; Davis would have to rustle them up himself!

Davis solved the problem by reverting to the age-old tried and true tactic of the "press gang." He "stole" eight hundred Marines, noting as he did so, "There is often a fine line between a medal and a court martial, but I did what had to be done." The larcenous battalion commander shanghaied several trucks and sent them out to do "the colonel's work." Large groups of newly arrived reservists dotted the landscape. As the trucks approached these Marines, an officer hailed them with, "Anybody want to go to Korea with 1/7?" Davis noted, "Soon truckloads of Marine 'volunteers' came back into Tent Camp Two. All in all, we fulfilled troop requirements in just eight hours of 'recruiting'!"

Davis personally welcomed the "volunteers," but he did not exactly overwhelm them. "I wore hastily acquired brand new utilities, and mentioned that I had been with a reserve battalion in Chicago." Lieutenant Bill Davis had misgivings. "Hell, we all thought he was an untried reservist who didn't know anything about combat." Thinking back on the incident, Davis remarked that "A Marine private or private first class needs all the reassurance he can get as he waits in his foxhole, preparing himself mentally and physically for hordes of North Koreans or Chinese Communists he has heard about." Lieutenant Joseph R. "Joe" Owen met Davis in the field. "The colonel, trim and of medium height, exuded boundless energy and had eyes that bored into you. He had a youthful appearance, although he had been a much-decorated battalion commander in the Pacific war."

Administrative clerks took over and searched through mounds of record books, which were simply piled on the parade ground under tarpaulins. Once they found the documents, the men were officially joined on the rolls. Old-time, by-the-book administrators looked on with absolute horror at this desecration of procedure. An unrepentant Davis proudly noted that "Without it [unorthodox recruiting], I would be leaving for Inchon, Korea, with less than half an infantry battalion." Needless to say, there were some snafus. One unit's records were inadvertently burned and another's payroll was delayed for two months. This recruiting and joining effort reduced Litzenberg's five-day schedule by two. Rifle practice, small-unit tactics, and a little exercise—hiking through the hot, dry Pendleton hills—took up days three and four.

On the evening of day four, Davis assembled the men for one last "this is the way it's going to be" talk. "We're going to war, and this outfit is going to be the finest in the division. When we work, we'll work harder than anyone else and when we fight, we'll go all out. There will be no slackers. We need to be ready to ship out at a moment's notice. If you have family nearby, you will have time for one farewell visit." As promised, the next day buses transported them to San Diego, where they boarded the USS *Okanogan* (APA-220), an assault transport—exactly five days after Litzenberg's "Where the hell have you been?" speech—and twenty-seven days before the battalion landed at Inchon.

Cross Country Interlude
Bob Barrow

The first day brought a welcome relief from the hustle and bustle of embarkation. Most of the company took advantage of the opportunity to "crap out," catching up on sleep and watching the passing scenery. By day two, boredom set in—and the inevitable card games started. For a few it was a real learning experience. Money changed hands rapidly in some of the high-stake games, although the players were careful to keep the green-backs out of sight. Gambling was forbidden, although several of the officers were known to try a game of chance now and again. Others broke out paperbacks, although the choice of reading material wasn't exactly college level—Westerns were the subject of choice.

They soon nicknamed their transportation "the little train that could," although, at times, the issue seemed in doubt. The steam engine was old and needed frequent replenishment of water and coal. One of the pit stops took them to a small, hard-scrabble town in central Georgia's red hills. It was the home of one of Barrow's men, and the townspeople got wind he was passing through with his friends. They arrived at the siding about noon to find the entire town and surrounding community turned out to greet them—and to treat them. They feasted on fried chicken, apple pie, corn of the cob, and all the trimmings—a real country home-cooked meal.

The company enjoyed itself immensely, but it was soon time to shove off. After thanking the community for its hospitality and, for a lucky few, lingering good-byes with newfound friends, they reboarded the train. Just as Barrow was boarding, "I felt a hand grip my arm. Now let me tell you, when your arm is gripped by a red-necked Georgia farmer, you turn and give him your full attention. I turned and looked into the deep grey eyes of . . . a man who made his living and raised his family in the red, clay hills of Georgia. Once the man had my attention, he spoke slowly: 'Captain, you take care of my boy; he's all that I have.' " Barrow never forgot that Georgia farmer when he led his men across Inchon's Blue Beach.

When Barrow arrived at Camp Pendleton, his company was redesignated Company A, 1st Battalion, 1st Regiment, 1st Marine Division and quickly brought up to strength by the addition of fifty reservists from the 20th Infantry Battalion and fifty regulars, mostly World War II vets, from various barracks and naval installations. Although he was in excellent personal shape, they hadn't trained together and had only a week to get ready. Most of the time was used for weapons familiarization, including the rocket section. Just before embarking, they received the new 3.5-inch rocket launcher, which his men got to fire one time for familiarization. The next time they fired them, at Yongdungpo, it was for real.

CHAPTER TWENTY THREE

THE GREAT GAMBLE

Eddie Craig

I n mid-July, Craig recounted, MacArthur "outlined to me his plan for the landing at Inchon ... 'The Marines were going to turn the tide of the Korean War,' and then he proceeded to outline in detail his plans for the landing. This landing, when it did take place, was more or less similar in all respects to the way he visualized it at the time."

MacArthur's genius was never more on display than his insistence on an amphibious operation even as the North Korean Army was on the verge of crushing U.S. and South Korean resistance and seizing all of Korea. The great Marine Corps historian Colonel commented to General Shepherd during an interview, "I think Inchon was MacArthur's greatest hour." Shepherd responded, "No question about it," and went on to say, "He [MacArthur] was, in my opinion, the greatest military leader of our century."

"The Worst Possible Place"

An amphibious assault is perhaps the most complicated of all operations in war. Of all the Korean west coast seaports, Inchon was probably the least desirable when considered strictly from the viewpoint of hydrographic conditions. In fact, there was great opposition to MacArthur's plan from all quarters. Rear Admiral James H. Doyle, perhaps the navy's finest amphibious practitioner, warned him, "General, I have not been asked, however, the best I can say is that Inchon is not impossible." Doyle's comment was made at the end of a very detailed brief for MacArthur, who responded, "If we find that we can't make it, we will withdraw. Doyle, a veteran of all the major World War II amphibious landings in the Pacific, responded, "No, General, we don't know how to do that. Once we start ashore, we'll keep going,"

Shepherd, no slouch when it came to landing on a hostile shore, was not happy and had reservations. "From the various reports that we had, it appeared that Inchon was a pretty damn tough spot to take. Initially I was lukewarm about making an amphibious landing in the center of a well-defended city. I was thinking about World War II, and the Japanese, and how they fought from house to house, and it was tough going. I was afraid we would run into similar difficulties at Inchon and that it would cost the lives of many Marines to take the city." Despite their misgivings, planning continued at a feverish pace; time was running out. MacArthur set D-day for September 15, when there was sufficient water to float the landing craft.

MacArthur viewed the Inchon-Seoul operation as the opening move in a strategic bid to crush the North Korean Army. The seizure of the seaport city, only twenty-five miles from Seoul, would enable him to move rapidly against the capital and cut the NKPA lines of communication and supply. Seoul was also the hub of an excellent railroad system and a road network that fanned north and south. Kimpo, the nation's best airport, lies between the two cities. Inchon was the key to the kingdom. No other port was satisfactory. Douglas MacArthur wanted the place—and being who he was, nothing was going to keep it from him—not hydrographic conditions, not opposition, and certainly not the North Korean Army. "We shall land at Inchon and I shall crush them!" After attending MacArthur's brief on Inchon, Chief of Naval Operations Admiral Forest P. Sherman is quoted, as saying, "I wish I had that man's optimism."

Lem Shepherd

Command of the operation, code-named Chromite, fell to MacArthur's chief of staff, Major General Edward M. "Ned" Almond, an officer with no experience in amphibious operations. The navy wanted Shepherd because of his background in landing on hostile beaches—but it was not to be. "MacArthur told me himself," Shepherd said, " 'Lem, I would like you to command this landing at Inchon. It's a Marine show, and you should be in command. But unfortunately, I have promised it to my chief of staff, Ned Almond. Since you can't command this corps landing, I want you to accompany me on my staff as my amphibious advisor.' " Shepherd was greatly disappointed but agreed to the temporary assignment, which gave him the opportunity to provide input on the landing plan.

Douglas MacArthur's dictate to seize Inchon on September 15 created almost impossible parameters for the planning staffs of Amphibious Group One (PhibGru-1) and the 1st Marine Division (1st MarDiv). They had only about twenty days to prepare, probably the shortest period ever allotted for a major amphibious assault. Inchon's natural conditions—extreme tidal range, torturous shipping channels, fast currents, mud flats, and high seawalls—gave them fits. Ned Almond and Major General O. P. Smith (commanding general 1st MarDiv) did not get along, which added to the difficulties. They were two different personalities. O. P. was a cautious individual, a fine staff officer who carefully considered every contingency before taking action. Almond, on the other hand, was aggressive and anxious for X Corps to push ahead faster than Smith wanted.

It seemed obvious to Smith that neither Almond nor his staff appreciated the difficulties inherent in the Inchon operation. In a letter to the commandant, Smith wrote, "It was only after a week of close study of all the factors involved that I was able to convince myself that the operation was feasible from the standpoint of the landing force." Colonel Alpha L. Bowser, Smith's operations officer, found, "They [X Corps staff] had no capability of understanding what we were doing or how we were doing it. They were standing around wringing their hands. I took the piece of paper that was brought to me by a corps staffer, folded it up very neatly, and stuck it through the front of his shirt and told him to blow . . . !" Shepherd tried to mediate between the two. "I talked to O. P. and told him to play the game. Don't get so mad with Almond; he's trying to do the right thing." Almond didn't help matters. The first time he met Smith, Almond addressed him as "son." There was only a year age difference separating the two.

Despite the friction, a landing plan quickly took shape. Inchon was divided into three color-coded landing beaches, Red, Green, and Blue. Two battalions of the 5th Marines would land over Red; one battalion at Green (Wolmi-Do); and the 1st Marines—two battalions abreast—over Blue Beach. The extreme tidal range—enough water to float landing craft—dictated two landings a day: one at first light and the other at twilight. It was a bold plan that depended on split-second timing and a hell of a lot of luck!

September 13 was a blustery, overcast afternoon when MacArthur's black 1941 Cadillac pulled up to the entrance of the Dai Ichi Building, MacArthur's headquarters in Tokyo. Three officers climbed in, MacArthur and Shepherd in the back—protocol required the most senior to sit on the right—and Almond in front. At a signal, the MP escort wheeled out of the driveway, sandwiching MacArthur's beflagged sedan between their vehicles. Shepherd made small talk with the "great man" during the drive to Haneda Airport. As they approached the gate, the clouds lifted briefly, revealing a rainbow. "Lem," said MacArthur, "there is my lucky rainbow. This operation is going to be a success. You know I commanded the Rainbow Division in France during World War I and I have always believed that a rainbow is my lucky omen."

Shepherd thought divine intervention might have played a hand. "It was an unusual coincidence that a rainbow should appear in the sky just prior to the general's embarkation on what was considered to be a hazardous amphibious operation with a typhoon threatening to disperse the convoy of ships enroute to Inchon. Although MacArthur placed a great confidence in his own decisions, I will always believe the rainbow that appeared in the sky at that psychological moment must have reassured him that the Inchon landing would be a successful operation." Just hours remained before naval gunfire began blasting the North Korean beach defenses.

Land the Landing Force

Alpha Bowser stood on the bridge of the *Mount McKinley* with his boss, O. P. Smith, watching the operation unfold. Inchon was his fourth combat landing, and he felt this one was the touchiest of all: "My heart was not only in my mouth, I think it was lying out on the deck!" Bowser was the division's principal planner for the operation and had had serious reservations from the beginning. He was quite concerned about the split-second timing that was required to pull it off. "I just felt that it would only take one major collapse to cause the whole thing to really shudder from stem to stern."

The long column of gunfire-support ships and transports was almost invisible in the moonless night as they carefully navigated Flying Fish channel toward Wolmi-Do. A bright glow on the horizon marked the shell-blasted island, still burning after two days of intense shelling and air strikes. Men on the open decks could smell smoke as the ships stood up the channel. Radarmen stared intently at the green-tinged scopes, calmly announcing bearings and course corrections to keep the ships in the channel. The narrow, winding passage, mud-banked flats, and fast current posed special challenges for the transports. In addition, the North Koreans had laid Russian sea mines, making navigation even more dangerous.

Early in the planning, it was decided to embark the Wolmi-Do assault battalion in smaller, more maneuverable ships—four transport destroyers (APDs) and one landing ship, dock (LSD). They were jammed—three hundred men per ship—which required special arrangements. Extra bunks were rigged, along with additional ventilation for the overcrowded troop berthing spaces. Despite this supplementary air, the spaces were miserable—stifling, stagnant air, rich with the pungent odor of unwashed bodies and stopped-up heads made the three-day voyage a memorable experience. Equipment, weapons, and transport packs cluttered every available space—including the bunks, which were stacked vertically from deck to overhead. Only twenty-four inches separated them, barely enough for a man to turn over.

By 5:00 a.m., the small armada had reached their assigned stations. Deck crews struggled to lower the fifteen-thousand-pound wooden LCVPs in the darkness, while heavily loaded Marines filled the passageways, waiting for the signal to form-up on deck. The LSD, USS *Fort Marion*, launched three landing craft, each loaded with three tanks. LPDs (landing ships, personnel, dock) *Bass*, *Wantuck*, and *Diachenko* successfully lowered seventeen LCVPs, which took position alongside their debarkation station. Marines climbed down cargo nets into the pitching landing craft.

At 5:40 a.m., a carefully timed bombardment commenced, covering the slow-moving landing craft as they moved to the line of departure. Thirty-five minutes later, LSMRs (landing ships, medium, rocket) spewed thousands of rockets onto the island. Cruisers and destroyers added to the furious barrage. This massive concentrated bombardment saturated the landing area, creating a dust and smoke cloud that reduced visibility to less than a hundred yards.

The flagship hoisted the pennant, "Land the landing force," the order that sent wave after wave of LCVPs surging toward the enemy beach. Shepherd peered through his binoculars, "watching the troops disembarking in small boats from the transports around us and their movement to the line of departure. It was overcast, and smoke from the burning city made it difficult to observe the final run to the beach. As H-hour approached, the crescendo of fire increased." MacArthur, Almond, and Shepherd stood on the bridge of the *Mount McKinley* as the assault elements of 3/5 stormed ashore on Wolmi-Do ("Moon Tip Island"). The island divided the harbor in two and blocked the way into Inchon. It was the first and most critical objective. Failure to seize the island would expose the landing craft to devastating North Korean anti-boat gunfire.

Eddie Craig

The 1st Marine Brigade almost didn't make the landing at all. General Walker wouldn't release it because, he said, "If I lose the 5th Marines I will not be responsible for the safety of the front." General Smith and Admirals Struble, Doyle, and Joy pressed Almond at the headquarters, but he refused, and the discussion grew heated. Finally, MacArthur was brought into the discussion. He sided with the Marines, "Tell Walker, he will have to give up the 5th Marines." Smith's division would now have two veteran regiments for the assault. His third, 7th Marines, was at sea and would not arrive until after the landing.

On September 6, Craig flew by helicopter to Pusan and established his headquarters in the rundown buildings of the local university. "Amphibious shipping had arrived and embarkation had commenced. I managed to get a number of truck loads of beer from the army . . . and soon my men had their first cold drink in over a month." Many of the parched Marines slaked their thirst with copious amounts of brew. A medical officer wrote in his diary: "Entries this date terminated early because, in addition to foul weather, it got considerably drunk out!"

The troops crapped out in large warehouses along the wharf, a far cry from muddy rice paddies, but still a long way from first-class accommodations.

The brigade surgeon bitched mightily, condemning the filthy sheds and rotten dock area. However, the navy tried to make up for it by throwing open the ship's galleys, in a magnanimous gesture of appreciation. The captain of the USS *Cavalier* (APA-31) offered Craig his cabin, with white sheets and hot coffee, all the comforts of home. "Never have I had a more sound and wonderful sleep."

The newly formed 1st Korean Marine Regiment was assigned to the brigade, minus weapons, which were furnished by the United States. Not one in ten had ever fired a weapon! Craig immediately assigned U.S. Marine instructors to teach them how to shoot and to train them for combat—in one week! Six days later the 1st Provisional Marine Brigade was disbanded and became part of the 1st Marine Division, with Craig as assistant division commander. They sailed for Inchon on the 14th. While at sea, Craig read a frantic NKPA message, "Enemy radio intercept states our convoy sighted and our intentions deduced; calls on all troops to repel our landing at Wolmi-Do and Inchon."

Craig received his marching orders from O. P. Smith. "I did not get to talk with General Smith before the landing; however, he sent me a message outlining my duties ashore on D-day. 'If everything goes all right on Wolmi-Do during D-day, I would like for you to go ashore on the evening tide and set up an advance CP. We will give you a dispatch to that effect some time during the day of D-day. I would expect you to function at discretion. There may be decisions to be made which you can best make on the spot. If there is time and you feel the matter should be referred to division, do so.'" Craig, along with his five-man personal staff, landed at H-hour on Wolmi-Do's "Green Beach." In a personal interview with the author, General Craig related that he was very proud of the fact that Smith gave him such latitude to "act as he saw fit."

Lem Shepherd

"It was a beautiful morning, and as the first pink streaks of dawn broke in the east my thoughts went back to other dawns when I had watched preparations for similar landings." Wolmi-Do belched fire as naval gunfire pounded the island. "I have never seen any better shooting. The entire island was smothered with bursting shells from the cruisers and destroyers."

Smoke obscured a portion of the denuded island—two days of napalm strikes had burned off the vegetation. Aboard the transports, Marines formed in ranks along the rail and, on the command "Land the landing force," started the long climb down the cargo nets. Private First Class Fred Davidson climbed over the rail and stepped down on the thick rope strand, remembering to "Buckle the helmet chin strap tightly so it can't fall on the men already in the landing craft. Second, climb down the boarding net, place hands on the vertical ropes so the man above doesn't step on them."

The flat-bottomed landing craft circled, wallowing heavily in the sea chop, waiting for the signal to run for the beach. Mal de mare raised its ugly head. Nervous stomachs reacted to the motion, spewing a disgusting, partially digested breakfast—powdered eggs and canned apricots—onto the plywood deck. The old salts stoically endured it; they had been there before—many were veterans of Pacific landings. Besides, as one wag described, seasickness makes us meaner—no one is going to force me back to those puke boats. First Lieutenant Ed Jaworski had a front row seat: "As we circled it was like watching a combined arms demonstration. It was like a continuous wave of fire. Wolmi-Do, this little island, literally exploded. Signal flags fluttered and the landing craft headed toward the beach." Shepherd "watched Wolmi-Do from the bridge of the Mount McKinley—a spectacular sight with Marine fighter planes zooming the island in close support of the infantry." Rifleman Davidson, much closer to the action, was overwhelmed with the din of the shellfire until suddenly, "It got quiet as hell; the only sounds were the LCVP's engine and the slap of water on the bow. The roar of the engines hit us like a bomb. Those Marine Corsairs came flying through the smoke toward the beach not more than thirty feet over our heads! Hot, empty machine-gun shells fell on us."

Shepherd tried to follow the line of landing craft, but "It was overcast and smoke from the burning city made it difficult to observe the final run for the beach." The assault troops scrambled ashore, across burned and blasted ground, shooting and grenading everyone and everything in their path. There was very little return fire, as the pre-assault bombing and gunfire had done its job. The North Koreans who survived the bombardment were in no condition to put up a stiff resistance. Lieutenant Colonel Bob Taplett, CO of 3/5 and a World War II veteran, "had never seen defenders in such a state of total shock . . . many of them staggered out of bunkers and holes in a total state of shock." Wolmi-Do was declared secure by 8:00 a.m., with only light Marine casualties. Taplett reported at 8:30 a.m., "Mission completed . . . Wolmi-Do secured. Casualties 17 WIA . . . dead, none."

Eddie Craig

As the afternoon high tide surged up Flying Fish Channel, LCVPs and amphibian tractors carrying the assault elements of the 1st and 5th Marines gunned across the line of departure toward their landing beaches. Close behind, two free boats carrying Craig, his personal staff, and a jeep and trailer broke off to land on Wolmi-Do. As his LCVP bottomed out, the ramp dropped and Craig stepped out on the sand. "I went ashore on the morning of D-day . . . established my CP near the shoreline, and went to the top of the hill . . . where I established an observation post (OP)." From here, he could clearly see Red Beach where Lieutenant Colonel Ray Murray's 5th Marines had stormed ashore. Craig inspected the North Korean positions, finding them heavily dug in. "Apparently this was done at the last minute . . . and it was a very thorough job. I believe that if our naval gunfire had not done such a fine job of shore bombardment, our casualties might have been very heavy. As it was, it was such an effective bombardment . . . that the island was practically denuded of cover and vegetation. There was very little that could live there when the Marines landed."

Smoke hid Blue Beach. All that Craig could see was a line of amphibian tractors floundering through the mud flats. Several tractors were stuck belly deep in the muck. However, just in front, movement caught his attention. Five North Koreans leaped out of hiding, fled across the causeway linking Wolmi-Do with the city, and escaped despite a flurry of rifle-fire, much to the chagrin of several sharpshooters. Late in the afternoon, Craig's five-man command group set up his CP tent on a flat area close to the beach. They erected the tent over a hole that they had laboriously dug for his protection. Craig turned in—but almost immediately exited, exclaiming, "The damn thing stinks like shit!" Upon closer inspection, it turned out the diggers had excavated a North Korean crapper! Craig slept in the trailer that night, while the others chose a less odiferous location.

In accordance with O. P. Smith's orders, Craig kept an eye on the beachhead's right flank. "Blue Beach, where the 1st Marines would land, could better be controlled by division headquarters on the command ship." However, the landing went so well that Craig had little to report, except to urge "that the army troops be landed at the earliest, in view of the fact that I envisioned a rapid advance from Inchon due to light enemy resistance."

The assault waves barely cleared Red Beach when the first of eight LSTs literally plowed into the seawall. The landing ships lived up to their nickname—"large slow target"—when the North Koreans started shooting them up. Craig was incensed to see "sailors manning the bow gun—a 40mm automatic cannon—fire directly onto the beach and hit some of our Marines. They then traversed the gun around and fired directly across our front. It was one of the instances of wild firing that I saw during that landing—and it was promptly stopped by the navy—but it did result in some of our men being injured." During the night, the landing force consolidated their lines and waited for the expected North Korean counterattack, which fortunately did not occur.

Lem Shepherd

After the initial landing, sometime in mid-morning, MacArthur insisted on going for a better look. The admiral's barge was called away. Shepherd, Vice Admiral Arthur D. Struble, commander Joint Task Force-7 (CJTF-7), and a few staff members hitched a ride. Shepherd vividly recalled the drama. "We all got in a boat together which took us to Wolmi-Do Island and then to the dock at Inchon to look that over. We then went around to another place [Red Beach] where there was a hell of a lot of fighting going on. Shells were falling all around the boat. I said, 'For God's sake, general. It's dangerous to get too close to the shore.' He didn't pay any attention and went right ahead. So I said to Struble, 'I don't think it's safe to take General MacArthur, the commander in chief of the theatre, in here and expose him to this rifle and mortar fire.' " The boat turned aside and escaped. MacArthur's luck held. The North Koreans were not aware of the lucrative target.

Struble caused hard feelings when he inferred that Shepherd was "scared of getting into the beach." Shepherd fumed, "Well, I wasn't scared;

it wasn't bothering me, but I felt a certain amount of responsibility of protecting General MacArthur from having a mortar shell hit the boat. So I never had a damn bit of use for Struble after that."

Later, Struble, Almond, and Shepherd set off again. As the admiral's coxswain lay alongside the Blue Beach seawall, a disheveled, dirt-encrusted Marine yelled out, "Lay off, you stupid bastards! We're going to blast a hole in the wall!" The coxswain replied, "This is Admiral Struble's barge." "I don't give a shit whose barge it is," said the Marine. "Get it clear before I blow the seawall!" "As we pulled out to sea," Shepherd recalled, "We could hear machine-gun and mortar firing all around the shoreline. The various fires were burning fiercely, and occasionally some oil storage would go off and flames would leap way up in the air. It was a terrific sight and one I shall long remember."

Shepherd watched MacArthur "hold court" in the admiral's chair on the bridge of the *Mount McKinley*. "His staff was grouped around him. He was seated in the admiral's chair with his old Bataan cap with its tarnished gold braid and a leather jacket on. Photographers were busily engaged in taking pictures of the general while he continued to watch the naval gunfire—paying no attention to his admirers." Reports flowed in describing a successful landing. MacArthur smiled at the reports and turning to Admiral Doyle, directed, "Say to the fleet, 'The navy and Marines have never shone more brightly than this morning.' " Shepherd was a very proud witness. "I was right there when MacArthur took his pen, and wrote it." After dictating the message, MacArthur turned to the group and said, "That's it, let's get a cup of coffee." General Smith was somewhat more cynical: "The reason it looked simple was that professionals did it."

Major General Frank E. Lowe, Truman's eyes and ears in Korea, reported, "In the last thirty-six hours [at Inchon] I have witnessed a miracle, no less; all calculated to the end we discussed in Washington and as a first objective, i.e., that no American troops shall be required to fight in the cold, the mud, and the filth of a Korea winter."

Army–Marine Friction

By 7:30 a.m. on D+1, the 1st Marine Division was clear of Inchon and advancing toward Seoul, twenty miles away. Almond was already pressuring

O. P. Smith to move quickly and seize the capital. "What Gen[eral] Almond tried to get me to agree to was that we would capture Seoul by the 25th of September. And, he explained frankly, that was exactly three months after the date that the North Koreans had invaded South Korea. They [MacArthur and Almond] wanted to be able to get out a communiqué saying that on September 25th, three months later, they'd [North Koreans] been thrown out." Smith was not happy with Almond's abbreviated time schedule and told him so. "I couldn't guarantee anything; that was up to the enemy. We'd do the best we could and go as fast as we could." Nevertheless, both Almond and MacArthur pushed for a quick resolution to the campaign. MacArthur believed the easy Inchon victory meant that Seoul would fall quickly. The Marines believed MacArthur's headquarters just wanted a public relations communiqué bolstering his reputation.

Continue the Attack

The division's attack started well. Puller's 1st Marines moved directly on Seoul along the main highway. The Korean Marines mopped up Inchon, while the 5th Marines on the left flank advanced past the city. Their orders were to advance to the northeast, seize Kimpo Airfield, cross the Han River, and attack Seoul from the west. A snag developed when six tanks and three hundred infantry from a battalion of the 18th North Korean Division counterattacked Dog Company, 5th Marines, early on the morning of the 17th. Corporal Okay Douglas took the lead tank under fire with his 2.36-inch rocket launcher, a weapon the army thought incapable of destroying a T-34. His first shot, at seventy-five yards, set it afire—and then all hell broke loose as other Marine weapons opened up. When the shooting stopped, all six tanks were destroyed and more than two hundred North Koreans killed.

Lem Shepherd

As luck would have it, MacArthur, accompanied by Almond and Shepherd, arrived on the scene within a half hour of the fight. Shepherd described the scene: "There were six tanks lined up on both sides of the road and burning with dead bodies laying half-cooked on top of several of the tanks. . . . The turrets had been punctured by clean hits. It was a very dramatic moment, and General MacArthur was truly impressed." Shepherd thought the army's antitank squads always shot too soon; they did not wait until the tanks were close enough. He took the opportunity to rub it in. "Well, General [MacArthur], that proves these 2.36-inch bazookas can knock out a tank." Almond almost choked. "You damned Marines! You always seem to be in the right spot at the right time! Hell, we've been fighting this battle with army troops, but MacArthur would arrive just as the Marines had knocked out six enemy tanks!" Shepherd responded rather tongue in cheek, "Well, Ned, we're just doing our job; that's all."

Eddie Craig

Craig watched the action. "I had my driver, Corporal Adams, take me to a small knoll overlooking the road. Sniping was heavy and the Marines were having a stiff fight at a small pass. One of our tanks was knocked out, when suddenly the enemy gave up the fight and retreated." As he watched the action, a mud-wattle hut beside him caught fire and erupted in flames. The fire set off a large quantity of ammunition the North Koreans had stored there. Craig jumped into a ditch. "Metal and debris were flying all around. Adams dashed over to the jeep and, as I yelled for him to take cover, he jumped in, started the motor, and drove it to safety."

That afternoon, after returning from the front, Craig passed through a small village. The road narrowed, and Adams slowed the jeep to pass a group of Korean peasants. An old man reached out to give something to Craig. "Without thinking, I reached out to take it. It was an American hand grenade. I quickly squeezed it to make sure the handle was not up or the pin pulled. The pin was still in, and I heaved a sign of relief. We stopped and the old man made gestures indicating he had found it by the road and was simply returning it. He was showing his goodwill and friendship for us."

Yongdungpo

While 5th Marines consolidated its position north of the Han River, the 1st Marines' early-morning attack was stymied by the high-banked Kalchon Creek, a network of dikes on the western outskirts of Yongdungpo. This formidable obstacle was heavily defended by North Korean infantrymen, supported by machine guns, mortars, and tanks. The attack ran into a storm of fire, which caused heavy casualties—2nd Battalion alone lost seventeen officers and two hundred men—and by late afternoon, the attack stalled. Barrow's company was ordered forward into Yongdungpo, a small city on the south bank of the Han River.

Eddie Craig

On September 20, the 5th Marines crossed the Han River in LVTs and by 5:30 p.m. were almost halfway to Seoul. Craig, as was his habit, was up front. "I had been checking the front of the 5th Marines, and on returning over the river on my way back to the division CP decided to make a hasty check of the 1st Marines. Arriving at the CP . . . I could see the city of Yongdungpo just ahead, and in the city many fires were burning as a result of our shelling."

As Craig's party made their way back to the CP in a jeep, they came under fire from several North Koreans. They bailed out and took up firing positions. First Lieutenant Jack Buck, the aide, and the driver, recently promoted Sergeant Dave Adams, set up the .30-caliber machine gun they always carried for just this sort of emergency. As the enemy came at them—probably expecting an easy victory—Buck and Adams opened fire with the machine gun, while Craig banged away with his .45. The heavy fire killed several. Three surrendered and were immediately stripped to ensure they weren't carrying concealed weapons. The prisoners sat on the hood of the jeep during the drive back, which cooled their ardor, if not their Communist ideology. Buck turned them over to the MPs, ending just another day with the ADC section.

Bob Barrow

Barrow's Able Company spent the night of the 20th on Hill 118 overlooking Yongdungpo. The next morning Barrow led them off the hill, keeping high ground between the company and the NKPA defenders—in effect concealing the move from the enemy. The company formed up behind the dike in a classic tactical formation, two platoons up and one back. The light machine guns were attached to each platoon. A section of heavy machine guns from Weapons Company, the company's 60mm mortars, and an assault squad followed in trace. On Barrow's signal, they crossed over the dike and plunged into a rice paddy. The uncollected rice stalks were chest high. Major Edwin H. Simmons watched them. "They were beautifully deployed. As they came through the dry rice paddy, I thought of the Marines coming through the wheat fields of Belleau Wood in 1918."

Barrow expected to be hit at any moment. He could hear the sounds of heavy fighting behind him on either side—small arms fire mixed with the heavy crump of exploding mortar and artillery fire. Aircraft passed overhead on bombing and strafing runs. Private First Class Morgan Brainard described the advance: "Somewhere off to our left, beyond a line of trees we could hear the rattle of rifle and machine gun fire where Baker Company was going in. To our immediate front, however, there was nothing but silence, as we continued to move forward through the field in perfect order, but my mind kept racing back toward the stories I had read as a boy of the Marines attacking through the wheat fields of Belleau Wood, and I expected our peaceful scene would be shattered in a similar manner at any moment."

Nothing happened. The company continued its advance. Barrow acknowledged that "We just happened to experience one of those rare fortunes of war, a momentary opportunity." They approached the last dike and stopped. Brainard was in the lead squad. "We passed over the top of the dike quickly, slithered down the other side, then inexplicably and stupidly stopped, facing a stream." The Company Gunnery Sergeant quickly ended their hesitation: "Get in the goddamned water!"

The two-hundred-man rifle company entered the nearly deserted city, astride the main east-west street. Barrow could hardly believe their good fortune. "It was eerie; we simply slithered into town undetected." They pushed several hundred yards into the heart of the city and by early afternoon were nearing the broad concrete highway that connected Inchon with Seoul. His lead platoon spied a large formation of enemy troops, chanting with patriotic fervor as they marched down the road. Barrow's men immediately opened fire with rifles and machine guns and watched as the unsuspecting North Koreans simply melted away under their concentrated fire.

Able continued to advance until it reached the far side of the city. By this time, it was late afternoon and the enemy was starting to turn its attention from the other units to this lone company so far into its rear. Barrow realized that it would not be "prudent" to continue, so he halted the column on an elongated, sausage-shaped embankment, 30 feet high and 150 yards long. From here, they could interdict the main North Korean lines of supply and reinforcement for the defense of the city.

The company quickly dug in, spurred on by the sounds of tanks in the vicinity and small arms fire that cracked over their heads. The deep, two-man foxholes formed a 360-degree circular defense on either side of the manmade dike. The men on the western side of the perimeter overlooked a large five-story building and a secondary road, while those facing east commanded the low ground and small airfield. Barrow placed his machine guns on the end positions, which generally ran north and south and faced more of the city and the road network. The position was a small island of Marines in the midst of a large enemy force. Barrow was confident, although he knew it was a difficult situation: "There wasn't any help coming; however, we felt strong. We were not 'The lost company.' "

In addition to being isolated, Barrow was having difficulty maintaining radio contact, not an uncommon occurrence, because the SCR300 radios they carried had a limited range. They were out of communications, and no one knew exactly where they were. In fact, higher headquarters had written them off, believing they would be annihilated by the superior number of North Korean troops in the area. The problem of communications was briefly solved when a Marine threw a hand grenade over the top of a large pile of coal. It set off an ammunition dump. The resultant explosion threw a large "mushroom-shaped cloud" into the air. Barrow just happened to be on the fading radio with the battalion operations officer attempting to describe their location. "Do you see that explosion?" "Yeh," the major responded, "it looks like an 'A' bomb; didn't know you had one with you." "That's our position; I'm about seventy-five yards north of there."

Shortly after dark, the telltale rattling, revving, and clanking of tracked vehicles reached the darkened perimeter. Private First Class Brainard crouched in his foxhole. "The squeaking and engine humming was drawing much closer, and I felt the ice-like shiver of pure fear." Five unescorted T-34 tanks edged slowly out of the city and onto the secondary road, which paralleled the dike. As the first tank started its run, a 3.5-inch rocket knocked its turret off, sending the vehicle lurching behind nearby buildings. The others began a series of firing passes—back and forth along the dike, with their 85mm guns and machine guns. At the ungodly range of only twenty-five to thirty yards, they could not miss—and neither could the outgunned Marines.

The North Koreans made the mistake of using armor-piercing shells, which buried in the soft dirt, causing only one casualty, a sergeant, who was knocked unconscious by a close hit. Barrow's men, on the other hand, fired rocket after rocket, hitting two more tanks and forcing them out of action. The remaining two were hit on their last pass and were not seen again. Barrow raved about the gunners. "One of the most courageous acts that I ever witnessed was those brave young Marines with the 3.5s."

Between 9:00 p.m. and 1:00 a.m., enemy infantry tried to accomplish what their tanks could not do. They launched four separate attacks against the northern end of the perimeter but were beaten off with heavy losses. At one point, an enemy officer prisoner escaped amid a hail of gunfire. He ran toward his own comrades yelling, "Don't attack. They're too strong; don't attack." He was unsuccessful, and they came again, after being harangued by a particularly loud-mouthed officer. After being repulsed, the officer again started a ranting tirade. Corporal Billy D. Webb, a fire team leader, grew tired of the man's cheek and slipped out of the perimeter, after cautioning his men, "For God's sake, don't shoot me when I come back. I'm going to get that son-of-a-bitch!"

Webb, a reservist from Tulsa, Oklahoma, made his way through a maze of burning buildings until he spotted the officer standing on the back of a truck. Taking careful aim in the semi-darkness, he ended the exhortation in mid-sentence. Webb escaped in the resultant confusion, earning praise from his platoon commander, who said of the incident, "That Gook literally talked himself to death!"

The death of this fiery officer signaled the end of the determined attacks. At dawn, Barrow counted more than 210 enemy dead, fifty automatic weapons, and four abandoned T-34 tanks. Countless other bodies were later discovered in abandoned buildings around the beleaguered perimeter. Barrow's daring advance through the city and spirited defense broke the back of the North Korean defense, and they withdrew from the city. He thought that "Yongdungpo did for A Company what no other thing could have done in terms of unifying it and giving it its own spirit—a spirit that said, 'We can do anything.' "

Crossing the Han River
Eddie Craig

Craig was concerned about crossing the Han River. "I knew we were going faster than had originally been planned, and we were making every effort to get to the river as quick as we could. The eyes of the world were upon us. It would have looked bad for the Marines, of all people, to reach a river and not be able to cross." It was the responsibility of X Corps to supply the pontoon bridging, and Craig was assured by the corps engineer officer that everything was ready—pontoons, powerboats, and so forth. Unfortunately, the equipment was not ready, adding to the Marines' disillusionment with Almond's command. One of the reasons the army was given the top job, rather than the Marines, was because they were supposed to be better at running a land campaign.

Craig had the division's Engineer Battalion break out their own equipment, which included pneumatic pontoon rafts and some bridging material. They constructed big rafts to ferry tanks and other critical material across, while the infantry crossed in amtracs and DUKWs. In the meantime, the army sweated getting enough material to construct a bridge—flying it in from all over the Far East—in time for MacArthur to enter the city. There was no airfield in Seoul, so he had to land at Kimpo and take a jeep.

Bob Barrow

Alpha's turn to cross over the river came when his company boarded open-hatched DUKWs. The five-minute, nerve-racking cruise—Would the damn things really float?—ended without incident. As they made their way to the battalion assembly area, Puller bluntly ordered them to "get in the attack." The entire 1st Battalion took off at high port, trying to pass through the lead battalion. Barrow double-timed past another company commander, who called out, "What the hell's going on?" Slightly out of breath, Barrow replied, "Take it easy, Johnny. This constitutes a passage of lines—Puller style."

Seoul

After the division crossed the Han River, there was increasing pressure to capture Seoul. MacArthur asked Shepherd every morning, "Lem, when are your Marines going to capture Seoul?"

The liberation of Seoul dwarfed, by far, any previous single Marine combat objective. The city was a sprawling metropolitan area with a population of more than 2 million people, including thousands of terrified refugees. The city proper consisted of solidly constructed multifloored office buildings that often fronted wide boulevards. The broad avenues offered excellent fields of fire for the defenders, who threw up barricades every four hundred to six hundred yards. They piled dirt- and rubble-filled rice bags eight feet high and six feet deep, reinforced with trolley cars, automobiles, and streetcar rails; anything to act as a barrier. They sowed mines around each barricade and supported them with machine guns and anti-tank weapons. The improvised strongpoints, stretching across the entire street, were centered on intersections for maximum effectiveness.

The makeshift barricades were almost impervious to machine gun and small arms fire. Their destruction took a coordinated effort by infantry, tanks, engineers, and supporting arms to destroy them. However, even successful attacks often left a trail of killed and wounded Marines. Rifle companies in both regiments melted away. In the close-quarter door-to-door fighting, it was shoot first, ask questions later. Private First Class Morgan Brainard described the stress: "The tension from these little forays whittled us pretty keen. I think if one's own mother had suddenly leapt out in front of us she would have been cut down immediately." Barrow's company quickly found another use for their new rocket launchers. "We employed it in a very effective manner in Seoul. In many instances [our] 3.5 [gunners] simply shot at some of those fragile houses, killing all the occupants." The civilian population was caught in the crossfire; Seoul became a killing ground. It would not, "be captured without great difficulty," as MacArthur, told Shepherd.

Battle of the Barricades
Bob Barrow

Barrow's scouts warily advanced parallel to the deserted streets, carefully avoiding the more obvious routes of approach. They cut through backyards and gardens, climbed fences, and ducked through houses, staying out of sight as they moved toward the high ground that ran through the western edge of the city. Luck favored the company—again—for by noon on the 24th, they sat on Hill 79, the battalion objective, with hardly a shot fired. From this vantage point, they could look out over the capital, which sprawled virtually to the horizon. Photographer David Douglas Duncan described the remarkable view: "The ground in front fell rapidly away to the freight yards of Seoul's main railroad terminal. The business and governmental districts sprawled around the base of the mountains to the left. Far back to the right stretched the broken bridges of the Han. Dead ahead lay another rather innocuous-looking residential district very similar to that surrounding the advance patrol." Barrow was more cautious; he described the situation as "ominous."

As the company moved into position, Barrow turned to an even more pressing matter. Early that morning, Puller had given him an American flag to raise on the regiment's first objective. The flag was tied to a pole, and a couple of troopers raised it over the roof of a school—the highest point on the hill. Duncan snapped the photo and later published it, enraging the 5th Marines, who cried "foul," because they had wanted to be the first to raise a flag. From that point on, according to Andy Geer, "Each unit obtained a supply of flags and the race was on."

Barrow, ever cautious, deployed his crew-served weapons along the edge of the ridge and ordered the fire support teams—mortar, artillery, and air-liaison officers—to look over the route he intended to follow. He was also concerned that Able Company was all alone—again—and he wanted to hold up until the flank units caught up. However, the battalion commander had other ideas and told him, in no uncertain terms, to move out. Barrow stalled; things just didn't "smell right." Suddenly, one of his men exclaimed, "Gooks," and half a dozen binoculars swung to where the man pointed. North Korean heads bobbed up along the railroad embankment and others appeared in the shadows of a building. As the Marines watched, a full platoon of North Koreans broke from the embankment and ran into a house.

Barrow calmly, in a matter-of-fact voice, directed fire on the enemy positions. The company machine guns and mortars were the first to fire, followed quickly by barrage after barrage of 105mm artillery. Marine Corsairs swept in, dropping bombs and canisters of napalm. The surrounding buildings caught fire, sending great columns of flames and smoke into the air. More and more enemy came out of hiding to escape the torrent of steel. Barrow saw "a mass scurrying, as literally hundreds scampered from behind the railroad embankment and we were killing them without loss to ourselves." Barrow reported the action, describing the one-sided battle in great detail, but he was still ordered to move. He refused, believing "If there was a place for fire support, this was it." He continued to pound the enemy positions. Still Barrow was pressured to advance, "But [the orders] sure as hell didn't make sense. . . . We thought we were having a turkey shoot," so he did the unthinkable and turned off his radio. In one last attempt to make them understand, he sent one of his best platoon commanders, as a guise to cover the "radio failure," to "respectfully" request that the battalion commander come forward. Forty minutes later, he arrived, saw what was going on, and happily joined in directing fire, ordering, "Get more mortars in there . . . get more artillery." The sudden communication failure was never brought up. The action was photographed and described by Duncan in an article for the New York Times titled: "Company Commander Defies Superiors." Fortunately, Barrow never heard another word about the incident or the article.

Barrow later discovered that his battalion commander was being pressured by higher headquarters to speed up the attack. He was incensed to learn that it all stemmed from MacArthur's push to liberate Seoul in three months. "It was a meaningless goal. It's easy to pass along pointless orders, except if you're the one who has to carry them out."

Night Attack
Lem Shepherd

"As the days passed it became increasingly difficult for me to answer MacArthur's question ['Lem, when are your Marines going to capture Seoul?']. I was in constant personal contact with General Smith and visited his command post daily. I knew the 1st Marine Division was making a determined effort to seize the city but were meeting determined resistance by its North Korean defenders, which I explained to Macarthur." General

Almond wanted Seoul wrapped up—and he wanted it by the 25th. At one point, he inferred that the 1st Marine Division might not be up to the task and the 7th Infantry Division might be sent in to help the Marines. O. P. Smith took great exception to Almond's threat.

Eddie Craig

"At about 20:00 on the [night of the] 25th, we received a dispatch from X Corps, saying that air reconnaissance had reported large groups of enemy moving out of the city and that enemy resistance in Seoul had ceased. We were ordered to attack immediately, 'NOW.' " Smith was incredulous; all his front-line units had been engaged all day and were expecting a counterattack. Craig was incredulous. "There was no doubt in our minds but that there was a strong enemy force still in front of us."

Smith called the X Corps chief of staff and complained. All he got for his trouble was, "After all, General Almond dictated that order, and he wants it carried out." Craig, a superb tactician, felt the order violated every tenet in the book: "A night attack requires at least a day's notice, careful observation of the terrain . . . and a thorough briefing of all small-unit commanders." Barrow was more direct: "It's a no, no!"

Nevertheless, an order was an order, and the two regiments were ordered into the attack. The indomitable Private First Class Brainard groused, "We were all rousted out and mustered down on the darkened street by platoons. Scuttlebutt said we were going into the heart of Seoul in a surprise night attack." Just as the order was relayed to Murray's 5th Marines, they were hit with a counterattack. Puller's 1st Marines delayed for a fifteen-minute artillery barrage and then requested a second—just in time to catch the North Koreans in a counterattack. Craig was elated. "This barrage caught them squarely. I believe the enemy had thought that after our first preparation, there would be no more . . . and started his attack."

All hell broke loose, when a reinforced battalion of the North Korean 25th Brigade hit 3/1's roadblock on Ma Po Boulevard. Ed Simmons, weapons company commander, heard the unmistakable sounds of tanks. Their first shot missed him by inches, but killed his radio operator, who had been standing by his side. The Marines opened up with everything they had: rifles, rocket launches, mortars, machine guns, and artillery, including three battalions of the 11th Marines. The area quickly turned into a night-marish scene of exploding shells and glowing tracers set against a backdrop of burning buildings. The attack went on all night, ending shortly before dawn. However, one North Korean self-propelled gun remained in the fight and continued to fire at Simmons' command post. He grew tired of the threat, brought up a 75mm recoilless rifle, and "gave the gunner a project." In the grey half-light of dawn, the crew spotted the vehicle and scored a direct hit.

In an interview with a correspondent from the *New York Times*, Almond allowed as how "Nothing could have been more fortunate than the tank-led enemy counter-attacks. It gave us a greater opportunity to kill more enemy soldiers and destroy his tanks more easily than if we had had to take the city house by house." While the Marines of the 1st Division were slug-ging it out in the nighttime battle, Almond sent a message to MacArthur, timing it to arrive just before midnight on the 25th. "Three months to the day after the North Koreans launched their surprise attack south of the 38th Parallel, the combat troops of X Corps recaptured the capital city of Seoul." Unfortunately, his message had little effect on the North Koreans. It took four more days of heavy combat—and five hundred Marine casual-ties—before Seoul was finally liberated. O. P. Smith recalled that Almond's headquarters "never admitted that the fighting went on after that."

Taplett's 3/5 won bragging rights by being the first unit to raise a flag over Government House. One of his companies spotted a large North Korean flag waving from a pole in front of the building. Several men ducked through a hole in the wall surrounding the burned-out building. The flag's halyards were snarled and wouldn't shake free, so three Marines stood on each other's shoulders, a la gymnastic act, and cut it down. They attached Old Glory to the shortened lines and with a shout, "Run her up," claimed victory over the 1st Marines.

Lem Shepherd

"Finally I decided to answer his [MacArthur's] question by simply replying, 'We will capture Seoul today, general,' which seemed to satisfy him." Fortunately, about midnight on the 28th he received a personal dispatch from O. P. Smith: "Marines of the 1st Marine Division have captured

Seoul." Shepherd was so elated by the news that he jumped out of bed in his pajamas and ran to MacArthur's cabin. "The general was pacing up and down, smoking his corncob pipe. Without apologizing for my informal attire, I said, 'General, we have captured Seoul. We've got it. I told you we would take Seoul today."

Liberation Ceremony
At 10:00 a.m. on the 29th, MacArthur's plane, named SCAP (acronym for Supreme Commander, Allied Powers), landed at Kimpo Airfield. An impeccably dressed MacArthur and his wife stepped onto the runway and climbed into the lead sedan. Other lesser dignitaries found room in one of the other four sedans or scrambled for space in one of forty jeeps that comprised the convoy. Elaborate preparations had been made to ensure not only the safety of the celebrants, but also the proper decorum of the proceedings. The latter rationale may have been the reason why the Marines were not invited to the party.

Eddie Craig
"The Marines were not represented in the ceremonies at the palace except General Smith, myself, Colonel Puller, my aide, and one or two other officers. You'd think that they'd have the decency to give some of the honor to the men who captured the place." The five Marines wore combat gear and one, Puller, had a hard time even getting in. An army MP, complete with white gloves and white bootlaces, barred his battered jeep from entering a "sedan only" entrance. Puller solved the dilemma in short order by ordering his driver to "run him over."

The National Palace still smelled of smoke and charred wood. The observers could clearly hear the sounds of distant small arms fire and artillery explosion. The interior was ringed with "a detachment of army military police wearing knife-pressed, tailor-made ODs [olive drabs] with gleaming black airborne boots laced with white nylon parachute cords." Their snazzy appearance was in sharp contrast to the "out of sight" grungy Marines who were really providing security. Craig said, rather tongue in cheek, "The MPs looked more or less out of place at that time." O. P. Smith commented dryly, "The Marines were a little caustic about it."

Jack Buck recalled that the palace had glass ceiling panels that were weakened after all the shelling. Shards of glass were constantly fluttering down onto the concrete floor, making a tinkling noise as they hit. Buck kept his helmet on, just to be on the safe side. He watched as MacArthur escorted Syngman Rhee to a small podium in front of the one hundred or so senior officer guests. MacArthur recited the Lord's Prayer and, after a short speech, turned to Rhee, saying, "Mr. President, I return your country to you."

After the ceremony, Craig and Buck stopped at what had been one of Seoul's better hotels. "It was a classic nice place," Buck recalled, "except for the dead North Koreans littering the winding staircase." Ever the explorer, Buck cautiously made his way to the basement. In the dim light, he saw a sight that would have made even the hardest gunnery sergeant smile with joy—stack after stack of the finest booze money could buy, or in Buck's case, what he could "appropriate." As the duly appointed representative of the assistant division commander, he loaded several cases of the hoard into his jeep and rode off into the sunset. Later, after a dinner of barely edible C-rations, Smith, Craig, and several of the division staff sipped an excellent cabernet, out of canteen cups.

CHAPTER TWENTY FOUR

NORTH TO THE YALU

With the liberation of Seoul and the restoration of the South Korean government, the only mission that remained was the destruction of the North Korean Army. Battered remnants of that army were desperately attempting to escape north across the 38th Parallel. MacArthur, basking in the glow of one of the most decisive operations in military history, was intent on crushing them. All he needed was approval to cross the boundary. On September 27, the Joint Chiefs of Staff, in the name of the president, gave its consent, with the proviso that "At the time of such operations there has been no entry into North Korea by major Soviet or Chinese Communist Forces, no announcement of intended entry, nor a threat to counter our operations in North Korea." There was great concern at the highest levels of the U.S. Government that either of the two countries might enter the war. MacArthur shared no such concerns.

On October 1, MacArthur authorized the release of a broadcast calling for the surrender of the North Korean Army, who did not dignify it with a reply. However, two days later, the Chinese forwarded their intentions through a third-party intermediary. The Indian ambassador in Peking met China's foreign minister in a hastily arranged meeting at his home over tea. After the usual small talk, the Indian ambassador was told, "If the Americans crossed the 38th Parallel, China would intervene." This message was immediately relayed to the State Department, but the secretary pooh-poohed it, because the Indian diplomat "was not a good reporter." Retired Admiral Kichisaburo Nomura, Japan's ambassador to the United States in 1941, said, "If you go north of the 38th Parallel, they'll come in.

They'll have to do that now to save face, live up to their own words." The 1st Cavalry Division crossed the 38th Parallel on October 9.

MacArthur's complicated strategy, OpnPlan 9-50, in which he assured the Joint Chiefs of Staff there was "no indication of Soviet or Chinese intervention," assigned Walker's Eighth Army the task of seizing the North Korean capital, Pyongyang. Almond's X Corps was directed to make an amphibious landing at Wonsan on the east coast and drive due west, linking up with Walker, thereby trapping the North Koreans between them. The plan further stipulated that at some future date, both commands would attack north to a line approximately fifty to one hundred miles south of the Manchurian border. O. P. Smith thought the plan was "really unrealistic because the central mountain chain was swarming with these North Koreans who were making their way north to reorganize and they had (all) their weapons with them."

The senior leadership of the division not only lacked confidence in the plan, but also with the corps commander. Almond was seen as a vain, overly aggressive officer, who let his ambitions overrule his judgment. O. P. Smith saw him as, "egotistical. He was a MacArthur man, and anything said, nothing could change it. MacArthur was God." Almond's aggressiveness would have serious consequences for X Corps in the drive north during the dead of a Korean winter. Smith was also very concerned "over the lack of realism in the plans of the corps and the tendency of the corps to ignore the enemy capabilities when a rapid advance was desired. I found in my dealings with the army, particularly with the X Corps, that the mood was either one of extreme optimism or of extreme pessimism. There did not seem to be any middle ground."

Wonsan
Ray Davis
"After the Inchon-Seoul-Uijongbu Campaign, we boarded Japanese LSTs in Inchon Harbor and sailed around to the east coast, where we steamed back and forth for five days while the navy cleared the approaches." The amphibious assault was quickly termed *Operation Yo-Yo*. The invasion fleet steamed back and forth while the navy cleared the estimated two thousand mines in the harbor and sea approaches. In the interim, South Korean

troops captured the city after a hard-fought battle. To add insult to injury, Bob Hope waited for the Marines on the beach, much to Davis' chagrin. "When we finally got ashore, landing in World War II–type assault waves in the event the enemy was still in the area, we were greeted by big signs inviting us to the Bob Hope show. He never let me forget that he was ashore when we landed."

A new radio operator, Corporal Roy Pearl, was assigned to Davis when he got ashore. Pearl, a reservist, was a World War II veteran, who left a wife and two small children at home in Duluth, Minnesota. His first impression of Davis did not inspire confidence. He was "an ordinary-looking man of average height who looked as though he would be comfortable in bib overalls. He was from Georgia and soft-spoken. No gruff, no bluff. Never talked down to you. Made you feel comfortable in his presence."

Eddie Craig

The Allied drive north was going so well; there was almost an end to the war atmosphere. *The Stars and Stripes*, an army-air force newspaper, quoted MacArthur as saying, "This war is definitely coming to an end shortly." Signs appeared throughout the area, "Drive carefully—the Marine you hit might be your relief." In fact, the division received a directive stating that when the war was over, the entire outfit, minus one regiment, would immediately return to the States. However, in the meantime, there were still armed North Korean troops in the area. "Shortly after our arrival," Craig related, "there were guerrilla activities to the south and west of us and it was necessary to send a battalion of the 1st Marines to Kojo and Majon-ni."

Majon-ni: Ambush Alley
Bob Barrow

Colonel Puller pulled Alpha Company out of the perimeter at Wonsan and assigned it to escort a resupply convoy to Majon-ni, twenty-eight miles away. The battalion defending this road junction was having a rough go of it because the North Koreans were ambushing the road. Marines had nicknamed it "Ambush Alley," because three attempts had failed to break through and each had been forced to turn back with heavy casualties. The defenders were now desperately short of food and ammunition. They were also burdened with hundreds of prisoners, whom they had caught attempting to hide among the hundreds of refugees flooding the area. The narrow, two-lane, mostly gravel track, was a perfect location for an ambush, as it twisted upward through hairpin curves and deep gorges to a mountain pass. Barrow thought, "It made no sense trying to block the North Koreans because they could simply go around," but he had his orders.

It was mid-afternoon before the convoy of forty-five trucks started out. As he expected, it ran into a very strong ambush, which could not be overcome. The steep terrain prohibited maneuver. Unwilling to lose men needlessly, Barrow attempted to bring in air strikes, but they were ineffective. By late afternoon, the attack stalled. It was obvious that the roadblock was not going to be taken before dark. They could see North Koreans working their way along the ridges to flank, so, reluctantly Barrow made a decision to return to Wonsan. By the sheerest of margins, and after much shouting, cursing, and hauling, the trucks were turned around safely on the narrow roadway. Enemy fire forced the convoy to drive without lights, until one carrying twenty men plunged over the side, down a thirty-foot embankment. Miraculously no one was killed, but sixteen were injured. Barrow decided enough was enough; it was better to drive with the lights on. Fortunately, they were able to complete the trip without further incident. The final tally for the day's fighting was eight wounded, sixteen injured, and five vehicles lost.

Upon reaching Wonsan, Barrow reported to the regimental commander. "No one would ever want to tell 'Chesty' Puller they were unsuccessful—but I had to do it." Puller's command post was located in the classroom of an abandoned schoolhouse. Barrow found him seated at the teacher's desk. "I stood in front of him, much like a recalcitrant child, or one who hasn't done what he was supposed to do, and said, 'Sir, I have failed you.' " It was an awful moment. Puller stared at him for a moment before responding, "No you haven't, Old Man," a term he used with someone he liked. "What do you need to get through?" A much-relieved Barrow responded, "More hours of daylight and a forward air controller."

Puller nodded, reached back and pulled a bottle of bourbon from a field desk. "Sit down," he said, "and have a drink." Barrow knew that Puller did not drink but believed there were occasions when a drink settled the nerves, and, obviously, he considered this was one of those times. "It was the last thing I wanted to do, but I couldn't refuse Chesty Puller, so I had a sip with him."

Barrow employed a new tactic the next day that was unusual but highly successful. He believed the North Koreans did not man the roadblocks until they heard vehicles, so Barrow dismounted a platoon and had them walk a thousand yards or more ahead of the convoy. The tactic worked to perfection. The lead platoon surprised a large force of North Koreans relaxing on the hillside, away from their weapons. The Marines immediately opened fire, killing and wounding a large number of the enemy, which allowed the convoy to pass without a single casualty.

The next morning, Barrow was faced with the problem of escorting more than six hundred prisoners back to Wonsan, a number three times the size of his company. He loaded them into the open trucks and covered them with tarps to prevent them from being seen as they traversed Ambush Alley. On the return trip, a convoy coming in the opposite direction was ambushed and lost quite a few men. Barrow arrived just after the fight and was very upset because, "They knew the technique we used and the success it brought but they chose to ignore it." He loaded the other company's casualties and took them back to Wonsan. Barrow reported to Puller that he had successfully completed the mission.

Chosin Reservoir

The entire division bivouacked among the low-lying hills and rice paddies west of Wonsan. There were a few buildings for the command posts, but most of the men lived in tents scattered over a distance of ten to twelve miles. On November 1, the division received orders to send a regiment "to relieve a South Korean unit in contact with enemy troops on the road leading to the Chosin Reservoir." The South Koreans were fighting hard but were forced to give up ground. There were rumors their attackers were Chinese "volunteers." The 7th Marines were given the mission of relieving the ROKS and immediately proceeded by truck and train to Hamhung. Before leaving, however, the regimental commander, Col. Homer L. Litzenberg, talked to his officers and NCOs. "We can expect to meet Chinese Communist troops, and it is important that we win this first battle."

Ray Davis

The battalion caught up with the South Korean soldiers in a wooded area south of Sudong. Roy Pearl watched the passage of lines. "The ROKs came down the slopes grinning and waving at us and pointing north. 'Many Chinesu,' they said. They were moving more smartly than any South Korean outfit I saw, before or since." "Colonel Litzenberg put my battalion in the lead, since we had been in the rear the previous campaign," Davis recalled. His mission was to secure the Changjin Power Plant above Chinhung-ni. "I made a jeep recon. We took three jeeps with communications, interpreter, and riflemen riding shotgun, and visited a number of villages and the power plant. My Korean Army interpreter talked at length with villagers and they reported that Chinese soldiers were in the area. I became concerned enough to want to move along to complete my travels before dark."

Roy Pearl was standing the midnight radio watch when, "I was yanked out of my reverie by the god-awfulest sounds—bugles and shepherd's horns and whistles—then saw the glow of flares descending in a neat row across the river." All at once the companies on both flanks were attacked. He heard Davis shout, "Listen up, Marines! The enemy is hitting the companies on the other side of the river. We are expecting an attack on this side momentarily. Get your weapons and ammo squared away and stand by. Good shooting." Suddenly, a T-34 tank rumbled into Davis' CP—the outpost thought it was a bulldozer! "He turned on his big light," Davis recalled. An NCO thought it was a Marine vehicle and shouted, "Turn that fuckin' light off." The tank opened fire with its machine gun. "Instantly every rocket launcher in the battalion went after him," Davis remembered. "They fired, but sandbags saved it." However, a 75mm shell hit the turret and set the sandbags on fire. The tank, trailing flames and sparks, clanked around a bend in the road and disappeared.

Davis yelled to the men in the CP, "Dig in and prepare to repel boarders!" Just as he called out the warning, an illumination round outlined four enemy soldiers heading toward his position. Someone shouted "Fire!" Three of the soldiers fell dead, and the fourth raised his hands in surrender. One of Davis' officers, who had served in China, interrogated the prisoner and confirmed that all four were Chinese. They were later identified as being members of the 124th CCF Division. "We now knew that Chinese Communist Forces [CCF] were all the way down here from the Yalu!"

The initial Chinese attack caused heavy casualties in Company A. Sergeant James I. Poynter was critically wounded but continued to fight hand to hand with a bayonet. He saw three enemy machine gun teams closing in and attacked them with hand grenades. Poynter killed two of the crews and disabled the other weapon before falling, mortally wounded. Staff Sergeant Archie Van Winkle, Company B, on the other side of the perimeter, rallied his platoon and led it forward, despite a bullet-shattered arm and a grenade that exploded against his chest. Both Marines were awarded the Medal of Honor.

The Chinese continued to attack, and Davis soon found out that "In addition to hitting Baker Company across the river, a third force was coming along the railroad tracks beside the river." Dawn revealed them moving toward a railroad tunnel. Davis described the resultant action as a "real turkey shoot." "They were near where we had set up our six heavy water-cooled machine guns. Not one of them made it. The final count was over six hundred dead!" Pearl stood next to Davis. "These people were only a hundred yards away. . . . It was unreal . . . our machine guns opened up and others joined in, including me. I was just getting warmed up when I felt a hand on my shoulder. It was Davis. 'You've had your fun, Pearl; now get back to your radio.' "

The Chinese slipped past Davis' right flank and hit Major Webb Sawyer's 2nd Battalion, setting in motion an ugly brawl for possession of the high ground, which lasted all the next day. By afternoon of November 3, the only Chinese in the regimental area were dead—or about to be. Litzenberg had his victory over the Chinese—but at a high cost. More than two hundred Marine battle casualties were evacuated. O. P. Smith remarked, "Litzenberg went on up the road and had quite a fight. He had forty-three killed and a couple of hundred wounded, but they absolutely decimated the 124th CCF Division." A young Marine put it more tersely: "We kicked the shit out of those bastards!"

Eddie Craig

"The first prisoners—Chinese prisoners—captured by the 7th Marines were within eighteen miles of Hungnam, and it was a definite Chinese division, the 124th. . . . There was no doubt in the minds of the Marines that there was an organized group of Chinese troops to our front. If higher headquarters did not realize there was a Chinese build-up in this area, I do not know why."

Martin Russ in his book, *Breakout: The Chosin Reservoir Campaign*, wrote that Almond did not even mention Sudong in his command diary. Willoughby, MacArthur's intelligence chief, announced on November 3 that there were only 16,500 to 34,000 Chinese "volunteers" in country. Captain Donald France, 7th Marines intelligence officer, told Almond, "General, there's a shitload of Chinamen in those mountains."

Lem Shepherd

Shepherd insisted that MacArthur continually asked, "Have you seen or heard anything of the Russians or the North Chinese?" As the months went by—October into November—without any proof of Chinese intervention, nobody paid much attention to the rumors that they would enter the war. Shepherd was visiting Smith after they captured several Chinese. "When I returned to Tokyo, I told General MacArthur about them. I had a long talk with him on the subject, so I think he realized the danger. He just took the chance on their not entering the war."

Ray Davis

"The battalion led the regiment's approach march north to Chinhung-ni. The division Reconnaissance Company was ahead of us. Suddenly they radioed they were in contact with tanks! Initially they reported one, then quickly, too quickly, four more, hidden in the brush off the road." Early in the war, there were stories galore about army troops running away, but not among the Marines. Davis almost got trampled. "Not only did the Reconnaissance Company call in air, but rocket launcher Marines from my battalion and from the battalions behind me came roaring up shouting, 'Where are the tanks!' "

Davis raced forward with his driver. "I had 'armed' my jeep with two land mines. At a very narrow spot in the road over a culvert I posted my Marine runner with a land mine and gave him instructions to arm it and place it where the tank's track would hit it—if one came down the road." Davis went forward to look at the battle site and then returned to advise his runner of the best escape route. The youngster looked a little unnerved and responded in a quivering voice, "My God, colonel, I thought you wanted me to hold the mine under the track!" Davis was taken aback. "The poor kid thought he was supposed to perform some sort of Kamikaze mission and get blown up with the tank." So many wanted credit for knocking out the tanks that Davis had to arbitrate before blood was spilled—between Marines. "I assigned and reported the kills: one to air, one to recon, one each of the two rocket teams. I also messaged regiment that I did not like to go hand-to-hand with tanks and asked, 'Where are our tanks?' "

Out on a Limb

On November 15, Almond ordered the 1st Marine Division to attack north to Yudam-ni, then west to assist the Eighth Army in its drive to the Yalu. He envisioned that the Army's 7th Infantry Division would cover the division's right flank. On that day, the 1st Marine Division was spread out from hell to breakfast. Litzenberg's 7th Marines had just reached the medium-sized town of Hagaru-ri at the base of the Chosin Reservoir; Murray's 5th Marines were spread along the MSR from Koto-ri to Majon-dong, a distance of twenty miles as the crow flies; and Puller's 1st Marines were still fifty miles to the rear.

Eddie Craig

"Before he left our command post, General Almond stressed the need for speed. We had reached Hagaru at the south end of the reservoir, and now he wanted Litzenberg to head northwest to Yudam-ni, fourteen miles away, while Murray was to take the 5th Marines up the east shore. 'We've got to go barreling up that road.' General Smith's involuntary response was NO! However, Almond pretended not to hear it. After he departed, General Smith said, 'We're not going anywhere until I get this division together and the airfield built.' " Smith admitted that "What I was trying to do was slow down the advance and stall until I could pull . . . our outfit together." He was so alarmed that he wrote a letter, out of channels, to the commandant: "I believe a winter campaign in the mountains of North Korea is too much to ask of the American soldier or Marine, and I doubt the feasibility of supplying troops in this area during the winter . . ." General Matthew B. Ridgway, who took over the Eighth Army, had high praise for Smith's protective tactics: "As it turned out, these textbook precautions were all that enabled this magnificent fighting force to battle its way out of the entrapment in one of the most successful retrograde movements in American military history."

Attack of General Winter
Ray Davis

"Before we went up the mountain on our Marine Corps' birthday, November 10, it was quiet enough for me to go swimming in the nearby stream—even though the water was a trifle cold for a guy from Atlanta!" Ten days later the temperature dropped below zero. "On our second or third day up on the plateau at Koto-ri, the Siberian winds struck, lowering the temperatures suddenly to sixteen degrees below zero. Vehicles died, everything froze, troops were frostbitten. It took two days to recover ([with] added clothing, heaters, warming tents, anti-freeze) before we were prepared to move north again."

The arctic-like weather struck so suddenly that it sent men into shock, and they had to be led, zombie-like, to shelter. Roy Pearl thought he could handle cold weather. "I grew up in Minnesota, so I was used to temperatures like that, but the thing that shocked me was the suddenness of it." Equipment just died, particularly the battery-operated radios. Vehicles would not start. The drivers soon learned to run them all night long. A little too much oil or grease on a weapon caused malfunctions; carbines, machine guns, and BARs were particularly susceptible. Artillery recoil mechanisms froze, and the cannoneers had to push the tubes back in battery by hand.

The men quickly adapted, however. They found that hair tonic, which had alcohol in it, proved to be an effective lubricant. Gasoline, purloined from an unattended vehicle, could be poured over dirt or gravel, producing enough heat to warm a ration. Unused mortar propellant charges were used to produce a quick flame. A canteen nearly full of water mixed with a couple of small bottles of sickbay alcohol would keep it from freezing—and made the purified water much more palatable.

The division was hard hit by frostbite. Davis recalled, "Troopers had their noses turn white, big spots on them. It was bad. My staff and I moved around among the troops, looking for characteristic candle-white splotches that signaled frostbite; and when we spotted it coming on, we would hustle the man to the nearest fire." Cold-weather clothing arrived just in time: heavy, knee-length, pile-lined, hooded parkas; wool caps; winter-weight, cold-weather trousers; flannel shirts; long johns; and heavy wool socks. To protect their hands, they had wool gloves and leather and canvas mittens with an ingenious "trigger" finger sewed into them. The new clothing was welcome, but it was not designed for humping the hills. After a few minutes, the men were sweating and overheated, forcing them to strip off a layer or two.

The newly issued shoepacs caused feet to sweat, but would not allow air to circulate. When the men stopped moving, the sweat-soaked felt inserts of the boots froze, causing frostbite. They were also heavy and, despite their cleated soles, clumsy for climbing and slippery on ice. The parka hoods kept ears from freezing, but cut down on peripheral vision and made it difficult to hear.

Turkey Hill

Thanksgiving caught 1/7 on the road south of Yudam-ni. A very gracious Litzenberg told Davis he could hold in place for a whole twenty-four hours—and "by the way, I'll send up the fixings for T-day." The "fixings" in this case included frozen turkeys—as in rock-solid hard. Davis just scratched his head. "I just could not see how the cooks could pull it off, when it was so cold by now. Winds coming from Siberia had lowered the temperature to minus eighteen degrees Fahrenheit." However, the troops needed the morale boost—and where there is a will, there is a way. Davis had a powwow with his mess crew. "We designed an innovative solution: two tents were erected one over the other for double thickness; two stoves were fixed up inside and the frozen turkeys were stacked around the stoves in the sealed tents." After several hours, they were ready and the troops were rotated, platoon by platoon, through the chow line.

Back in the rear, Almond's holiday meal included all the appointments, including a cocktail bar, white tablecloths and napkins, china, silverware, and place cards. Up north, it was still cold enough to do damage to a brass monkey. One Marine remarked, "The gravy froze first, then the potatoes. Boy you ate fast. And all the time the snipers were shooting at us!" Despite the circumstances, Davis looked back at the meal with something akin to fondness. "This was to be our last hot meal for seventeen days, though we didn't know it at the time."

Lem Shepherd

Shepherd continued to send staff officers to visit the division. "Judging on past experience, much can be gained by sending out FMF [Fleet Marine Force] senior staff officers to observe operations at first hand in order that they may become familiar with your problems and in turn be better prepared to advise me in providing for your administrative and logistic support. I trust that visitors from my staff do not cause you too great an inconvenience and take this opportunity to express my thanks to you for looking after them so well." Shepherd also wanted Smith to keep him informed. "I know you are extremely busy with your many problems. I would appreciate, however, your dropping me a personal note from time to time to keep me informed of matters which you are unable to include in official dispatches, especially in regard to anything my Headquarters can do to support the Division." In short, Shepherd wanted to maintain a Marine "back channel" communication link with Smith to run interference if Almond misused the division.

Eddie Craig

Craig was not happy about Almond's orders to move north. "I was very jittery about the situation up there. When I spoke to General Smith about it, all he said was, 'It's what the army wants.' The whole setup looked bad to me."

On the 26th Craig received a Red Cross message, "Father not expected to live . . ." O. P. Smith sent a "dispatch to General Shepherd at Pearl Harbor and said unless I [Smith] receive an answer within twelve hours I am going to grant Craig leave to go home." Both officers were aware that Craig was very close to his father, a well-known retired army doctor. They were also aware that in World War II, Craig's corps commander had refused him leave to attend his dying wife. Smith, hearing nothing, granted his assistant ten days' emergency leave, starting on the 27th.

Crisis at Yudam-ni

X Corps ordered the division to advance along the road from Yudam-ni, west to Mupyong-ni, cut the railroad, and attack north to the Manchurian border. 1st Marine Division Operation Order 23-50 ordered Litzenberg's 7th Marines to seize and occupy Yudam-ni. Ray Davis' 1st Battalion took the lead, advancing along the desolate road, past booby-trapped, unmanned roadblocks. Resistance was light, only the occasional squad of enemy soldiers, who were easily brushed aside. The battalion reached its objective on the 25th and took up positions on the high ground overlooking the forlorn hamlet of Yudam-ni. Major Thomas Tighe, the operations officer, thought one of the huts looked occupied. He had an interpreter order everyone out under threat that the hut was going to be burned down. Three Chinese soldiers timidly emerged with their hands over their heads. Under interrogation, the three freely admitted to being riflemen in the 60th Chinese Division. They also volunteered that two other divisions were in the area. The information was passed up the line. Lieutenant Colonel Frederick Dowsett, 7th Marines executive officer, said, "All this was very interesting, but we doubted that ordinary private soldiers could be privy to such high-level information, so we didn't put much faith in what they told us. . . ."

Ray Davis

Early on the 26th, O. P. Smith dropped in to talk with Litzenberg—and drop he did. His helicopter tried to hover in the thin mountain air; instead, it dropped like a stone for the last ten feet. Davis saw the "crash" and ran over. Smith emerged, nodded, and asked courteously where the regimental CP was. "Right over there, general." Davis pointed and asked, "Are you all right?" "Fine," Smith nonchalantly replied, and strode off. Late in the afternoon, the vanguard of the 5th Marines reached Yudam-ni. Two companies of 2/7, Dog and Easy, also arrived and were immediately attached to 1/7, giving Davis five companies. The arrival of the other two battalions the next day brought Marine strength to five infantry and three artillery battalions—a little more than eight thousand men and forty-eight artillery pieces. Concealed in the mountains around the Marine positions were eighty thousand to ninety thousand Chinese infantrymen. First Lieutenant Joseph Owen recalled, "Yudam-ni, that's where the shit hit the fan."

Before dawn on the 27th, Davis sent a patrol from Baker Company to search the hills to the south and southwest. The other two companies were held in reserve. The men of Baker were glad to be moving, after suffering through an impossibly cold night. Temperatures bottomed out at twenty-five degrees below zero around midnight. Marines on the perimeter rotated through warming tents, which gave them an opportunity to thaw out and get something hot to drink, but it was still damn cold! One officer commented, "It was a clear, starlit night, like a Christmas-card scene with the mountains and the evergreens and the snow. But that wind was a killer."

By early afternoon, the weary Baker Company patrol was climbing one of the many ridges in the area. The point spotted enemy soldiers on the ridgeline ahead. As they continued to climb, other groups appeared. Suddenly, heavy firing broke out from all directions, and Marines began to fall. Davis learned of the ambush over the radio net. "Captain Wilcox, commander of Baker Company . . . was shot in the mouth while talking to me on the radio! I ordered Baker Company to break contact." He received permission to lead Charlie Company to the rescue. The patrol was able to break contact under cover of darkness and reached the road just as the relief force arrived. Davis "fired mortar illumination rounds to mark the way . . . and used truck lights to guide them into our position." The wounded were loaded in empty trucks and sent to Hagaru for treatment. It was the last convoy to get through before the Chinese cut the road. Litzenberg ordered Davis to leave Charlie Company on Turkey Hill, named for the turkey bones that littered the ground, to guard the road.

Meanwhile, Dog and Easy Companies in the hills above Yudam-ni were fighting for their lives. Captain Walter Phillips' Easy Company reported that it was barely holding on. "We've taken too many casualties. We're holding, but we can sure use some help." Davis recalled, "They came under heavy attack by waves of Chinese. Their situation turned desperate soon after dark. Communications were difficult; I was not fully aware of their situation or precise deployment." Roy Pearl remembered, "It looked like the enemy was breaking through between the two hills to the north, and the battalion command post was in danger. Colonel Davis ordered [everyone] into a makeshift defense line around the headquarters tents."

Davis stayed in the tent, ignoring the danger. Pearl stayed with him. "He [Davis] was very busy assessing the overall situation as reports came in by radio, phone, and runner. The only time he raised his voice in all the weeks I served with him was when Captain Hull reported by radio that Dog

Company was no longer on the hill. The colonel's voice got loud: he told Captain Hull to get his people together and retake that hill and stay up there!" Davis recalled, "I don't hesitate to say I was tormented for hours by the situation: Easy Company barely holding onto [Hill] 1282, Dog Company driven off 1240 . . . Only one of my companies . . . was in anything other than an emergency situation." Captain Hull gathered the remnants of his company. "Okay, let's go get the bastards." At dawn reinforcements arrived to find sixteen survivors on top of the hill. One of them asked a wounded rifleman where the company was. "This here's it," he croakily replied. "This here's Dog Company, 7th Marines."

Roy Pearl monitored a radio in the backseat of a jeep with Davis at the wheel. "I kept picking up this faint transmission. . . . I thought I could hear gunfire in the background and someone shouting." He asked Davis to stop the jeep and turn off the motor. "I finally determined that the signal was from the Charlie Company radio operator. He said Charlie was surrounded and needed help." Davis learned that "With darkness came many, many Chinese Communist soldiers. Apparently our troops climbing from the main supply route up onto Turkey Hill in the darkness met Chinese coming down the hill." Pearl handed Davis the handset. "I could hear the relief in the man's voice when he realized he was talking to his battalion commander." Davis recalled, "I don't recall exactly how the conversation went . . . but I got across the basic message: Hang on! We're on the way."

"It didn't take us long to get saddled up," Davis remembered. "I told the two company commanders . . . to strike off down the road very fast. . . . I sent Able Company up the slope, keeping Baker below." Tom Tighe worried about the way Davis exposed himself. "From the ditch beside the road I suggested that the colonel take cover. Davis smiled and explained that he could better coordinate the tactical moves from the road, where he could see the situation as it unfolded. It may have been foolhardy of him, but the men of 1/7 were glad to have the battalion commander up front like that, sharing the danger and risk." The coordinated attack worked, and the enemy was caught in a crossfire. Pearl saw "the Chinese break up into small bands, running every which way."

Small arms fire peppered the road around Davis. "A jeep driver ran up to me and said, 'Colonel, won't you at least get down behind the jeep?' It was bothering him so much that I decided to do as he requested, and I continued my radio conversation crouched next to one of the rear wheels." Charlie Company was finally extracted and the force pulled back to Yudam-ni. Davis was dejected. "I've always thought a better job could have been done supporting those Marines out there."

While Davis struggled to hold the vital hill positions, the Chinese hurled its infantry against the Marine positions on the high ground, threatening to engulf the entire perimeter. The battlefield echoed with the sounds of whistles, bugles, and weird oriental chants as the enemy advanced. The Marines had their backs to the wall; the Chinese were determined to chop them up. A political commissar wrote, "Kill these Marines as you would snakes in your homes!" The two regiments held, but the furious two-day assault cost them more than 1,200 casualties. O. P. Smith noted that, for the 5th and 7th Marines, "The only feasible thing to do was to pool their resources. The two regimental commanders drew up a joint plan . . . which was flown to me by helicopter and which I approved." Smith added that "an ADC (Craig) would have come in handy at this point." The 7th Marines were to lead out from Yudam-ni to Hagaru-ri, while the 5th Marines covered the rear.

Bowser told his assistant to start planning. "My God," he exclaimed. "It never occurred to me that the Marine Corps would be involved in a retrograde movement." As the plan evolved, someone brought up the word *retreat*. Smith responded, "Well, really, in the tactical situation in which we find ourselves, having to fight forward . . . this is really not a retreat, because in every case we must attack." At a news conference the next day, a reporter asked, "What do you think of this, because the Marine Corps is retreating?" Smith bristled and replied, "Retreat hell, we are simply attacking in another direction."

On the 30th, Almond flew in to talk with Smith. He authorized the destruction of the division's equipment and supplies. Smith replied, "I would have to fight my way back and could not afford to discard equipment. . . . I intended to bring out the bulk of my equipment." The vehicle train—trucks, jeeps, and artillery prime movers—moved within this defensive bubble, with the wounded, extra ammunition, and supplies. The road back led through a high mountain pass that was being held open by one valiant Marine company.

Fox Hill

Captain William E. Barber's Fox Company, 7th Marines, held the vital four-thousand-foot Toktong Pass, which dominated the division's main supply and withdrawal route from Koto-ri to Yudam-ni. At 4:30 a.m. on the 27th, an estimated one company of Chinese infantrymen overran the center platoon, killing or wounding twenty-four of its thirty-five Marines; three others were missing. The fighting quickly spread until the entire perimeter was under attack. At daybreak, the Chinese broke off the attack, leaving more than 450 dead on the battlefield. Hundreds of grotesque shapes covered the ground, many within feet of the Marine positions. The battered Fox Company survivors crawled through the cordite-stained snow into the killing zone to retrieve frozen Chinese bodies, stacking them in gruesome layers like sandbags around their foxholes.

Isolated and surrounded by overwhelming force, Fox Company began a heroic five-day ordeal by fire. Four attempts were made to reach them, but each failed under withering Chinese fire. The company was in desperate shape, numbed by days and nights of heavy combat and terrible cold, no sleep, little if any food, and heavy casualties.

Toktong Ridge Runners
Ray Davis

"It was midday when Litz sent for me. He had just moved his command post south of Yudam-ni close to me. He was most concerned about Fox Company. 'Nothing works,' he said, referring to four prior efforts to get them out. 'You have got to get to them. Come back here in twenty minutes with a plan!' " Davis had been over the road and around the area enough to know that a road approach was a nonstarter. The Chinese had established roadblocks covered by fire from positions along the ridges. Instead, he planned a bold, night cross-country march over the ridges to the high ground overlooking Fox Company's position. "I went back to Litzenberg and briefed him on my plan."

Lieutenant Colonel Fox Parry, CO of the 3rd Battalion, 11th Marines, happened to be in Litzenberg's small CP tent when Davis presented his plan. "The regimental commander was sitting on his cot, the battalion commander on the ground, holding a map. My principal recollection of this meeting is of Ray's cool determination and his matter-of-factness. Ray was as self-possessed as if he were about to set out on an evening stroll. Neither man raised his voice nor did a hint of passion insinuate itself into the tiny command tent. They were two men going about their business. Litzenberg was taking a terrific gamble. He was sending Davis off into the frigid gloom away from the main body . . . the chances of a mishap were everywhere. Davis' map was primitive. Maintaining companies in close contact and headed toward the objective through snow, ice, darkness, and treacherous mountain slopes would require a heroic effort. If he got in trouble, he was on his own. With an everyday farewell and a shyly confident smile, Ray got up and headed quietly down the hill. . . ." Davis recalled that Litzenberg, with characteristic bluntness, growled, "Plan approved, go!"

Davis called his company commanders together for a briefing. He took a stick and drew the plan of attack in the snow, pointing out the three hill masses. "Surprise will be our essential weapon," he said. "Marines don't ordinarily attack at night, so the Chinese won't be expecting us. We'll move out in single file, along an azimuth of one hundred and twenty degrees. Every three minutes a star shell will burst along the azimuth to guide us." He ordered all wounded and disabled to stay behind with the column on the road. Gun crews were doubled up. He left half the heavy machine guns and mortars behind. Extra ammunition was piled on stretchers and passed out to individual riflemen to carry in the big pockets of their parkas. The men were free to choose their own rations. Most selected canned fruit, crackers, and candy that would not freeze and could be eaten quickly.

With the battalion ready to go, Davis "got in touch with Litzenberg and found him in an impatient mood. He said we had to go *now*. He pointed out that it was so cold, and getting colder, that if we let our men sit around much longer they'd freeze to death." Litzenberg assigned How Company to clear a path for 1/7 through the Chinese perimeter. Their attack bogged down and Davis was forced to deploy two of his companies before breaking through to the jump-off point. As they reorganized in the dark, a freezing wind struck the column. Davis estimated that "In the wind on our mountain top it could have been seventy-five degrees below zero, with the wind

chill! We would freeze if we did not move. So, I called the company commanders together and told them, 'We're going now—we're just going.' "
Roy Pearl was ready: "We had perfect confidence in Colonel Davis."

Davis turned to Lieutenant Chew-Een Lee, Baker Company platoon
commander, and ordered, "Move out smartly." At the same time, he tried not
to think of the consequences. "I was trying not to worry about the weakness
of the battalion's radios or about how we were going to deal with casualties
on the steep icy slopes in the dark." The point moved out, followed by a single file of men that soon formed a column half a mile long—five hundred
men striking out into a desolate no-man's-land of ice and snow. Davis turned
to his radioman. "Come on, Pearl. We're going for a little stroll."

As the point moved out, it had to break a trail through the knee-deep
snow, slowing the column movement and forcing frequent rotation of
the exhausted men. The newly formed path froze and became ice-glazed. The
treacherous footing caused serious falls among the exhausted, heavily
loaded men and made it especially difficult to climb the snow-covered
slopes. Often they were forced to crawl upward on their hands and knees,
clutching bushes and roots to keep from sliding back down the icy trail.

The exertion caused them to start sweating. The many layers of
clothing trapped the moisture and kept it from evaporating, increasing the
risk of frostbite if they did not keep moving. Men stumbled into each
other or fell in the snow, creating gaps, which had to be closed. The column stopped and started, accordion-like, while unit leaders struggled to
keep the men moving.

Darkness and blowing snow hid Hill 1520, their first objective, 1,500
long yards away over the forbidding terrain. Lieutenant Lee, at the head of
the column, needed a direction to guide on. "At one point," Davis
described, "I got myself all hunched down in an abandoned Chinese hole
with my map, compass, and flashlight. Naturally, we didn't want the enemy
to know we were there, so before I turned on the flashlight I made sure I
was tucked in under a poncho. I then got oriented to the azimuth in rela-
tion to the next hill mass, turned off the light, and climbed out. The three
company commanders were standing there shivering, waiting for orders—
and suddenly I couldn't recall what I had done down in the hole!" He had
to repeat the process, this time with another officer. "Everybody had to

repeat back to you two or three times to be sure of what was supposed to happen. We were absolutely numb with the cold. It was hard to believe."

Despite the low-hanging clouds and swirling snow, Davis could see a few stars, one of which seemed to be in the general direction of their objective. He had Lee guide "toward that star" and, as an added precaution, arranged for artillery to fire star shells and white phosphorus rounds to mark the direction of march. However, as the point descended into a valley, it lost all sense of direction. Lee whispered to Lieutenant Joe Owen, "Haven't seen a star burst in ten minutes. Tell them back there that we can't go any faster unless we want to walk in circles—or over a cliff!" The column started drifting south, toward the road and the Chinese positions, which had been targeted for artillery bombardment.

Davis sensed the deviation, but could not raise Lee because the radios were frozen and useless. "I passed the word to stop the column to get everyone back in line. No response." He sent his runner forward and still nothing happened. In desperation, Davis and Pearl left the trail and beat a parallel track toward the head of the column. As he pressed forward, he found out why the men had not reacted to his orders—with parka hoods tied tightly around their ice-covered faces, they simply could not hear. "I made quite a racket thrashing through the snow," Davis recalled. "That drew complaints. 'Quiet! Knock off the noise!' I could hear Corporal Pearl behind me explaining that it was the battalion commander who was making all the commotion." At one point, he collided with Owen, who was horrified that he had knocked his battalion commander to the ground. Davis finally reached the head of the column, out of breath—"I could hardly breathe"—and exhausted by the effort. Lieutenant Bill Davis remembered, "We couldn't believe it. Here was Colonel Davis going up and down the column. I was in good shape, and I was dying. He was phenomenal."

Quickly recovering, Davis redirected the point just as the Chinese on the north slope of Hill 1520 opened fire. Baker and Charlie Companies deployed in two columns and began their assault, supported by 81mm mortars and four heavy machine guns. Exhausted Marines somehow found the strength to push forward. A cacophony of sound erupted, shattering the stillness with the roar of rifle and machine gun fire, shouted commands, oaths, and tension-releasing bellows of the attackers. Exploding grenades and mortar

rounds flashed in the darkness. Marines closed with the Chinese, who, surprised and overwhelmed by the violence of the assault, died in their holes,
except for a few who escaped or were taken prisoner.

A big NCO called Davis over to look in one of the foxholes. Reaching
down, he dragged a Chinese soldier out of the hole, totally frozen, except
for his eyes, which showed a flicker of movement. A half-dozen more were
found frozen to death, their winter uniforms unable to keep them alive in
the terrible cold. Davis saw that "The men of Baker Company had already
taken care of ones still hanging on."

As the combat-induced adrenaline rush wore off, the Leathernecks
started dropping like tenpins, completely spent after twenty exhausting
hours on the move. Davis called a halt for a few hours of sleep, but there was
no way to get warm. Private First Class Theodore B. Hudson recalled,
"When we stopped for our break, I got chilled pretty bad and started shaking all over. There was no way to get out of the wind." Davis had two-man
teams of officers and NCOs move along the perimeter, trying to keep one
man in four awake, which was difficult despite the occasional small arms
fire. After contacting regiment with a situation report, he settled down next
to a small rock formation for a short nap. "As I was getting settled, I saw one
Marine sitting on a rock twenty feet away. I sat up to tell him to get down,
and just then a bullet tore through my hood and skinned my forehead."
Major Thomas Tighe, the operations officer, watched as "Colonel Davis
turned over on his side and, in that nerveless way of his, fell asleep immediately." Later a chunk of shrapnel bounced off Davis' helmet. Others were
less fortunate, joining the wounded after being patched up and stuffed into
sleeping bags. Two hours later, at first light, the battalion moved out toward
its final objective, Hill 1653, about 1,500 yards north of Barber's position.

The advance proceeded without contact until it approached the hill.
The Chinese opened up with long-range small arms fire from all four directions. A group also threatened to overrun How Company and the
wounded, but it was beaten off, and the casualties were brought forward
for better protection. Charlie Company jumped off in the attack, seizing a
spur, which covered Able Company's drive on Hill 1653. As Davis
reached the spur, he saw Fox Company's perimeter. "There it was, plain as
day, about eight hundred yards off." Pearl called out to him greatly excited,

"Colonel, I've got Fox 6 [Barber] on the radio!" After trying to reach Fox Company for two days, they finally got through. Pearl said that Davis stood there smiling.

This first contact was an emotional experience for both officers, particularly Barber's offer to send a patrol out to lead his rescuers in. "Our radio got the F Company commander, Captain Bill Barber, and I got all choked up as he said, 'Well, I'll send a patrol to show you the way in.'" Tears came to his eyes as he thought about how this beat-up Marine company—118 casualties out of 220, six of seven officers wounded, and the company commander being carried on a stretcher—still maintained its esprit de corps.

Baker Company completed the link-up at 11:25 a.m. on December 2. Joe Owen was astonished at the sight. "The snowfield that led up to the embattled company's position was covered with hundreds of Chinese dead. Many of them seemed asleep under blankets of snow, but their bodies were frozen in spasms of pain. There were jumbles of corpses in padded green uniforms." One Fox Company Marine noted, "We saw a column of Marines straggling in toward us, but when they got here we realized that they were in just as bad shape as we were." "People," another of Barber's Marines shouted, "You look like shit!" A rescuer saw "Dead Chinese . . . piled up like sandbags to form barricades and gun pits. Dead Marines were neatly piled to one side of the aid tent, wounded on the other side." Pearl "stood around with a grin frozen on my face, until I saw a sight that wiped it off real quick: the stack of dead Marines between the aid tents." The effort was too much for two of Davis' Marines. O. P. Smith remembered, "When he [Davis] made that trip across country to relieve Toktong Pass, two of his men just couldn't take it. They were out of their heads and [we] had to put them in improvised straightjackets. The two died after reaching Fox Company's position."

Eddie Craig

The flight to San Antonio took five days, and during that time, Craig was out of touch and did not learn about the Chinese intervention. "It was a great shock to me when I did see them [newspaper headlines], 'Eighth Army in Retreat; Marines Still Trapped.' . . . The newspapers unanimously predicted the destruction of the 1st Marine Division." The commandant called Craig and ordered him back to Korea, immediately. O. P. Smith thought that "Almond, or somebody else in the army chain of command, wired the commandant to complain about only one general officer in the division." Craig left on the 7th—his father died two days later—and reported back to the division on December 11, too late to participate in the withdrawal. To his dying day, Craig deeply regretted being absent during the division's fight from the Chosin Reservoir.

In Tokyo, Snedeker got the word. "I received orders to get back to the division very quickly and I returned the day the orders were received. I'll always remember going down to see Admiral Arleigh Burke, who was then the operations officer for the commander Naval Forces in Japan, to tell him good-bye. I'd known him for some time then. Things were so serious then that he didn't say good-bye. He looked up and shook my hand, and the way he looked, it seemed like he was saying, 'Well, you old bastard, I'll never see you again.' "

Attack South
Ray Davis

Davis continued with the mission to clear the passes. "I formed two task forces. My operations officer, Major Tom Tighe, took one force to clear the southern passes and I took the other to clear the northern passes. At the same time, I moved my people toward Hagaru-ri to get a head start. I also had the troops build fires around the area to draw the Chinese out." The next morning, December 3, Davis led the remnants of 1/7 and the survivors of Fox Company off the hill and joined the head of the column on the road. Behind him stretched the regimental trains of the 5th and 7th Marines: hundreds of trucks, jeeps, artillery prime movers—an assortment of battered and shot-up vehicles loaded down with wounded and dead Marines. Hundreds of lightly wounded and frostbitten survivors shuffled alongside them, while the remnants of infantry battalions attacked along the ridges, keeping the Chinese at bay.

Davis was up front, with the lead platoon. Five hundred yards from the perimeter at Hagaru-ri, he stopped the column. "You people will now shape up and look sharp," he shouted. "We're going in like United States Marines!" Others picked up the order, even the lightly wounded and frostbitten men who could walk. They got into formation, rifles slung, heads up, backs straight, and stepped out. A former drill instructor called cadence, in the distinctive voice that all Marines come to know. Shoepacs pounded the road in unison as they marched forward. Davis led the way. "By the time we reached the checkpoint we were parade-ground Marines—stepping smartly . . . singing the 'Marines' Hymn.' " A doctor who witnessed the column's arrival exclaimed, "Look at those bastards! Those magnificent bastards!"

Lem Shepherd

Shepherd flew into Koto-ri for a firsthand appraisal of the withdrawal. The old war-horse decided to walk out with the troops and mentioned it to Smith. "I had known O. P. since the end of the First World War, and I thought he would welcome me as someone who could take some of the responsibility off his shoulders. Well, I was wrong. O. P. didn't like the idea at all. 'General,' he said, 'please don't march down with us. No one wants to see a lieutenant general of Marines killed or captured.' " A chastened Shepherd reconsidered and decided to honor Smith's request. As he was about to board the plane, a very angry Marguerite Higgins, the well-known reporter for the *New York Herald Tribune*, showed up under escort. She wanted to walk out but Smith nixed the idea, which did not sit well with her. "This is the biggest story of the war," she pleaded. "I don't want to miss it, general." Shepherd, an old friend, tried to calm her down, with little effect. She wrote a scathing article claiming O. P. was prejudiced—but the story was squelched.

Before the plane could take off, fighter-bombers had to work over surrounding hills to knock out Chinese machine gunners. Shepherd and Higgins were crammed together in the cockpit of the overloaded aircraft. As it flew over the Communist gunners, Shepherd playfully remarked to Higgins, "Won't it be scandalous if we crash in each other's arms." Marguerite's crass rejoinder would have done credit to a Marine gunnery sergeant.

Bob Barrow

Halfway down toward Funchilin Pass, the Chinese had blown a critical bridge built over four huge penstocks where the water from the Changjin Reservoir passed down toward a power plant near Dudong, cutting the road and making it impassable for vehicles. The bridge spanned a sheer drop that totally cut off any chance to get the vehicles out. It was decided to air-drop eight steel treadway sections to bridge the gap. However, the Chinese, in large numbers, were on top of Hill 1081 overlooking the cut. It was doubtful if the engineers could replace the bridge if the Chinese remained in control of the high ground.

Barrow's company was ordered into the attack. At midnight, they started up the base of the hill, a thousand meters of steep, ice-covered slopes. Barrow took the lead, sometimes on hands and knees, using rocks and bushes to pull himself upward. There was no room for maneuver; the company had to go straight into the enemy's defenses. Fortunately, a snow squall covered their movement until the very last, when it momentarily lifted, "just for a second," giving Barrow a chance to see the Chinese. "I brought in artillery and mortars by sound, first to the right, then north onto the target, and finally down, three sides of a box, and then I gave the signal to attack."

Up they scrambled, yelling and shouting. "The 2nd Platoon suffered heavy losses," Barrow recalled, "but they would not be denied! As they closed with the enemy, they began to yell as if on signal. There was a crescendo of shouting, grenade explosions, and rifle fire, [and] when it was over I don't think a single Chinese was left alive in those bunkers." The quick victory cost Barrow seven men killed in action and eleven wounded.

Darkness prevented the company from continuing the attack. Barrow consolidated the position, had his men dig in, and prepared for the expected enemy counterattack. Just after midnight, a Chinese platoon attacked. Barrow radioed the results of the contact. "We killed them all." The enemy was not the least of their problems. The temperature dropped like a rock, reaching twenty-five degrees below zero. Barrow struggled to keep his men from getting frostbite. "We found out later that those two days and nights were the coldest of the entire campaign. It's easy to say that a man should change his socks; but getting him to do so when the temperature is twenty-five degrees below is another matter. I found it necessary to stay with the individual until he actually took off his boots and changed his socks and put his boots back on."

Barrow gave his sleeping bag to his radio operator, "not as a noble gesture, but because I was damn sure that if I had no bag there would be no temptation to goof off. We needed all the alertness we could muster. I spent the remainder of the night moving from man to man and stamping my feet to keep the circulation going."

The next morning, it was bitterly cold, but clear. Barrow watched the semi-circle of enemy bunkers on a higher crest as air strikes and artillery pounded them. The preparation fires stopped and his Marines assaulted behind a shower of hand grenades. Barrow remarked, "We did better than the Chinese with grenades, not only because we were better throwers, but because we had a better grenade." As they neared the summit, one of his men shouted out, "Look, there's the rest of the division." Despite the heavy firing, Barrow looked to the northwest. "There, off in the distance, snaking along the road, I could see the long column of Marines. That really motivated us; what we were doing was absolutely critical." By noon, the shell-battered, blackened crest was theirs.

That night Barrow slept with his legs partially inside a caved-in bunker. His feet remained warm. The next morning, the company gunnery sergeant looked inside and saw a half-dead enemy soldier. "Introduce me to your friend," he asked his surprised commander. Bob Barrow's depleted rifle company stayed on the hill for two more days. As the last element of the division crossed over the bridge, it was blown. The sound of explosions was still echoing across the ridge when Alpha slithered down the hill to join the rear of the column. "We knew, all of us, that we had been involved in something historic."

In 1981 the first delegation of high-ranking Chinese generals visited the Pentagon. The Chairman of the Joint Chiefs of Staff hosted them at a luncheon and invited each of the service chiefs, along with several interpreters. Bob Barrow, then Commandant of the Marine Corps, remembered the lunch being pleasant but very formal. The Chief of Staff of the Air Force, in an effort to keep the converstion going, pointed to Barrow and mentioned he participated in the Chosin Reservoir Campaign. Barrow said, "There was a very audible inhalation of breath by all the Chinese generals." The whole mood changed, and the Chinese focused their attention on Barrow with respect, "Kind of like, 'you mean you were one of those fellows at the reservoir?' They knew what the Marines had accomplished."

Evacuation

The 1st Marine Division received word that they would be evacuated, rather than defend Hungnam. The Marines were not happy. They were prepared to defend the port city. In Shepherd's opinion, "The 1st Marine Division and the rest of X Corps could hold on to the port and airfield indefinitely." Puller was more pithy: "Why the hell they withdrew, I'll never know. . . . Not all the Chinese in hell could have run over us."

Eddie Craig

"Thousands and thousands of Koreans were endeavoring to board the ships at Hungnam and be evacuated before the arrival of the Communists. It became difficult for me to look these poor refugees in the eye. I was ashamed that we were leaving them behind." In a massive effort, the navy evacuated more than 91,000 refugees, 105,000 military, 17,500 vehicles, and thousands of tons of cargo.

Lem Shepherd

Shepherd released a statement for the press upon his arrival back in Hawaii, in which he dismissed their accounts that the Marines were trapped and had to retreat. "The opposing Chinese forces were so punished by the Marines as to constitute no further threat. . . . I believe that by no stretch of the imagination can this be described as a retreat, since a retreat presupposes a defeat—and the only defeat involved in this battle was the one suffered by the Chinese. Furthermore, when the Marines arrived in Hamhung, they had their arms, equipment, vehicles, and supplies with them. Their spirits were high and they were proud of their accomplishments."

EPILOGUE

MacArthur made periodic reports to the United Nations. In report number eleven, he gave an account of the Chosin Reservoir operation: "In this epic action the Marine Division and attached elements of the 7th Infantry Division marched and fought over 60 miles in bitter cold along a narrow, tortuous, ice covered road, against opposition of from six to eight Chinese Communist Force Divisions, which suffered staggering losses." Smith was complimentary to MacArthur but could not say the same for Almond's

leadership of X Corps. He was too much of a gentleman to disparage publicly his boss, but that did not hold true of Puller. A *Time* magazine
reporter asked Puller, "What is the most important lesson that the Marines
have learned in Korea so far?" Puller did not bat an eye: "Never serve
under X Corps!"

Between the Wars
Lem Shepherd

*After completing a two-year tour as commanding general, Fleet Marine Force,
Pacific, Shepherd was appointed as the twentieth Commandant of the Marine
Corps. He retired in 1956 after thirty-nine years of service.*

Eddie Craig

*On January 24, 1951, Craig was promoted to major general and ordered back to
Washington, D.C., as the director of the Marine Corps Reserve. He left Korea
feeling that "If those in Washington wanted to win the Korean War that sufficient
troops could have been sent out to win. I felt that my men had been let down. I
was even more certain of that when I later arrived in Washington for duty." Craig
was unhappy with the assignment. He had notebooks filled with recommendations
on tactics and equipment, but no one at headquarters seemed to be interested.
After Truman relieved MacArthur, Craig became embittered with the administration, "knowing that it did not intend to win but only reach a stalemate."*

*Finally, in disgust, Craig decided to retire. "I felt that justice was not being
done for the men in Korea, and that I did not want to be part of the Washington
scene." The commandant and the Secretary of the Navy tried to talk him out of
it, but to no avail, and accordingly, on June 1, 1951, after thirty-four years of
service, Major General Edward A. Craig retired. Jack Buck, his aide and
longtime friend, said Craig always regretted the decision because he loved the
Marine Corps. Because of his wartime service, Craig was advanced to the rank
of lieutenant general.*

*Eddie Craig lived a full, active life, maintaining a vigorous correspondence
with old friends and comrades. He was often cited as reference for official Marine
Corps publications about World War II and Korea. He passed away in 1994—
at the age of ninety-eight. Jack Buck took him to lunch on the last day of his life.
Upon returning home, Craig went into his room and sat on the bed. Buck followed.*

Craig turned to him and said, "I think the end is near. I'm just waiting for the bugler to sound Taps."

Ray Davis

Davis returned home in May 1951. He was assigned to Marine Corps Headquarters in G-3 (Plans, Operations, and Training). While on a trip to observe maneuvers in Turkey, he was notified that President Truman would present him the Medal of Honor. Excerpts from his citation read: "Always in the thick of fighting, Lieutenant Colonel Davis led his battalion over three successive ridges in the deep snow in continuous attacks against the enemy and, constantly inspiring and encouraging his men throughout the night. . . . By his superb leadership, outstanding courage and brilliant tactical ability, Lieutenant Colonel Davis was directly instrumental in saving the beleaguered rifle company from complete annihilation and enabled the two Marine regiments to escape possible destruction. . . ." He later served in various staff assignments at Marine Headquarters and Quantico. In 1963, he was promoted to brigadier general and assigned duty as assistant division commander, 3rd Marine Division, Okinawa. At the end of that tour of duty, he returned to headquarters, where he was promoted to major general. In the spring of 1968, he was ordered to the Republic of Vietnam.

Bob Barrow

After being stateside for only a short time, Barrow volunteered for a one-year special duty assignment with the Central Intelligence Agency, training Nationalist Chinese agents to infiltrate the mainland. Upon completion of the assignment, he returned to headquarters. While in Washington, he completed a bachelor of science degree from the University of Maryland. Subsequent assignments included an eighteen-month tour with 2nd Battalion, 6th Marines, Camp Lejeune; Marine officer instructor, NROTC Unit at Tulane University; editor and chief writer, Publications Group, Quantico; G-3, III Marine Expeditionary Force (III MEF), Okinawa; and G-3, Headquarters, Fleet Marine Force, Pacific, Hawaii. During this time, he also attended the Senior Course at Quantico and the National War College. In the summer of 1968, he received orders to the Republic of Vietnam.

PART FIVE

VIETNAM

CHAPTER TWENTY FIVE

PROVISIONAL CORPS VIETNAM (PCV)

The Old War Horse
Ray Davis

Ray Davis strode along the remote jungle pathway with his young aide-de-camp in tow. Suddenly, the older man stopped and peered intently into the thick green foliage. The aide, sensing danger, brought his rifle up and slipped off the safety. After a few minutes, Davis turned and said, "Dick, this reminds me of a command post I had on Guadalcanal." The aide mumbled, "Yes, sir," surreptitiously fingering the safety to the "on" position. "Christ," he thought to himself in awe, "I was only two years old at the time of Guadalcanal. This is the old man's third war!" (The author was that aide. "At the time, I was a twenty-five-year-old captain and had just recently been assigned as General Davis' aide-de-camp, after serving six months as a company commander and battalion assistant operations officer.)

Provisional Corps Vietnam (PCV)

In December 1967, a major North Vietnamese buildup began in and around the I Corps Tactical Zone, which comprised South Vietnam's five provinces that abutted the Ben Hai River, the boundary between the two Vietnams. Quang Tri and Thua Thien, the northernmost provinces, were bordered on the east by the South China Sea, on the west by Laos, and to the south by Quang Nam Province. Within its boundaries lived some five hundred thousand people, mostly in the coastal lowlands. West of this rich delta was the sparsely populated Piedmont, a strip of low rolling wasteland covered with scrub growth. Bordering on the west with Laos was a belt of mountainous terrain, roughly fifteen miles wide.

To counter this buildup, the Commander U.S. Military Assistance Command, Vietnam (COMUSMACV), General William C. Westmoreland, directed the establishment of a tactical corps headquarters, designated Provisional Corps Vietnam (PCV), in the Hue-Phu Bai area under the command of Lieutenant General William B. Rosson. This command was subordinate to the III Marine Amphibious Corps (MAF) located at Danang. In addition to the corps headquarters, the army sent two of its elite divisions north, the 1st Cavalry Division, which was often called the 1st Air Cav because it was an airmobile division, and the 101st Airborne Division. (The Screaming Eagles of the 101st were also a helicopter-heavy airmobile division.) The PCV headquarters was activated on January 29, 1968, just in time for the nationwide North Vietnamese Tet Offensive.

Ray Davis

Davis was serving as G-1, manpower coordinator, at Headquarters Marine Corps, when a request came in to provide a deputy for PCV. He immediately went to see Commandant Leonard F. Chapman, Jr. "I told General Chapman I had the ideal man for the job, Raymond G. Davis." Chapman informally floated his name through channels and found that the army, particularly Rosson, would be happy with Davis' selection. The approval was a mere formality because Davis and Rosson were close friends and had attended the National War College together. In fact, Davis thought highly of the army commander. "Bill was, in my view, the ideal type of commander who was really out with the troops, getting the most out of his forces all the time, day and night."

When Davis arrived in Vietnam, the complex command structure between III Marine Amphibious Force and Provisional Corps Vietnam was a source of contention. While PCV was subordinate to III MAF, the two army divisions that were assigned to the army corps were not directly under the command of the III MAF commanding general or the "control" of the III MAF staff, as were the 1st and 3rd Marine divisions. PCV had its own staff and was commanded by its own army three-star general.

Davis, however, was not concerned. "I did not see having a senior army command in the Marine zone as a vote of no confidence . . . vis-à-vis Marines at Danang [III MAF headquarters] . . . the army had put its best and most important forces forward . . . these were the best the army had, and they were in an all-helicopter posture . . . so I can see how the army would be ticklish about turning them over to Marines." General Davis' aide-de-camp, agreed saying, "The Army did not want direct Marine control of its elite units. And I can understand that, after seeing the caliber of some of the Marine commanders . . . until Gen. Davis arrived." Other senior Marine commanders were not convinced. Major General Rathvon McClure Tompkins, who commanded the 3rd Marine Division, had deeply resented the establishment of MACV (Forward), the predecessor to Provisional Corps Vietnam, the previous year. "I thought it was the most unpardonable thing that Saigon did. You don't move a MACV (Forward) up in a combat area unless you're very, very, very worried about the local commander. . . . It's tantamount to . . . the relief of a commander." The issue remained a serious bone of contention, even with Westmoreland's letter of instruction, which outlined specific responsibilities for the two headquarters. III MAF headquarters never completely trusted the arrangement.

The deployment of the 1st Cavalry Division seemed to justify the army's concern when the division commander complained that the Marines were not providing enough air support. General Westmoreland "blew his top" and moved to centralize control of air operations under a single manager, the Seventh Air Force—an anathema for the Marine Corps, which considered its aviation assets to be an integral part of its air-ground team. The fight intensified when General William W. Momyer, who commanded Seventh Air Force, called upon General Rosson to solicit support for the concept. Rosson was well aware of Marine sensitivity and, unknown to Momyer, invited Davis to sit in on the meeting. To say that the air force officer was disconcerted upon seeing to the Marine general would be an understatement.

The two army divisions, particularly the 1st Cavalry, were organized on the concept of high mobility, using helicopters as their primary mode of transportation. Infantry, artillery, aviation, and engineers were molded into a finely tuned, highly mobile force that added a new dimension to the war in the northern I Corps. Davis saw that "Out in the mountains in the western part of Vietnam there were no flat landing zones, so through necessity the army started knocking off the tops of the hills and hummocks and making places for helicopters." Infantry "air assaulted" into these hilltop positions and fanned out quickly to locate the North Vietnamese. After securing the immediate area, follow-on troops arrived to prepare command-and-control bunkers, artillery positions, and ammunition and supply dumps. Often a small bulldozer was heli-lifted in to assist with the preparations. The entire evolution was often completed in a matter of hours, depending on the scale of the operation.

The army was critical of how the Marines used helicopters, according to Davis. "We had our operations usually tied to selecting an ideal place for a helicopter to sit down as opposed to sitting down where you can best defeat the enemy. Being oriented towards helicopters already and watching this with Rosson, I learned the lesson of operating with helicopters on high ground as opposed to the way the Marines had been doing it in flat landing zones."

McNamara's Folly

Conversely, Davis found the Marines tied down to fixed installations. In the spring of 1968, the bulk of the 3rd Marine Division's 24,000 men were spread out in a series of strong points and base camps south of the Demilitarized Zone (DMZ) in Quang Tri Province. Organized into one artillery regiment, five infantry regiments, and supporting units, the division's scheme of maneuver was extremely limited because of a political decision to build a barrier of strong points, manned with Marine infantry. McNamara's Line, as it was called, spread across the top of South Vietnam. Davis believed this strong-point defense was faulty. "We weren't fighting guerrillas; we were fighting North Vietnamese Army (NVA) units. The strong points were too far apart to protect the line, and it was tying down our forces." The freedom to maneuver belonged to the NVA, who regularly ventured south across the DMZ to attack specific targets along the barrier and then withdrew north to rest and refit. The McNamara Line policy gave the initiative to the enemy by keeping Marine infantry inside fixed installations. Defense became the name of the game, and with it came a corresponding loss of offensive spirit.

In the "Leatherneck Square," a quadrangle bounded by Con Thien, Gio Linh, Cam Lo, and Dong Ha, it was commonplace for a single battalion to operate all alone because of the need to man the barrier positions. Given the mission to conduct sweep operations to locate and disrupt the infiltrating NVA, the Marine unit would often make contact with the superbly camouflaged and entrenched enemy whose strategy was to let the lead elements in close before initiating contact. The opening burst of fire was designed to cause casualties close to their position to nullify American artillery and close-air support. This placed the unit commander on the horns of a dilemma: either attack head on into prepared lanes of fire to rescue the wounded or withdraw to call in fire, leaving the casualties to fend for themselves. The outcome was often numbing: heavy casualties with little to show for the effort. No exploitation of the contact, no pursuit, no overwhelming concentration of force, just "soldier on," day after day, contact after contact, until relieved by another one of the strong-point battalions. Battalion after battalion rotated through this "meat grinder."

Morale within the infantry battalions dropped precipitously as casualties and frustration mounted. In 1967, five thousand Marines were killed or wounded, with almost one thousand in September alone, in and around the DMZ, including the Leatherneck Square area. One long-suffering unit, 1st Battalion, 9th Marines, which was intimately familiar with combat in the Leatherneck Square, earned the macabre nickname, "Walking Dead." Continued heavy fighting promised more of the same. In the first three months of the New Year, the 3rd Marine Division averaged 170 Marines killed and almost 1,200 wounded a month.

The 3rd Marine Division G-2 estimated that, at one time or another, elements of five NVA divisions operated against the Marines: the 324th, 325th, 308th, 307th, and 320th divisions, together with several separate battalions—some 20,000 men. A "front" headquarters was located north of the DMZ to control these forces. It maintained pressure on the Marine positions by direct infantry attack and by indirect fire from artillery, rockets, and mortars. All the major Marine bases in the central and eastern DMZ could be hit by NVA artillery located north of the Ben Hai River.

The NVA's 1968 Tet Offensive throughout South Vietnam marked a renewed effort by them to win the war. The U.S. news media were filled with accounts of the fighting, including the dramatic sapper attack on the U.S. Embassy in Saigon. In the north, the battles of Hue City and the Siege of Khe Sanh captured the public's attention.

Ray Davis

General Rosson furnished Davis a helicopter on a daily basis to visit PCV's area of operations area, which included the two northern provinces. Davis thought, "It was an ideal way to get oriented and attuned to the entire situation . . . in terms of evaluating the readiness and effectiveness of [our] forces." One PCV officer commented that senior officers of Rosson staff would "take turns having dinner with him [Davis] every night in the headquarters mess, giving him our ideas on mobile warfare, and during the day we flew around with him." During this period, he got to meet the principal commanders—General John J. Tolson of the "Cav," the 101st Airborne's General Olinto M. Barsanti, General Rathvon Tompkins of the 3rd Marine Division—and established not only a professional working rapport, but a personal, first-name-basis friendship. The author (General Davis' aide) noted a marked difference between the two spirited army generals and the "played out" Marine. Tolson and Barsoanti were vibrant, enthusiastic troop leaders. Tompkins, however, seemed worn out, with no enthusiasm. He had been at war too long.

From the very first, Davis started a routine that became standard throughout his tour in Vietnam—up at dawn, short situation brief, followed by helicopter visits to units in the field, returning late in the afternoon. In this manner, he was able to keep his finger on the tactical pulse of the units, as well as gain insight into the abilities of his commanders.

The army commanders encouraged him to attend briefings and participate in their high-mobility operations. On one momentous occasion, Davis watched the "Cavalry" air assault into the notorious A Shau Valley, a huge NVA supply area and base camp in the western mountains of Thua Thien Province. Davis flew over the valley in an Air Cavalry helicopter, a UH-1H Huey, piloted by the division commander. As the lead troop aircraft approached the landing zones, black puffs of 37mm antiaircraft fire darkened the sky. Several helicopters were hit, including a "flying crane," ferrying a sling-loaded bulldozer. The aircraft went straight in, hitting the ground with a huge explosion. There were no survivors. Tolson described the NVA's defenses as "very sophisticated and damn good antiaircraft forces . . . by far the hottest place we've ever gone into, and the most losses we've taken in a single day." The Cav lost thirty helicopters the first day of the operation. General Davis' aide remembers that "The sky was literally filled with helicopters, as wave after wave of "sky troopers" entered the valley, in a carefully choreographed air-assault. The general's [Tolson's] aircraft flew at ten thousand feet, which allowed us to see the entire operation. It was unlike anything I have ever seen—quite beyond the capability of the Marine Corps at that time." Despite the losses, the operation was termed a success because a large amount of weapons and ammunition was captured or destroyed, and the flow of supplies was disrupted for months. When Davis landed in the valley, the first thing he saw were "Sky Troopers" driving Russian trucks filled with NVA weapons. Several 37mm antiaircraft guns were captured and one was prominently displayed outside the division headquarters.

Davis was extremely interested in the high mobility operations of the Air Cavalry. He proposed "an article for the *Marine Corps Gazette*, highlighting the lessons learned from the army." Clearly, Davis wanted the article to be a guide for future Marine Corps operations, because Marine mobility in I Corps was severely limited. A prime example of this occurred in late April when the Marine Special Landing Force, Battalion Landing Team 2/4, engaged elements of the 320th NVA Division near Dai Do, about three thousand meters north of the 3rd Marine Division Headquarters at Dong Ha. Rosson and Davis happened to be on a routine visit. Tompkins gave them a brief on the division's activities. He barely mentioned Dai Do and did not seem particularly concerned about the action.

The two returned to Dong Ha the following day. As the helicopter approached the base, evidence of heavy fighting could be seen around Dai Do. Plumes of greyish smoke marked bomb and artillery strikes. Supply and medical evacuation helicopters busily scurried back and forth. They could see the occasional flash of sunlight reflecting off a diving aircraft. By now, it was obvious that 2/4 was in heavy combat with a major enemy force—and yet Tompkins did not reinforce them. In fact, the battalion fought alone until the NVA withdrew across the border to lick its wounds. (To this day, Brigadier General William Weise, who was the 2/4 battalion commander at

Dai Do, blames Tompkins for not properly supporting his battalion.) Davis said that Rosson "was disappointed with the Marines because they didn't apply all their forces to the situation. I could feel Rosson was concerned about the immobility of the Marines in Quang Tri Province . . . and I agreed with that. I tried to understand that when forced into a defensive situation involving the manning of strong points for so long a period, one can become less aggressive in the pursuit and destruction of the enemy." Rosson's aide, army Major Ken Leur, said privately, "His boss was so upset with Tompkins that if he hadn't been a Marine (a la Smith versus Smith of World War II controversy) he would have been relieved."

Shortly after Dai Do, a brigade of the 101st Airborne Division, in coordination with the 1st ARVN Division's Black Panther Company, trapped a North Vietnamese battalion near the small village of Phuoc Yen. Davis met General Barsanti at the brigade headquarters and, after a briefing, flew to the scene of the action. They were met by a very excited paratrooper commander, who escorted them around the battlefield. "Bomb and artillery craters covered almost every square foot of ground; bunkers were demolished; trench lines destroyed; and the ground littered with the remains of the 8th Battalion of the 90th NVA Regiment." The group had to jump a trench that ran through the center of the position. Fifteen dead NVA lay crumpled along its sides, the smell of death poisoning the air.

The official party, including the two generals, aides, and participants, numbered more than a dozen. As they approached a small stream, one of the Black Panthers leaned over the bank and fired his carbine, on full automatic. It caused quite a stir among the aides, who, among other jobs, provided protection for their bosses. A collection of pistols and various other weapons immediately materialized—pointing directly at the bemused trooper. The two old war-horses, Davis and Barsanti, did not bat an eyelash. Several excited Vietnamese jumped into the water, reached into the stream bank, and pulled two "newly shot" enemy soldiers from their camouflaged hideaway. One quivered and gagged as blood poured from his mouth in the final throes of death.

The operation was a classic encirclement operation, employing the rapid deployment of infantry by helicopter. Radio intercepts told of frantic

NVA radio traffic trying to contact this "lost" battalion. The paratroopers counted three hundred enemy dead and more than a hundred prisoners, up to that time the largest number captured during a single engagement.

Three days after the battle, General Rosson the PCV commander, visited the scene. One could smell the sickly odor of decay even as the helicopters flew over the site. Several decomposing bodies still lined the trench. The smell was overpowering, causing more than one onlooker to wretch. The corpses were so maggot-infested that they looked like they were crawling! Local Vietnamese were hired to bury the remains and cover them with lime.

A month after submitting the high-mobility article, Davis received a travel-worn package from the editor of the *Marine Corps Gazette*. It contained the article, along with a rejection slip. The accompanying note simply stated that "As the article did not contain anything new in the way of innovative tactics, the *Gazette* did not feel it was worthy of publication." The editor was savvy enough to include the comments of the editorial board, some of whom were senior aviators. One rather terse comment simply stated, "Nothing new here, the Corps has been doing this for years." Davis was upset. "I called Lieutenant General Bill Van Ryzin, chief of staff at Marine Corps Headquarters, who had just returned from Vietnam, and said, 'Bill, you know what's real; those guys don't.' It became the bible for the first few months of my oncoming 3rd Marine Division command."

The Dai Do, A Shau Valley, and Phuoc Yen operations firmly convinced Davis that Marines had to revise their tactics. "The way to get it done was to get out of those fixed positions and get mobility, to go and destroy the enemy on our terms—not sit there and absorb the shot and shell and frequent penetrations that he was able to mount." He went on to say that "The Marines 'invented' the troop-carrying helicopter, but we failed to exploit it. The army came along . . . and had greater mobility." Davis observed their high mobility for two months, particularly Operation Pegasus, the army's relief of Khe Sanh. "They applied forces directly responsive to the enemy's dispositions and forgot about real estate . . . forgetting about bases, going after the enemy in key areas . . . this punished the enemy most. Pegasus demonstrated the complete decisiveness of high-mobility operations."

Davis developed such a professional rapport with Rosson that he had total confidence that he would be supported. "Rosson . . . guaranteed me that when we'd go into tactical operations, I never needed to look back over my shoulder a single time and wonder if I was going to be supported. I knew that they were going to give me the helicopters I needed."

Thirty days later, Davis received orders to take command of the 3rd Marine Division at Dong Ha. He looked back at his time with PCV as extremely valuable in preparing to take over the division. "The assignment as Marine deputy in Provisional Corps Vietnam allowed me to do something I had never done before or since, and that was to move in prepared in the first hours to completely turn the command upside down."

CHAPTER TWENTY SIX

ASSUMPTION OF COMMAND: MEN, MACHINES, AND MANEUVER

Men

A t 11:00 on May 21, 1968, a small group of onlookers, mostly off-duty staff, and a small contingent of troops gathered around the division landing zone near the underground combat operations center at the Dong Ha combat base. Davis and Tompkins stood in front of a line of staff officers. The division colors were brought forward and presented to General Tompkins, who turned and presented them to General Davis; signifying the formal change of command. The two exchanged places—Davis on the right, the commander's position. The two officers spoke briefly, and then General Rosson stepped forward. He ended the ceremony by praising the abilities of both men and the 3rd Marine Division.

Immediately after the change of command, all key staff officers and regimental commanders were assembled in the division conference room. He started the meeting by waving a copy of his "yet to be published high-mobility article." He announced, "From this point on, the division would use it as a guide." He told them that no longer would infantry guard fixed installations. "I didn't ask or plead with them. I ordered: 'Before dark, these things will happen.' I laid out my scheme, what were later called my 'before dark dictates.' " After he departed, several of the more senior officers groused about these new precepts. "Who does he think he is?" "Wait until he finds out what it's really like." Davis' aide observed, "It did not take the staff long to understand that Ray Davis meant exactly what he said. He never raised his voice and was always courteous. I never heard him swear. However, his strength of character, powerful intellect, and tactical mastery communicated a determination that did not brook opposition.

The next day during the morning intelligence brief, a South Vietnamese Army (ARVN) officer pointed out the location of two major North Vietnamese units on the map that covered one wall of the general's plywood office. The officer started to move on, when Davis interrupted him with several questions. The ARVN officer was stunned; no one had ever asked a question during any of his previous briefs. His information was always treated perfunctorily. It took a moment for him to gather his thoughts before answering. He traced a line on the map east of Route 1, along the Cua Viet River toward Dong Ha. Davis listened intently and nodded, as if to say, now I have an opportunity to take on the division's old nemesis who escaped earlier in May at Dai Do. (Davis had a habit of indicting acceptance by nodding his head. He was such a quick study that often he had formulated a plan by the time of the acknowledgment.) "It [the 320th NVA Division] was gone just nine days and came back to welcome me the night I took command."

Davis turned to his aide and told him to order up his helicopter for a flight to the 2nd ARVN regimental headquarters. Twenty-five minutes later, he landed in their command post, completely unannounced. The compound exploded as frenzied Vietnamese rushed to greet the two-star visitor. Lieutenant Colonel Vu Van Giai, the regimental commander, met Davis, verified the intelligence report, and added more details. The larger unit comprised the command element of the 52nd Regiment, 320th North Vietnamese Division. Davis asked him "if he could support an operation against them with two battalions?" Giai nodded assent, and Davis departed for a flight to the 9th Marines' command post (CP).

(Colonel Giai was an impressive officer with a good command of English. He was a slender, wiry Vietnamese who had a well-documented record of bravery. One story had him leaping from a helicopter in the DMZ to grab weapons and equipment of NVA soldiers he had just killed. He was tough, combat hardened, and respected by Davis for his tactical and leadership skills. Giai was eventually promoted to major general and placed in command of the 1st ARVN Division. During the 1972 NVA offensive, his division was routed and defeated. Giai escaped to the United States upon the fall of South Vietnam.)

The 9th Marines "owned" the "Square" area, but never had more than a bob-tailed battalion to operate in the area, as the rest of the regiment guarded base camps. The regimental CP was located in a large sandbagged bunker less than a hundred meters from the 3rd Division CP. The division commander's aide remembers, "Davis and I walked over and entered the CP, unannounced, surprising hell out of the regimental commander. It was my job to ensure this did not happen. The colonel was not happy and, if looks could kill, I'd have been a dead man!" After greeting everyone, Davis immediately stepped to the tactical map that covered one wall. In typical fashion, he pointed to the suspected enemy location and quickly briefed the commander, Colonel Richard B. Smith, ordering him to coordinate an attack on the enemy force. The quizzical look on the officer's face spoke volumes—"Where the hell am I going to find an extra Marine?" Smith believed that his Marines were "sitting in defensive positions up there playing strictly defensive combat. Marines are always supposed to be in an assault over a beach, but this just isn't the name of the game out there."

The stunned look was quickly replaced with astonishment as Davis informed him that two battalions of ARVN soldiers would join his command within an hour, a Marine battalion was flying in from Khe Sanh, and another was force-marching to join him at that very moment. Four battalions encircled the unsuspecting NVA force and pounded it with "massive supporting arms. The 9th Marines Command Chronology noted, "On one occasion, the encircled enemy attempted to escape across the trace; however, artillery . . . gunships, fixed wing [aircraft], and tanks were brought to bear . . . with devastating effect." The two-day fight was bloody—twenty-three Marines killed in action and seventy-five wounded, while the NVA lost 225 dead and three prisoners. An entire battery of 12.7mm machine guns was also captured. Unfortunately, many of the NVA escaped because the Marines were slow in completing the encirclement. However, Davis was pleased with the results because the operation introduced the concept of generating overwhelming force by stripping the fixed positions of their infantry.

With the success of this first operation, Davis "directed that each of the four or five forward positions where we had a battalion holed up—or hiding out, as I called it—would now have only one company, and the other three rifle companies and the headquarters would deploy as a mobile force to seek out the enemy." He changed the division's tactical disposition to take the fight to the enemy. Lieutenant Colonel Max McQuown, Battalion Landing Team 3/1, stated that prior to Davis taking command there were "a myriad of static defensive positions of little tactical value. These positions and the rigid control the division exercised over every combat unit, fragmented battalions, reduced their combat capability, and severely limited their freedom of action. . . . The initiative passed to the NVA by default." Tompkins' defenders pointed out, however, that Khe Sanh had been the division's main focus of attention. In addition, he was hamstrung by the requirement to maintain and man McNamara Line.

However, the infantry had other problems. Soon after taking command, Davis stood on a ridge reviewing the next day's helicopter assault with a battalion commander. He pointed at the objective and said, "I want you to sweep that entire area with artillery before you land." The next day, the lead company was shot out of a hot zone. One helicopter, carrying a dozen Marines, crashed and tumbled down the slope of a hill, killing everyone onboard. The day after the aborted assault, Davis called his aide into his office and asked him to verify his orders [to use artillery] to the battalion commander. "I remember [General Davis] watching me intently as I recited the conversation. After finishing, he nodded and said, 'He killed my Marines.' I found out later that [Davis] relieved the battalion commander."

Davis believed that Vietnam "demanded superior quality commanders, even more than Korea and World War II. There were just too many near impossible things that had to be done. In other words, the very good to excellent officer can perform most things, but when you've got Marines' lives at stake, you need an . . . officer who can ensure that the task gets done with the least casualties. I guess I relieved as many battalion commanders as anybody . . . but it was never because of any flush, immediate judgment. It was because of performance over a period where they were getting too many Marines killed, not responding to the kind of operation that we wanted to conduct, or some other good, substantial reason."

One of the difficulties Davis encountered was the constant rotation of battalions among the regiments. This system broke down the traditional relationship between a battalion and its parent regiment. One commander described its shortfall. "The regiment had little interest in the logistics, personnel, supply, and maintenance fields of the battalion." On the other hand, "Battalions felt . . . they were commanded by strangers." Bob Barrow was equally concerned. "Every unit has a kind of personality of its own, often reflecting the personality of the commander, so you never got to know who did what best, or who you would give this mission to." Davis reorganized the division so that regiments controlled their own organic battalions. He felt this restructuring created "a greater awareness on the part of the staff officers in the regiment and their counterparts in the battalions about one another's capabilities and personalities. Unit integrity is essential for high-mobility mountain warfare—very complex, very fast-moving operations where you must depend on people knowing each other and being able to respond. It was crucial in the kind of war I wanted to fight."

Machines

A key decision in this reorganization was the closing of the Khe Sanh Combat Base. When the news leaked out, Davis was asked by several newsmen: "How can you abandon Khe Sanh after you paid so much for it?" He replied, "I can manage that whole area with a couple of mobile battalions better than it was managed with five fixed, in place, battalions." A news blackout was clamped over the closing to protect the lives of the remaining garrison. Major General Carl Hoffman's Task Force Hotel began an orderly withdrawal, until a correspondent broke the story. Hoffman blamed John S. Carroll of the *Baltimore Sun* for breaking the blackout. Along with Carroll's story, the *Baltimore Sun* published an aerial photo of the base, which showed the position of every trench, bunker, and installation. Immediately after the story was published, there was a dramatic increase in shelling, which cost the lives of several Marines. Although it was a small punishment considering the crime, Carroll's press credentials were suspended for six months.

The first part of the Davis strategy was implemented, but the second would have to wait for helicopter assets to arrive in country. "Fortunately, I arrived at a time when our resources were fully generated; the new model of the CH-46 helicopter was available, with greater power and lift capacity. Whereas it would pick up a platoon, the old 46 would hardly pick up a squad." Soon we were knocking the tops off little mountain peaks, putting our forces up there to move down against the enemy." Provisional Marine Air Group 39 (Prov MAG-39), comprising three squadrons of CH-46 helicopters, was formed to support the division from Quang Tri.

Davis placed increasing demands on MAG-39 to support his high-mobility concept. Much to Davis' chagrin, the group commander, a colonel, did not have the "horsepower" to change rigid operational procedures. On one particularly frustrating day, helicopters were actually in the air when they were called back to base because the pilots were about to exceed their daily flight hours. In another instance, Davis' scheduled daily helicopter failed to show. After repeated calls, a beat-up "hangar queen" arrived—no doors, oil leaks, unbriefed flight crew. An investigation discovered that the squadron commander, a lieutenant colonel, had taken the general's bird for his own personal use. It was the last time he made that mistake!

The MAG commander finally assigned Davis his own helicopter, a Huey UH-1E. Unfortunately, "it couldn't hack it" in the mountainous terrain of the division's area of operations. It lacked the lift capability of the army's H model, which Davis had used at PCV. An H model's increased power would have allowed him to get into "all of these out of the way places and these hilltops, and through all this weather." In the Marine bird he "got flopped down two or three times. . . . On one memorable occasion, the aircraft hit the ground at full power, tearing up shrubbery and creating a huge dust storm as it bounced over the landscape. When it finally stopped, Davis calmly unbuckled and exited the rocking aircraft—immediately followed by his frenzied aide.

Davis "went to war" with the III MAF and 1st Marine Air Wing (MAW) in an effort to gain more helicopters. This lack of support was particularly galling, because the 3rd Division "established all kinds of records, in terms of helo lift, support, and utilization rates—but something is wrong with the system. It has led us to too many bad days." Davis thought the allocation of helicopters "was so centralized that you have got to work out in detail the day before exactly what you want and schedule it. There's no way a ground commander can work out a precise plan for the next day's operation unless the enemy is going to hold still." He wanted a system that was "totally flexible and responsive to the ground commander's needs."

The system was partially fixed when Brigadier General Homer Dan Hill, assistant wing commander, came north to keep an eye on "that infantry ruffian." Hill turned out to be Davis' right-hand man—he was an aviator who made things happen—and damn the torpedoes! "Homer Dan," Davis said, "brought authority from the wing commander to not only offer professional advice to me, but to run our air operations. He gave us great flexibility." Hill commented that since the temporary assignment, he had participated in about seventy-five "highly successful helicopter heli-borne assaults in and around the DMZ." Hill attended all division briefings and went with Davis "on many of his helo rides to his units talking to our FACs [forward air controllers] and ALOs [air liaison officers] as well as regimental and battalion commanders."

Unfortunately, Hill "was recalled down below the pass, and the longer he stayed away, the more problems were generated." Davis was forced to deal with officers who were not in a position to make decisions without going to Danang for approval. He viewed this as unworkable. Lieutenant Colonel Richard E. Carey, a staff officer with the MAW, said that while Hill was with Davis the relationship "was superior, simply because he spoke for the wing and worked so closely with the division commander. [Hill] maintained a constant dialogue on both fixed-wing and helo support for the division. It was not uncommon for him to be on the phone at all hours of the day and night working closely with us on the details of the required support. After he left, work had to be conducted through an intermediary, which really slowed down the decision process. We also lost the pulse of the dynamic, fast-moving General Davis."

Another aviator chipped in, Brigadier General Earl E. Anderson: "Ray Davis has really been shot in the fanny with the army helicopter system; although I frankly believe that it's more the result of the large numbers of helicopters available to the army units, together with the fact that the ground officer has greater control over them than does the Marine commander." Davis fired back that this was exactly the problem. He complained that after the initial planning, the infantry commander played a secondary role. "The helicopter leader with his captive load of troops decides where, when, and even if the troops will land."

The allocation of helicopters was never satisfactorily resolved and remained a constant source of irritation. The bottom line, as Davis told III MAF, was, "If I don't get this helicopter support that I'm asking for . . . from you, I'm going to get it from the army. The devil take the hindmost!"

Maneuver

All through the summer and into the fall, North Vietnamese attacks slacked off. However, it did not "smell" right. The Division G-2 reported increased enemy activity along the Laotian border, thirty-five miles due west of Hue City, the same area they used to stage for the 1968 Tet Offensive. There was some concern the North Vietnamese were going to launch another offensive, "Tet '69." Signal intelligence picked up increased radio traffic on the recently reopened Route 922, which ran from Laos toward the A Shau Valley. Reconnaissance aircraft sighted scores of trucks, sometimes as many as a thousand per day. The road was protected by 12.7mm, 25mm, and 37mm antiaircraft guns. In mid-January, a 37mm gun shot down an A-6 Intruder, with the loss of its two-man crew. The NVA definitely did not want aircraft nosing around.

Davis knew something was up and "had to know what was going on in those mountains. The NVA logistics system was designed to support not only his main force . . . but also his local forces through propositioned supplies. He (NVA) would start down through Laos or the DMZ and establish concealed bases about every ten miles. Each of these bases was prepared with bunkers, tunnels, and hideaways, so that his porters could leave their supplies and dodge our air attacks." Most enemy porters relied on guides instead of maps, and used well-marked, high-speed trails. "We came to realize," noted Davis, "that if we were able to keep Marines on these trails, even from time to time, and were able to clean out his way stations periodically, that we could severely limit his activity."

With the enemy playing a deadly game of hide and seek, Davis ordered reconnaissance teams into the mountain fastness—up to twenty teams at one time—to locate enemy base camps. He was deadly serious about this. "Every day at our staff briefing, my officers knew I would ask the same question: 'How many patrols do we have on the ground?' If we had less than twenty, they would have until noon to get twenty on the ground." The division G-3, Colonel Alexander L. Michaux, said the mission of these teams was "not to call in fire or anything . . . just find them and tell us where they [the NVA] are." Davis emphasized that "Every indication of enemy activity from whatever means is explored by the insertion of reconnaissance teams . . . everywhere . . . on a continuing basis, a massive reconnaissance team effort is maintained."

The four-man teams were inserted by helicopter, with enough food and water for several days. Stealth was their primary defense against the heavily armed North Vietnamese. However, it did not always protect them. One team, call sign "Amanda," ran into trouble immediately upon insertion. They heard movement and almost simultaneously began receiving a heavy volume of small arms and automatic weapons fire. The team returned fire and called for help. An aerial observer came up on station and directed air strikes. By this time, the hard-pressed Marines were trading hand grenades with the NVA, who were only fifty feet away. Air strikes were brought in close; dirt clods from a bomb explosion hit one of the team members. The situation was desperate; Amanda was in danger of being overrun and needed immediate extraction.

A last air strike was called in to clear a path to a landing zone seventy-five meters away. The team made a mad dash, as four helicopter gunships swooped in, guns blazing, to cover the extraction bird. The CH-46 touched down, the team scrambled on board, and the helicopter leaped back into the air, taking hits as it passed out of range. Team Amanda was lucky; they survived the experience. Ground troops were inserted to exploit the contact, in accordance with Davis' precepts. "Where we found activity we went in and smashed them. . . ." However, the 3rd Marine Division "never launched an operation without acquiring clear definition of the targets and objectives through intelligence confirmed by recon patrols. High-mobility operations [were] too difficult and complex to come up empty or [end] in disaster."

Ray Davis

Within weeks of taking command, Davis sketched out his concept for a dedicated force to exploit intelligence reports. "Every time a needle flickered on a sensor, we put Marines in the field." Initially he identified 2/9 as his dedicated battalion. Lieutenant Colonel Frederic S. Knight related a conversation on the subject. "General Davis dropped in at my headquarters. 'Fred . . . I have decided to make you my swing battalion.' I asked him what a swing battalion was. He responded, 'Whenever anyone finds the enemy, I'm going to drop you right on top of them!' " Davis wanted the capability to commit up to a regiment, if necessary. After carefully screening the division's regiments, he settled on the 26th Marines, who were just pulling out of the abandoned base at Khe Sanh. Unfortunately, before he could officially designate them, they were transferred to the 1st Marine Division.

Davis received notice that III MAF intended to further reduce his forces. "It is obvious that a severe draw down on 3d Mar Div capability at this time will seriously limit my ability to maintain the present flexible, mobile posture which I feel is necessary if I am to continue the effective suppression of enemy activity in this area." Lieutenant General Richard G. Stilwell, Rosson's replacement, took up the issue with III MAF and, after some hard bargaining, got a commitment from them to maintain 3rd Marine Division at twelve battalions, nine Marine and three army. The III MAF acquiesced after PCV, now XXIV Corps, proposed a boundary shift, which decreased the area of operations of the 1st Marine Division. With that commitment, Davis selected the 9th Marine Regiment as his swing force, but he needed a commander who could lead them.

Davis recounted, "I received a roster of senior officers that were slated for duty in the next few months. I noted that Colonel Robert H. Barrow was being assigned to the 1st Marine Division. I resolved to have his orders changed to the 3rd Marine Division."

Bob Barrow

"In the spring of 1968 I was told I was going to the 1st Marine Division as the G-3. It was a little bit of a disappointment because I would have liked to have a command, but orders are orders, so I reconciled myself to the staff assignment. At the time, all colonels and above going to Vietnam had to stop off in Hawaii for briefings and to pay a call on the FMF PAC commander, Lieutenant General Henry Buse. I knew him well. He has a delightful sense of humor, likes to tease people, but I was not prepared for his sense of humor. He asked, 'Now, where you going?' and 'What are you going to do there?' I told him and he replied, much to my surprise. 'Well, you're not going. I just visited Ray Davis. He spoke of what he planned to do. . . . That is quite different from what his predecessors had been doing. He said, 'I need a swing regiment and you have a fellow coming out here that I want to command that regiment—and that's Bob Barrow,' so that's where you're going."

Ray Davis

"I wanted to bring back unit integrity. This whole business of rotating units in and out of fixed positions just served to disrupt the organization. . . . The regimental commander didn't know his own regiment at all . . . half their battalions belonged to them and the other half were somewhere else." By reducing the fixed positions to company-size units, Davis was able to generate a mobile force of several battalions and keep them together, along with their supporting units—artillery, engineers, and communications. He was convinced that "Unity integrity is essential for high-mobility mountain warfare—very complex, very fast-moving operations, where you must depend on people knowing each other. . . ." The 9th Marine Regiment, "Striking Ninth," was his swing force, and Bob Barrow was going to lead it.

CHAPTER TWENTY SEVEN

SWING FORCE

Welcome to Vietnam
Bob Barrow

Barrow flew into Danang aboard a military transport aircraft, after spending the night on Okinawa. He and the other passengers made their way to the large, metal-paneled III MAF transit facility to check in and arrange for transportation. Inside, bored clerks processed the new arrivals, stamping orders and issuing instructions. The metal building was hot as hell, particularly for the new men, who sweated completely through their starched, stateside utilities. Rivulets of sweat-laced starch coursed down overheated bodies, increasing their misery factor. A layer of fine dust covered the concrete deck, benches, countertops, and every flat surface. It stuck to sweat-soaked utilities and lightly caked faces and hands. Mouths felt gritty and lips dried out.

Dozens of Marines in faded jungle utilities and worn boots lounged around in studied idleness, watching the "new meat," while waiting for their "freedom bird" and the glorious flight stateside. Periodically, conversation stopped as fighter-bombers roared aloft at full power. The overpowering stench of JP-4 avgas wafted through the building, despite the almost total absence of any cooling breeze. Outside, the blinding sunlight was almost painful after the building's protective shade. A metal water buffalo close to the entrance offered tepid liquid that was almost unfit to drink. Welcome to Vietnam!

Two days later Barrow reached the 3rd Marine Division Headquarters (Forward) at Dong Ha and reported to the division commander, who "Immediately took me on an aerial reconnaissance all around the area." The tour gave Barrow an opportunity to see, first hand, what Davis had in store for the "Striking Ninth." Once Barrow was established with the regiment, this aerial tour became standard procedure for every new field-grade officer who reported to the division. Davis would drop the officer off at the 9th Marines CP, where Barrow would take him in tow for a little chat. If the officer passed muster, he stayed; if not, he was loaded back aboard a helo and assigned elsewhere.

Davis had great confidence in Barrow. He was the man for the job. Likewise, Barrow "knew Ray Davis. He was one of our great thinkers, a doer, a real hero, with a Medal of Honor, Navy Cross—a very distinguished record of service. He was also very aggressive" and wanted to "do things quickly." A day after Barrow arrived in Dong Ha, he took command of the 9th Marines. After a short, simple ceremony, he turned to the operations officer and said, "Saddle up the headquarters." The look on the officer's face was priceless. "Where to?" he asked incredulously. At that time, the regiment had almost a permanent base camp, with all the amenities of home. They had gotten comfortable or, as Barrow noted, "Even though they were good guys, they had lost touch with the men in the field. They were used to putting up antennas and staying in contact with subordinates—at some distance." Barrow responded, "We're going to C-2," an artillery position below the DMZ.

Some hours later, they finally squeezed aboard the trucks for the motor march to C-2. One of Barrow's friends observed the evolution: "My God, Bob, they look like Cox's Army!" The men and trucks were festooned with personal gear. Barrow replied, "After I move them three or four times, they'll get rid of that stuff." He also noted his boss watching. "Being the man that he was, Davis just smiled in his quiet, taciturn manner; he knew what the results would be." In the coming months, Barrow was true to his word. He displaced the command post fourteen times, getting the relocation down to a fine science. "I'd say, 'Let's move this afternoon.' We'd get a couple of helos and, in no time at all, we'd be gone." The regiment flew to the sound of the guns.

Dewey Canyon

As an independent regimental operation . . . it may be unparalleled.
—Lieutenant General Richard G. Stilwell, USA,
Commanding General, XXIV Corps, Vietnam

In early January 1969, Davis ordered a pre-emptive strike into the A Shau Valley: Operation Dewey Canyon. Barrow's Swing Force was given the mission to interdict the enemy's supply route and capture and destroy his equipment. "In five days we conceived, planned, and launched a regimental-sized force, totally dependent on helicopter resupply, in and around the A Shau Valley, thirty miles from the nearest friendly force." A Shau was one of the strongest enemy bases in South Vietnam. It was located only six miles from the Laotian border near the Ho Chi Minh Trail network, the major enemy supply route that provided access into the two northern provinces.

Hundreds of trucks convoyed supplies and equipment east, along Route 922, into the southern end of the valley, where it was stockpiled in camouflaged dumps. "No army fights without logistic support," Barrow declared. "The NVA laboriously and surreptitiously built-up its supplies in South Vietnam before its troops arrived. The [enemy's] first order of business was to move all the things of war; all their logistics forward from the sanctuaries of North Vietnam, just across the DMZ, or from Laos. We must do everything we can to find that stuff, wherever it exists, and obviously destroy it."

A Shau itself was a deep valley twenty-two miles long, sandwiched between two heavily forested mountain ranges. Thousands of North Vietnamese porters and support troops maintained the road network and supply caches. Battle-tested NVA of the 6th and 9th Regiment provided security. Three abandoned airstrips and the remnants of an old Special Forces camp—overrun in a savage battle—bore mute testimony to the enemy's fighting capabilities. Barrow knew they were tough opponents. "The enemy bore no resemblance to the little fellow with black pajamas; they were a really first-class army."

In the early morning hours of January 22, artillery and air strikes pounded the 9th Marines' first objective, a hill mass three kilometers inside the A Shau Valley. Immediately following the prep fires, two companies of the 2nd Battalion conducted a heliborne assault onto the hill. Teams of engineers closely followed and began clearing trees to form a landing zone for a 105mm artillery battery. It was not an easy task—trees three to four feet in diameter had to be cut down. Bulldozers were helilifted in to help clear the area, as well as dig gun pits, ammunition berms, and command bunkers. Within twenty-four hours, Fire Support Base (FSB) Razor was up and running and prepared to support the next helicopter assault. (Barrow recalled that FSB Razor was named after General Davis from a nickname given him in the early 1960s by Major General James M. Master, Sr., when both served on Okinawa: "The razor cuts to the root of the problems.")

Without incident, Fire Support Base Cunningham, a 1,100-meter-long razorback ridge in the center of the regiment's area of operations, was opened next. The two FSBs were mutually supporting—within artillery range of each other—so that if one was attacked, it could call on support from the other. The concept required that FSBs be established no more than 8,000 meters from each other in order to provide mutual support—plus an additional 3,000-meter overlap, the range of North Vietnamese mortars.

Soon, five artillery batteries were in position to support infantry patrols into the surrounding jungle. Almost immediately, a company discovered a four-strand telephone line that ran for miles through the jungle, from Laos to Quang Tri Province. It was strung from tree-mounted insulators under the jungle canopy, effectively concealing it from air observation. A special five-man army and Marine intelligence team tapped into the wire and monitored North Vietnamese transmissions.

Infantry patrols, operating under the protective artillery fans of the two FSBs, searched for signs of the enemy. Barrow described the effort. "Each battalion has four companies operating out of company operating bases, each separated from the other by about 2,000 to 3,000 meters. A company will spend, characteristically, two, three, or four days in one of these operating bases and conduct extensive patrolling by platoon or squads in all directions . . . so that after three or four days the area extending in a radius of a couple of thousand meters out from the operating base has been covered. The operating base represents a place of resupply and for a patrol that has been out perhaps for two days to rest for a day, preparatory for renewing its patrolling activities."

The patrols quickly ran into small groups of enemy soldiers. The deadly encounters were often at close range—a few meters in the dense foliage—and usually resulted in casualties on both sides. The enemy was trying to slow the Marine advance, so they could evacuate or conceal their supplies and facilities. It was not enough. One patrol discovered a complete field hospital, consisting of eight large wooden buildings capable of housing

150 patients. In addition, large quantities of Russianmade surgical instruments and medical supplies were captured.

Enemy resistance stiffened as the Swing Force advanced toward the southern end of the valley. North Vietnamese Army 122mm artillery shelled Cunningham from inside Laos, killing and wounding ten Marines and temporarily disabling a 155mm howitzer. Counterbattery fire proved ineffective because the Marine guns were outranged. The only solution was to use air. Barrow noted, "Counterbattery was a simple thing of always having an AO [aerial observer] up." Failing to knock out Cunningham by indirect fire, the NVA tried another tactic. In the early morning hours of February 16, elite sapper teams from the 812th Regiment attacked the fire support base.

Under cover of a thick blanket of fog and a heavy mortar barrage, three teams—fifty sappers—breached the defensive wire and fought their way inside the perimeter. Chaplain David Brock was startled awake. "During the early moments of the attack, an NVA soldier stuck his head into the tent . . . but fortunately did not throw a grenade inside. A grenade was thrown into a small bunker a few feet away, killing two men." An officer crawled out of his partially collapsed bunker, to face an enemy soldier. He leaped on the surprised North Vietnamese and bludgeoned him to death with a hand grenade. The company gunnery sergeant killed several sappers, in hand-to-hand combat, with his K-Bar fighting knife.

Dawn revealed a gruesome aftermath: dead sappers strewn amid shell-blasted bunkers and gun pits. The penetrating odor of cordite and smoke hung in the air. Another smell, a mixture of blood and decomposition, mingled with the stench, leaving a never-to-be-forgotten memory for the survivors. Casualties totaled thirty-seven North Vietnamese, four Marines killed in action, and forty-six wounded. Barrow praised the actions of the Marine defenders: "They'll [NVA] probably think twice from here on out before taking on another Marine headquarters group. These lads did a fantastic job. . . . They were 100 percent professional fighting men; good Marines all the way."

Bad weather accomplished what the NVA could not do: force Barrow to curtail operations. Heavy rains alternating with drizzle and dense fog grounded the helicopters. He ordered the infantry battalions to regroup near the two FSBs where there were supplies of food and ammunition.

However, one company had endured an extraordinarily grueling ordeal. Company G ran into a large enemy force and, in the ensuing firefight, lost five Marines killed and seventeen wounded. Without helicopter evacuation, they were forced to carry them for three days through almost impassable terrain. The company commander, Captain Daniel A. Hitzelberger, described the ground: "At this time the stretcher cases were moving up and down slopes in excess of seventy degrees. We had to use six, eight, and, at times, ten men to carry a stretcher and it would take us over thirty minutes to move one stretcher case over one bad area." At one point, they had to lower the stretchers on ropes down the face of a rock cliff.

Company G finally reached a flat area. Two CH-46 medical evacuation helicopters, in a heroic display of airmanship, flew through dense fog and enemy small arms fire to evacuate the company's wounded. A day later, their battalion commander watched the battered but unbroken company enter friendly lines. "They were smiling and laughing. Their clothes were torn, and in some cases completely off them, but they were ready for a fight." Barrow believed, "Well-trained, well-led men with character do what is expected, independent of orders, because they do not want to let their comrades down."

The weather cleared and the 9th Marines pressed the attack. Enemy resistance stiffened, desperate to keep the Marines from advancing on Route 922. In one action, Company C fought through an NVA position and discovered two Russianmade 122mm field guns and a five-ton, tracked prime mover. (General Davis couldn't find a legal way to ship one of the captured weapons back to Quantico, so he simply had it loaded aboard a Marine C-130 and directed a sergeant to make sure it arrived safely. The NCO successfully carried out his orders, and the weapon is on display at Quantico Marine Base.) First Lieutenant Wesley L. Fox's Company A continued the attack, seizing another truck and a large amount of artillery ammunition. Each day brought new discoveries, as Marines uncovered supply caches, weapons, and ammunition, often cleverly concealed in the bottom of bomb craters, caves, and jungle hideouts. The Swing Force was well on its way to completely interdicting the NVA's supply network in South Vietnam. The enemy, however boldly continued to exploit its road network across the border.

Ray Davis

The persistent shelling of Marine positions from Laos and continued heavy NVA traffic across the international border caused Davis to request a cross-border operation. "From the present position of the 9th Marines, a raid by a force of two battalions could be launched quickly and effectively to cut Road 922 and mov[e] rapidly back to the east, destroy[ing] artillery forces,and other forces and installations which threaten us." His request was denied. However, the rules of engagement permitted commanders to take "counteractions against VC/NVA forces in the exercise of self-defense and to defend their units against armed attacks with all means at their disposal."

Bob Barrow

Barrow echoed Davis' request. "During the day the AOs [aerial observers] were reporting fresh vehicle tracks, including tracked vehicle tracks on the road, and as our forces moved further south, we could hear vehicles on the road. This was a pretty unacceptable situation, and it cried out for some sort of action to put a stop to it." Captain David F. Winecoff's company watched an enemy convoy drive slowly down Route 992 on the Laotian side of the border. He called in several fire missions with unknown results. His troops wanted action. "The company was talking about let's get down on the road and do some ambushing. I don't think they really thought that they were going to let us go over into Laos."

Winecoff's heart went into his throat. His radio operator had just deciphered a priority message from Barrow: "Ambush Route 922 tonight!" "No way," he thought. "We're not ready" and immediately requested a twenty-four-hour delay. "No way," Barrow replied, "and by the way, be back in South Vietnam before 0630 tomorrow morning." Winecoff with two platoons—one stayed behind to provide security—climbed down the steep slopes to their ambush position. After a harrowing four-hour trek through thick jungle foliage, they halted while a two-man reconnaissance team scouted a good ambush site. As they waited, six trucks and a tracked vehicle mounting a spotlight passed by, shining its light on both sides of the road. At one point, it played over the lead elements of the company but did not spot them. The recon team returned and led the company into position. Winecoff put the two platoons on line, in a hasty linear ambush. Several enemy vehicles passed by before they were finally ready.

Bob Barrow

"I made a decision to ambush the road despite the rules of engagement (ROE) that prohibited the use of ground troops in Laos. I thought it was essential to protect the lives of my men and accomplish the mission." Winecoff's men were five hundred meters inside Laos, when Barrow alerted his nominal boss at Task Force Hotel—Davis was on R&R with his son, who was recovering from wounds—over an encrypted radio. "Where are they?" his superior exclaimed. "Are you crazy?" Then, more threateningly, "There were some of us who thought you had a future in the Marine Corps." Barrow would not back down. He took full responsibility for the decision—and waited for the axe to fall.

Ambush

An NVA soldier strode into the ambush site aimlessly firing his AK-47 into the underbrush. He did not hit anyone and was allowed to pass by. At 2:30 a.m., a line of trucks drove up and stopped, three of them in the kill zone. Fearing they would be discovered, Winecoff triggered a Claymore mine, which detonated with a huge blast, sending hundreds of deadly steel balls into the second truck—killing its three occupants. The company opened fire with a vengeance: "Everybody had been waiting a long time and the excitement was keen!" Winecoff ordered a cease-fire and then swept through the zone, checking it for prisoners and anything of intelligence value. They discovered eight bodies and three destroyed trucks. There were no Marine casualties. Winecoff radioed a brief status report and "proceeded in column right back in the same direction we came."

Bob Barrow

Every echelon in the chain of command seemed to be monitoring Winecoff's transmission. Regiment notified division, who in turn, notified III MAF and on up the chain of command. The next morning, Barrow sent a formal request "stating why we had done what we had done, reiterating the success achieved, and then my final paragraph made an urgent request for authority to maneuver into Laos. . . ." Faced with a fait accompli, MACV acquiesced, letting Barrow off the hook. Davis found out about the ambush while on R&R. He responded "Great!" when asked what he thought of it. Barrow "had no concerns. I had great confidence in him [Davis] and definitely knew he would approve."

Uncommon Valor

Lieutenant Fox unknowingly triggered the last major firefight of Dewey Canyon, when he okayed a working party to get water from a nearby stream. The twenty-man water detail started filling their canteens. Suddenly, they came under heavy mortar and machine gun fire. Fox ordered his first platoon to cover their withdrawal. It immediately ran into a buzz saw and started taking heavy casualties from a reinforced NVA company in a well-prepared, well-camouflaged, and heavily fortified bunker complex. The triple-canopy jungle and dense underbrush kept Fox from employing supporting arms, and he was forced to attack head on into the teeth of the enemy fire. As the Marines fought their way into the complex, a mortar round landed in the middle of the Company A command group, killing and wounding everyone, except one officer. Although painfully wounded, Fox continued to lead his casualty-riddled company through the bunker complex. At the end of the action, 11 Marines had been killed and 72 wounded. The North Vietnamese left 105 bodies on the battlefield.

Ray Davis

"I had an announced 'law' that nobody could lose a skirmish with the enemy. Any time an outfit got chopped up pretty bad, the first question that I wanted to know from the battalion commander was how many rounds of artillery they fired; and if they didn't fire enough, then he was criticized." Davis ordered an investigation into the bloody fight. It was determined that Fox's actions were fully justified, and he was subsequently awarded the Medal of Honor. Davis felt that "When you've got Marines' lives at stake, you need an excellent to outstanding officer who can ensure that the task gets done with the least casualties." Davis relieved several battalion commanders for incompetence, "But it was never because of any flush, immediate judgment. It was because of performance . . . where they were getting too many Marines killed."

Dewey Canyon marked the high point of Davis' high-mobility concept. He felt that "Bob Barrow and the 9th Marines worked together as a team, and it was just an absolutely superb performance. . . ."

The Challenge

By defeating the NVA, the local Vietcong guerrillas, who depended on them for support, were destroyed. Davis directed the 3rd Marine Division to "go into the villages and get the Vietcong out." He claimed, "Eventually we had total pacification," and issued a challenge to any visitor: "You can point anywhere in this province, day or night, and we'll land there and I'll take off my pistol and we'll walk around there alone." Davis claimed, "Quang Tri Province was much safer than the streets of most American cities."

Ray Davis

In April 1969, Davis was ordered to the Marine Corps Development and Education Command (MCDEC) as the director of the Education Center. Three months later, he was appointed by the president to the rank of lieutenant general and was given command of MCDEC. On March 12, 1971, he was nominated for a fourth star and upon confirmation by the Senate, became the Assistant Commandant of the Marine Corps. He retired one year later after thirty-four years of service. His wife, Knox Davis, remembered that at her husband's retirement ceremony at the Marine Barracks, she asked the band not to play "Auld Lang Syne" because, "I knew I could not get through it without crying." Instead they played, "Georgia on My Mind." "At least," she chuckled, "it wasn't 'Ramblin Wreck [from Georgia Tech]'!"

When asked to sum up his three decades of service, Davis simply stated, "I wouldn't know how to do any better than I did. I went from a poor country boy in Georgia up to four stars in the most elite organization in the world."

After the Wars
Ray Davis

In his long retirement, Davis worked tirelessly for veteran causes, including several trips to North Korea in an attempt to recover the remains of U.S. MIAs. His final legacy was the Korean War Veterans Memorial, in which he was the driving force behind its design and construction. On September 3, 2003, eighty-eight-year-old Ray Davis died peacefully in his sleep. His old friend Bob Barrow described him as "the finest man I've ever known, a Marine's Marine."

Bob Barrow

Upon returning from Vietnam, Barrow was promoted to brigadier general and assigned to Camp Butler, Okinawa. He was subsequently promoted to major general and took command of the Recruit Depot at Parris Island, where he worked tirelessly to improve the quality of Marines entering the force. As a lieutenant general, he served as deputy chief of staff, Headquarters Marine Corps and commanding general, Fleet Marine Force, Atlantic. On July 1, 1979, he became Commandant of the Marine Corps, the first Marine to serve, by law, a regular four-year tour as a full member of the Joint Chiefs of Staff. General Barrow retired in 1983 to his home state of Louisiana. He now lives in Cashiers, in the western mountains of North Carolina.

BIBLIOGRAPHY

Published Works

Alexander, Col. Joseph H. *Battle of the Barricades: U.S. Marines in the Recapture of Seoul.* (Washington, DC: Marine Corps Historical Center, 2000)

Alexander, Col. Joseph H. *Closing in: Marines in the Seizure of Iwo Jima.* (Washington, DC: History and Museums Division, Headquarters, U.S. Marine Corps, 1994)

Alexander, Colonel Joseph H. *The Final Campaign, Marines in the Victory on Okinawa.* (Washington, DC: History and Museums Division, Headquarters, U.S. Marine Corps, 1996)

Appleman, Roy E. *South to the Naktong, North to the Yalu.* (Washington, DC: Center of Military History, U.S. Army, 1992)

Asprey, Robert B. *At Belleau Wood.* (New York: Putnam, 1965)

Astor, Gerald. *Operation Iceberg: The Invasion and Conquest of Okinawa in World War II— an Oral History.* (New York: Donald I. Fine, 1995)

Bartley, Lt. Col. Whitman S. *Iwo Jima: Amphibious Epic.* (Washington: Marine Corps Historical Branch G-3, 1954)

Bayler, Walter L. *Last Man off Wake Island.* (Indianapolis: Bobbs-Merrill Co., 1943)

Bergerud, Eric M. *Fire in the Sky: The Air War in the South Pacific.* (Boulder, CO Westview Press, 2000)

———. *Touched With Fire, The Land War in the South Pacific.* (New York: Penguin, 1996)

Berry, Henry. *Semper Fi, Mac, Living Memories of the U.S. Marines in World War II.* (New York: Arbor House, 1982)

Boyle, Martin. *Yanks Don't Cry.* (New York: Bernard Geis Associates, 1963)

Carl, Marian, and Barrett Tillman. *Pushing the Envelope: The Career of Fighter Ace and Test Pilot Marion Carl.* (Annapolis: Naval Institute Press, 1994)

Cass, Bevin, ed. *History of the Sixth Marine Division.* (Nashville: Battery Press, 1987)

Chapin, Capt John C. *Fire Brigade: U.S. Marines in the Pusan Perimeter.* (Washington, DC: U.S. Marine Corps Historical Center, 2000)

Clark, George B. *Devil Dogs, Fighting Marines of World War I.* (Novato, CA: Presidio Press, 1999)

Conner, Howard M. *The Spearhead: The World War II History of the 5th Marine Division.* (Washington, DC: Infantry Journal Press, 1950)

Conroy, Michael R. "Sapper Attack in the A Shau," undated, http://1stbattalion9thmarinesfirebase.net/documents/Story%20-%20Sapper%20Attack%20In%20The%20A%20Shau.pdf

Craig, Edward A. *Incidents of Service 1917–1951.* (self published, circa 1968)

Davis, Raymond G. *The Story of Ray Davis.* Fuquay-Varina, NC: Research Triangle Publishing, 1995)

Davis, William J. *Chosin Marine.* (self-published, 1986)

Davis,Burke. *Marine: The Life of Lt. Gen. Lewis B. (Chesty) Puller, USMC (Ret).* (Boston: Little, Brown, 1962)

Detzer, David. *Thunder of the Captains: The Short Summer of 1950.* (New York: Thomas Y. Crowell, 1977)

Dingwall, Bill. "More Dead than Alive, Corps Said," *Pensacola News-Journal,* September 20, 1970.

Duncan, David Douglas. *This is War.* (New York: Harper, 1951)

Feifer, George. *Tennozan, The Battle of Okinawa and the Atomic Bomb.* (New York: Tickner & Field, 1992)

Foster, John. *Guadalcanal General: The Story of A.A. Vandegrift USMC.* (New York: Morrow, 1966)

Gaily, Harry. *The Liberation of Guam.* (Novato, CA Presidio Press, 1988)

Garand, George W., and Truman R. Strobridge. *History of U.S. Marine Corps Operations in World War II, Western Pacific Operations.* (Washington, DC: Historical Division, Headquarters, U.S. Marine Corps, 1971)

Geer, Andrew Clare. *The New Breed: The Story of the U.S. Marines in Korea.* (New York: Harper & Brothers, 1952)

Gow, Ian. *Okinawa: Gateway to Japan.* (London: Grub Street, 1986)

Griffith, Samuel B. II. *The Battle for Guadalcanal.* (Philadelphia: Lippincott, 1963)

Guttman, Jon. "Three-War Hero," *Military History,* December 1997.

Hallas, James H. *The Devil's Anvil: The Assault on Peleliu.* (Westport, CT. Praeger Publishers, 1994)

———. *Killing Ground on Okinawa: The Battle for Sugar Loaf Hill.* (Westport, CTConn.: Praeger, 1996)

Heinl, Robert. *Soldiers of the Sea: The United States Marine Corps, 1775-1962.* (Baltimore: Nautical & Aviation Pub. Co. of America, 1991)

———. *Victory at High Tide, the Inchon-Seoul Campaign.* (Philadelphia: Lippincott, 1968)

Henderson, Brig. Gen. F. P. "Roy S. Geiger: The First Air-Ground General," *Marine Corps Gazette* April 1995.

Hoffman, Lt. Col. Jon T. *Chesty: The Story of Lieutenant General Lewis B. Puller, USMC.* (New York: Random House, 2001)

Johnson, Lt. Col. Edward C. *Marine Corps Aviation: The Early Years 1912–1940.* Washington, DC: History and Museums Division, Headquarters, U.S. Marine Corps, 1977)

Keene, R. R. "Pistol Pete, Akio Tani, the 'Mantis,' Sent Marines Scrambling," *Leatherneck,* October 1992

Knox, Donald. *The Korean War: An Oral History, Pusan to Chosin.* (San Diego: Harcourt Brace Jovanovich, 1985)

Krulak, Lt. Gen. Victor H. *First to Fight, An Inside View of the U.S. Marine Corps.* (Annapolis: Naval Institute Press, 1984)

La Bree, Clifton. *The Gentle Warrior: General Oliver Prince Smith, USMC.* (Kent, OH: Kent State University Press, 2001)

Lamont-Brown, Raymond. *Kempeitai, Japan's Dreaded Military Police.* (Stroud, England: Sutton Publishing, 1998)

Lea, Tom. *Peleliu Landing.* (El Paso: Carl Hertzog, 1945)

Leckie, Robert. *Challenge for the Pacific: The Bloody Six-Month Battle of Guadalcanal.* (New York: Da Capo, 1999)

———. *Conflict: The History of the Korean War, 1950-53.* (New York: Da Capo, 1996)

———. *Helmet for My Pillow.* (New York: Bantam, 1979)

———. *Okinawa, The Last Battle of WW II.* (New York: Viking Penguin, 1995)

———. *Strong Men Armed: The United States Marines Against Japan.* (New York: Da Capo, 1997)

———. *The Wars of America,* 2nd rev. and up. ed. (New York, HarperCollins, 1992)

Lodge, Maj. O. R. *The Recapture of Guam.* (Washington: Historical Branch, G-3 Division, Headquarters, U. S. Marine Corps, 1954)

Mackin, Elton E. *Suddenly We Didn't Want to Die*. (Novato, CA: Presidio Press, 1993)

McMillin, Captain George J., USN. "The McMillan Report." Center for Research, Allied POWs Under the Japanese. http://www.mansell.com/pow_resources/guam/mcmillan-rpt.html

McMillan, George. *The Old Breed: A History of the 1st Marine Division in World War II*. (Washington, DC: Infantry Journal Press, 1949)

Miller, Thomas G. *The Cactus Air Force*. (New York: Harper, 1969)

Millett, Allan R. *In Many a Strife, General Gerald C. Thomas and the U.S. Marine Corps 1917-1951*. (Annapolis: Naval Institute Press, 1993)

Montross, Lynn, and Nicholas A. Canzona. *U.S. Marine Operations in Korea, 1950-1953, Volume I: The Pusan Perimeter*. (Washington, D.C.: Historical Branch, G-3, Headquarters, U.S. Marine Corps, 1954)

———. *U.S. Marine Operations in Korea 1950–1953, Volume II: The Inchon-Seoul Operation*. (Washington, D.C.: Historical Branch, G-3, Headquarters U.S. Marine Corps, 1955)

———. *U.S. Marine Operations in Korea: The Chosin Reservoir Campaign*. (Washington, DC: Historical Branch, G-3, 1957)

Nichols, David. *Ernie's War: The Best of Ernie Pyle's World War II Dispatches*. (New York: Random House, 1986)

O'Brien, Cyril J. *Liberation: Marines in the Recapture of Guam*. (Washington: History and Museums Division, Headquarters, U.S. Marine Corps, 1994)

O'Sheel, Capt. Patrick, and Staff Sgt. Gene Cook, eds. *Semper Fidelis: The U.S. Marines in the Pacific, 1942–1945*. (New York: William Sloane Associates, 1947)

Owen, Joseph R. *Colder Than Hell: A Marine Rifle Company at Chosin Reservoir*. (Annapolis: Naval Institute Press, 1996)

Parry, Francis Fox. *Three-War Marine: The Pacific - Korea – Vietnam*. (Novato, CA: Presidio Press, 1987)

Potter, E. B. *Bull Halsey*. (Annapolis: Naval Institute Press, 1985)

Prados, John, and Ray W. Stubbe. *Valley of Decision: The Siege of Khe Sanh*. (New York: Houghton Mifflin, 1991)

Proehl, Carl W. *The Fourth Marine Division in World War II*. (Washington: Infantry Journal Press, 1946)

Ross, Bill D. *Peleliu: Tragic Triumph: The Untold Story of the Pacific War's Forgotten Battle*. (New York: Random House, 1991)

Russ, Martin. *Breakout: The Chosin Reservoir Campaign, Korea, 1950*. (New York: Penguin Books, 1999)

Sarantakes, Nicholas Evan, ed. *Seven Stars: the Okinawa Battle Diaries of Simon Bolivar Buckner, Jr., and Joseph Stilwell*. (College Station: Texas A & M University Press, 2004)

Schiani, Alfred. *A Former Marine Tells It Like It Was, and Is*. (New York: Carlton Press, 1988)

Schom, Alan. *The Eagle and the Rising Sun: The Japanese-American War, 1941–1943: Pearl Harbor through Guadalcanal*. (New York: Norton, 2003)

Sherrod, Robert. *History of Marine Corps Aviation in WW II*. (Washington, DC: Combat Forces Press, 1952)

Shulimson, Jack, et al. *U.S. Marines in Vietnam: The Defining Year, 1968*. (Washington, DC: History and Museums Division, Headquarters, U.S. Marine Corps, 1997)

Simmons, Walter. *Joe Foss, Flying Marine: The Story of his Flying Circus*. (New York: Dutton. 1943)

Sledge, E. B. *With the Old Breed at Peleliu and Okinawa*. (Novato, CA: Presidio Press, 1981)

Smith, Charles R. *U.S. Marines in Vietnam: High Mobility and Standdown, 1969*. (Washington, D.C. : History and Museums Division, Headquarters, U.S. Marine Corps 1988)

Smith, Holland M., and Percy Finch. *Coral and Brass*. (New York: Charles Scribner's Sons, 1949)

Smith, S. E. *The United States Marine Corps in World War II*. (New York: Random House, 1969)

Soule, Thayer. *Shooting the Pacific War: Marine Corps Combat Photography in World War II*. (Lexington: University Press of Kentucky, 2000)

Staff of the 9th Marines. *The Ninth Marines: A Brief History of the Ninth Marine Regiment*. (Washington: Infantry Journal Press, 1946)

Taplett, Col. Robert D. *Darkhorse Six, A Memoir of the Korean War 1950-1951*. (Williamstown, NJ: Phillips Publications, 2002)

Toland, John. *In Mortal Combat, Korea, 1950–1953*. (New York: Morrow, 1991)

Vandegrift, Gen. Alexander A. *Once a Marine: The Memoirs of General A.A. Vandegrift*. (New York: Norton, 1964)

Waldron, Maj. Miles D., and Spec 5 Richard W. Beavers. *The Critical Year 1968, The XXIV Corps Team*. (APO San Francisco: 31st Military History Detachment, Headquarters, XXIV Corps, 1969)

Weathersby, Katherine. "Soviet Aims in Korea and the Origins of the Korean War, 1945-1950: New Evidence from Russian Archives," Cold War International History Project, Working Paper No. 8, November 1993

Weintraub, Stanley. *MacArthur's War: Korea and the Undoing of an American Hero*. (New York: Free Press, 2000)

Willock, Roger. *Unaccustomed to Fear: A Biography of the Late General Roy S. Geiger*. (Princeton, New Jersey: privately published, 1968)

Wise, Col. Frederick. *A Marine Tells It to You*. (New York: J. H. Sears and Co., 1929)

Witty, Robert M., and Neil Morgan. *Marines of the Margarita*. (San Diego: Frye and Smith, Ltd., 1970)

Yahara, Col. Hiromichi. *The Battle for Okinawa*. (New York: Wiley, 1995)

Zimmerman, Maj. John L. *The Guadalcanal Campaign*. (Washington, DC: Historical Division, Headquarters, U.S. Marine Corps, 1949)

Archival Sources

Located at Quantico, Virginia, the Marine Corps University archives, which are maintained by the Alfred M. Gray Marine Corps Research Center, provide a rich source of material for researchers of Marine Corps history including nearly 4,000 collections of papers donated by active duty and former officers and enlisted, documenting every conflict involving Marines. Of particular importance to this book were the oral histories that have been conducted by the Marine Corps History Division over the years.

Barrow, Gen. Robert H. interview by Peter Soderbergh, tape T-121, T. Harry Williams Center for Oral History, Louisiana State University.

——— Marine Corps Historical Division. Oral History Interview.

Craig, Maj. Gen. Edward A. "Pusan Perimeter through Pohang Commitment," Historical Division Interview, Headquarters, U.S. Marine Corps, May 1951.
——— Marine Corps Historical Division. Oral History Interview, May 16, 1968.
Geiger, Gen. Roy S. personal papers, Gray Research Center archives, Quantico.
Honsowetz, Col. Russell E. Marine Corps Historical Division. Oral History Interview, 1990.
Jones, Lt. Gen. Louis B. (ret). Marine Corps Historical Division. Oral History Interview.
Shepherd, Gen. Lemuel C. Marine Corps Historical Division. Oral History Interview.
Silverthorn, Lt. Gen. Merwin. Marine Corps Historical Division. Oral History Interview, 1973.
Smith, Gen. Julien. Marine Corps Historical Division. Oral History Interview, 1973.
Smith, Gen Oliver P. personal papers, Marine Corps Historical Division archives.

Unpublished Materials

Barrow, Lt. Gen. Robert H. Commanding General FMF Lant, comments at 2nd Division Officer's Ball, November 1977, Goettge Field house, Camp Lejeune, N.C.
Colt, C. C. "Farewell General Geiger," unpublished memorial
Craig, Lt. Gen Edward A. personal interview with author, summer 1983.
———. personal interview with author, June 5, 1995.
Davis, Gen Raymond G. personal interview with author, June 12, 1969.
Geiger, Roy S. letter to Alexander A. Vandegrift, June 26, 1945.
———. letter to the Major General Commandant, 1 July 1920.
Perrett, Marvin J., USCG. personal interview personal interview with author, March 11, 2005.
Quagge, Maj. Timothy E. "General Roy Stanley Geiger, USMC: A Professional Biographical Study," dissertaion, U.S. Marine Corps Command Staff College, 1996.
Shepherd, Gen, Lemuel C. personal interview with author, May 19, 1984.
———. personal interview with author, June 30, 1985.
———. personal interview with author, July 10, 1985.
———. personal interview with author, July 15, 1985.
Simmons, Brig. Gen. Ed. personal interview with author, December 4, 2004.
U.S. Naval Group, report, February 6, 1945: Observations of Chinese Guerrilla.
U.S. Naval Group, China report dated February 6, 1945.
V Amphibious Corps, Assistant Chief of Staff, G-3 (Operations), Special Action Report, Iwo Jima Campaign, March 31, 1945.
Vandegrift, Alexander A. letter to Roy Geiger, July 6, 1945.